THE
National Pastime

A REVIEW OF BASEBALL HISTORY

THE NATIONAL PASTIME (ISSN 0734-6905, ISBN 0-910137-68-4), Number 17. Published by The Society for American Baseball Research, Inc., P.O. Box 93183, Cleveland, OH 44101. Postage paid at Birmingham, AL. Copyright 1997, The Society for American Baseball Research, Inc. All rights reserved. Reproduction in whole or in part without written permission is prohibited. Printed by EBSCO Media, Birmingham, AL.

Editor
Mark Alvarez

Copy Editor
A.D. Suehsdorf

Designated Reader
Dick Thompson

SABR Publications Order Form

Baseball Research Journal

The *Baseball Research Journal* is the annual publication of the society featuring some of the best research done by members. Articles range from statistical in nature to biographical sketches, plus nearly every other topic in baseball.

*	1975 (112 pp)	
____	1976 (128 pp)	...................$4.00
____	1977 (144 pp)	...................$4.00
____	1978 (160 pp)	...................$4.00
____	1979 (160 pp)	...................$5.00
____	1980 (180 pp)	...................$5.00
____	1981 (180 pp)	...................$5.00
*	1982 (184 pp)	
*	1983 (188 pp)	

larger format

____	1984 (88 pp)	...................$6.00
____	1985 (88 pp)	...................$6.00
____	1986 (88 pp)	...................$6.00
____	1987 (88 pp)	...................$6.00
____	1988 (88 pp)	...................$7.00
____	1989 (88 pp)	...................$8.00
____	1990 (88 pp)	...................$8.00
____	1991 (88 pp)	...................$8.00
____	1992 (96 pp)	...................$7.95
____	1993 (112 pp)	...................$9.95
____	1994 (112 pp)	...................$9.95
____	1995 (144 pp)	...................$9.95
____	1996 (154 pp)	...................$9.95

Baseball Historical Review
____ 1981; Best of the '72-'74 BRJs $6.00

Index to SABR Publications
____ 1987 (58 pp) $1.00
TNP, BRJ & SABR Review of Bks. v. I

Baseball Records Update 1993
____ 1993 ....$4.95
Changes to the Statistical Record found by the SABR Baseball Records Committee

Home Runs in the Old Ballparks
____ 1995 ....$9.95
.....member price, $5.95
Listings of top 5 HR hitters in parks no longer in use.

Award Voting
____ 1988 (72 pp) $7.00
History & listing of MVP, Rookie of the Year & Cy Young Awards

The National Pastime

The National Pastime features articles by members more general in nature, although some volumes are arranged around a theme, as noted below.

____	#1 Fall, 1982 (88 pp)	......$5.00
*	#2 Fall, 1983 (88 pp)	
____	#3 Spring 1984 (88 pp)	
	19th Century Pictorial	......$7.00
____	#4 Spring 1985 (88 pp)	......$6.00
____	#5 Winter, 1985 (88 pp)	......$6.00
____	#6 Spring, 1986 (88 pp)	
	Dead Ball Era Pictorial	......$8.00
____	#7 Winter, 1987 (88 pp)	......$6.00
____	#8 Spring, 1988 (80 pp)	
	Nap Lajoie Biography	......$8.00
*	#9 1989 (88 pp)	
____	#10 Fall, 1990 (88 pp)	......$8.00
____	#11 Fall, 1991 (88 pp)	......$7.95
____	#12 Summer, 1992 (96 pp)	
	The International Pastime	.....$7.95
____	#13 Summer, 1993 (96 pp)	........$7.95
____	#14 Summer, 1994 (112 pp)	........$9.95
____	#15 Spring, 1995 (156 pp)	........$9.95
____	#16 Spring, 1996 (144 pp.)	........$9.95

The Federal League of 1914-15
____ 1989 (64 pp) $12.00
Baseball's Third Major League

The Negro Leagues Book
____	1994 (382 pp, softcover)	....$29.95
____	1994 (382 pp, hardcover)	....$49.95
____	1994 (382 pp, limited edit.)	...$149.95

(Leather bound, slipcase, autographed)

Cooperstown Corner
Columns From The Sporting News *by Lee Allen*
____ 1990 (181 pp) $10.00

Run, Rabbit, Run
Tales of Walter "Rabbit" Maranville
____ 1991 (96 pp) $9.95

SABR Review of Books
Articles of Baseball Literary Criticism
____	Volume 1, 1986	......$6.00
____	Volume 2, 1987	......$6.00
____	Volume 3, 1988	......$6.00
____	Volume 4, 1989	......$7.00
*	Volume 5, 1990	

* - out of print

SABR's Books on the Minors

Minor League Baseball Stars
____ Volume I, 1978 (132 pp)
over 160 player records $5
____ Volume II, 1984 (158 pp)
175 players + managers $5
____ Volume III, 1992 (184 pp)
250 players $9

Minor League History Journal
a publication of SABR's Minor League Committee
____ Volume 1 (40 pp) $6
____ Volume 2 (54 pp) $6
____ Volume 3 (72 pp) $7

SABR's Books on the 19th Centur

Nineteenth Century Stars
____ 1988 (144 pp) $10
Bios of America's First Heroes (Non-Hall of Fam

Baseball's First Stars
____ 1996 (183 pp) $14
More Bios, including the Hall of Famers

Base Ball: How to Become a Player
by John Montgomery Ward *(reprint of 1888)*
____ 1993 (149 pp) ......$9.

Baseball's Regional Flavor

Saint Louis's Favorite Sport
____ 1992 Convention Publication (64 pp) $7

A History of San Diego Baseball
____ 1993 Convention Publication (40 pp) $7

Texas is Baseball Country
____ 1994 Convention Publication (48 pp) $5

Baseball In Pittsburgh
____ 1995 Convention Publication (64 pp) $7

Unions to Royals: *The Story of Professional Baseball In Kansas City*
____ 1996 Convention Publication (64 pp) $7

Book Shipping Costs
1 book	$1.50
2-3 books	$2.50
4-5 books	$5.00
6-10 books	$7.50
11+ books	$9.00

Book delivery is usually 3-6 weeks.

Membership Dues	_____
Book Total	_____
Shipping	_____
TOTAL	_____

Discover, Master Card & Visa Accepted

SABR members receive *Baseball Research Journal, The National Pastime,* one or more special publications, a membership directory, and *The SABR Bulletin,* SABR's newsletter. Additional membership benefits include access to a National Convention and regional meetings, research exchange and research paper collection, the SABR lending library, occasional discounts on baseball trade publications and 6,000 other baseball enthusiasts like yourself around the country and the world.

To join SABR, send check, money order, Visa, Master or Discover Card in US funds or equivalent (dues are $35 US, $45 Canada, Mexico; $50 Overseas) to SABR, PO Box 93183, Cleveland OH 44101.

Name: _____

Address: _____

City, State, ZIP: _____

Card # _____

_____

Exp Date _____

TNP17

George Davis

William F. Lamb

Late in the morning of October 17, 1940, a failing 70-year-old mental patient was found dead in his bed at a Philadelphia asylum. The old man's passing went unnoticed by the public and in little more than twenty-four hours his widow had him buried in an unmarked grave at a nearby suburban cemetery. For a quarter century thereafter, he would lie there in total anonymity.

Things, however, had not always been like this for the deceased. In his heyday at the turn of the century, the man had been perhaps the best all-around baseball player in America. A potent switch hitter at the plate, a superb shortstop in the field and twice player-manager of the renowned New York Giants to boot, the old-timer had compiled the kind of record that turns today's major league players into first-ballot Hall of Famers. In 1903 his obdurate refusal to comply with directives assigning his services to the Chicago White Sox had almost wrecked the fragile peace agreement that had been reached between the established National League and its fledgling rival, the American. The name of this famed-in-his-time but now forgotten figure is George Davis and he deserves a better fate.

George Stacey Davis was born in Cohoes, New York, on August 23, 1870. He was the fifth of seven children born to Abraham (or Abram) Davis, a Welsh immigrant who had settled in Cohoes, and his English-born wife, Sarah Healy Davis, a neighbor of Abraham's prior to their marriage in the late 1850s. At the time of George's birth, Cohoes was a small but bustling upstate mill town and transportation center situated on

the Hudson River. It also lay within the Albany-Troy-Schenectady triangle, then a hotbed of the newly popular sport of baseball.

Apart from the fact that George Davis was raised and presumably schooled in Cohoes, little is known of his early life. Although there is no hard evidence, it seems safe to assume that a future baseball star like the young Davis would have followed the fortunes of Troy's National League entry of 1879-82. While not a pennant contender, the Trojan squad featured such destined Hall of Famers as Roger Connor, Tim Keefe, Mickey Welch, and Buck Ewing. Buck, considered by some the greatest player of the nineteenth century, would figure prominently in several important events in the later career of George Davis.

In the early 1880s, however, Ewing, Connor, Keefe and Welch were just starting their playing days. The dominant force on the Trojan team was veteran player-manager Bob "Death to Flying Things" Ferguson, himself a significant figure in the early years of professional baseball. Interesting from the Davis perspective is the fact that Ferguson is generally regarded as the major leagues' first switch hitter. Whether this influenced Davis, a natural lefty with the bat, to become a switch hitter himself is unknown but not implausible.

Davis' career in organized baseball began in the outfield of an 1889 team of amateur and semipro players based in Albany. Upon a recommendation by Albany manager Tom York, himself a veteran of 15 National Association and National League seasons, Davis was signed by the NL Cleveland Spiders for the 1890 season. Like many others that year, the 19-year-old Davis owed his quick ascension to the majors to the forma-

William F. Lamb *is a veteran assistant county prosecutor. He lives with his family in Monroe, New Jersey.*

tion of the Players' League. Established stars and lesser lights alike were drawn to John Montgomery Ward's brainchild that season, leaving the sixteen teams of the rival National League and American Association to scramble for replacements. The Spiders' situation was typically dire, Cleveland having lost a number of regulars, including its entire 1889 outfield.

Davis quickly established himself. As a rookie, he hit a solid, if unspectacular .264 with a team-leading 73 RBIs. Davis upped his offensive numbers the following year (.289 BA with 89 RBIs plus 115 runs scored and 42 stolen bases) while placing second among league leaders in doubles (35) and fourth in hits (165). Fleet afoot, with a powerful arm, Davis was outstanding defensively in center field, leading all major league outfielders with 35 assists during the 1890 season. His innate athleticism, however, soon permitted player-manager Patsy Tebeau to move him all around the field. He even took the mound for the Spiders on occasion, albeit with underwhelming results (an 0-1 record with one save and a 15.75 ERA in three 1891 season appearances).

On the verge of stardom, Davis played poorly in 1892. His batting average plummeted to .241 and his fielding became erratic. The cause for this drop-off in performance is unclear. Frequent position changes—Davis rotated around the outfield, saw action at third base and shortstop and filled in at second that season—may have been unsettling. Or perhaps the brawling, umpire-baiting style of play inspired by Tebeau did not agree with Davis, a clean, scientific type of player. Or maybe Davis had a minor but nagging injury or just encountered the subpar season that all fine players occasionally suffer. In any event, he saw only sparing action in Cleveland's 1892 postseason championship series loss to Boston, going 1 for 6 in three games at third base.

New York stardom—Prior to the start of the 1893 season, John Montgomery Ward, newly installed as manager of the Giants, shocked New York fans by trading the redoubtable but graying Buck Ewing to Cleveland for the now 22-year-old Davis. In Gotham for the next nine seasons, Davis played superbly. Benefitting as did all batters from the elimination of the pitcher's box and the newly created 60'6" pitching distance, Davis turned in a sensational year at the plate. His batting average soared to .355, fifth best in the league, with sixty extra-base hits, an impressive 11 homers and 119 RBIs. Among league leaders, Davis' 27 triples (still an all-time single season record for a switch hitter) and his .554 slugging average were second best, while he placed fourth in hits with 195, and third in total bases with 304. He also had a then-record 33-game hitting streak.

In 1894 Davis proved that the previous season had been no fluke. While offensive statistics that season were truly remarkable—the league as a whole posted a .309 batting average and hit 627 home runs—Davis' numbers were again outstanding. He batted .352 with 53 extra-base hits, 120 runs scored, 91 RBIs and 40 stolen bases. Davis and his Giant mates, moreover, enjoyed the postseason satisfaction of routing the league champion Baltimore Orioles in the inaugural Temple Cup series. So overpowering was New York's offense—a .393 team batting average and 33 runs scored in just four games—that Davis' 5 hit, 5 RBI contribution actually made him one of the Giants' lesser weapons in the series.

As the 1895 season approached, the Giants stood poised for another serious run at the league pennant. Then disaster struck in the form of a demoniac Tammany Hall lawyer named Andrew Freedman. Soon after Freedman acquired a controlling interest in the New York franchise, manager Ward resigned to make use of his freshly minted Columbia Law School degree. Casting about for a new field leader, Freedman seized upon Davis, now playing third base. Intelligent, well spoken and a keen student of the game, the great young player appeared a sound choice. But Davis was never to be a success as a manager. When the Davis-led Giants struggled out of the gate with a 16-17 record, the mercurial Freedman installed first baseman Dirty Jack Doyle, who went 32-31 before parting ways with Freedman. The unknown Harvey Watkins finished the season at 18-17.

Under their three managers, the Giants fell to ninth place in what was then a twelve-team league. But little of this was the fault of Davis who, his travails as skipper notwithstanding, turned in another fine season. Playing in only 110 games due to shoulder miseries, Davis still scored 108 runs and drove in 101 more. His .340 batting average included 50 extra base hits and a 6 for 6 day on August 15. Davis also stole 48 bases.

Although left off the club's reserve list that winter, Davis returned to the Giants for the 1896 season. New York began the campaign under the stewardship of former NL infielder Arthur Irwin, but after a 38-53 start, Irwin was gone. His replacement was hard-hitting third baseman Bill Joyce, recently acquired from Washington. Upon his arrival, Joyce shifted Davis over to shortstop and thus began a remarkable mid-career transformation. Although not much more than adequate at third, Davis quickly proved a natural at short, where his great range and strong arm could be put to optimum advantage. The shift to short also permitted the heady Davis to assume a leadership role in the infield.

Under Joyce's command, the Giants closed with a 26-14 spurt to finish 64-67 overall—not bad considering that Freedman's abusive treatment of star hurler Amos Rusie had prompted the big Hoosier to sit out the entire season. As for Davis, he turned in yet another outstanding season at the plate: a .320 batting average, 98 runs scored, 99 RBIs, and 48 stolen bases.

The 1897 season saw the 27-year-old Davis at the pinnacle of his career. His play, both in the field and at bat, was simply awesome. Playing in all but one of the Giants 131 games, Davis batted .353. His 51 extra-base hits included 10 homers, second best in the league, and his 136 RBIs topped the circuit. Throw in a .509 slugging average (fifth best) and 65 stolen bases (fourth best) and a brilliant offensive season is complete. Then add a comparable effort in the field. In his first full season as a shortstop, Davis led the league in putouts (337) and double plays (67), while his overall fielding percentage of .926 placed him third in league standings.

Uncharacteristically stable with Joyce still holding the managerial reins, and boosted by the return of Rusie (28-10), the Giants posted a fine 83-48 record, good for third place. But from this point, the Giants fortunes would descend rapidly as Freedman continued to change managers at a pace that has been likened to George Steinbrenner's. Davis' offensive production also began to slacken. He hit only .307 with reduced power in 1898, and .337 in an injury-plagued 1899 season. The Davis stat lines, however, reflect a league-wide trend. From the high-water marks of 1894 (.309 BA with 627 homers), the league norm had fallen to a .271 batting average with only 299 home runs by 1898.

In Davis' case, he at least partially compensated for the reduction in his plate numbers with sterling play in the field. He led NL shortstops in chances per game in both 1898 and 1899, as well as fielding percentage in the latter season. In fact, *Total Baseball* rates Davis' work at short as having saved the Giants an extraordinary 86 runs during that two-year period. His efforts, however, availed the Giants little. By the end of the

A young George Davis in his earliest years in the majors.

Transcendental Graphics

1899 season New York had slid all the way to tenth place.

The Ewing controversy—Misfortune would continue to follow the Giants in 1900 and envelop Davis in the first of the two controversies that punctuated his career. Unhappy with the results of the previous season, Freedman enticed Buck Ewing to manage the team in 1900. Ewing knew baseball and had proven managerial skills, having just produced five consecutive winning seasons at the helm in Cincinnati. But he would have little success in New York and would later place most of the blame for this at the feet of George Davis.

The Ewing-Davis relationship started well enough with Buck citing Davis' baseball acumen and his easy manner in dealing with umpires when he appointed Davis the team's field captain that spring. The Giants, however, were soon riven by dissention, with the team dividing largely into two camps: New York's holdover players and the men imported from Cincinnati by Ewing.

The Giants staggered to a 21-41 record and Ewing resigned under pressure in mid-July. In explaining his departure, Ewing blasted Davis as the leader of the holdover clique and accused him of undermining Ewing's efforts to upgrade the team's talent, particularly at third base where Charley "Piano Legs" Hickman had proved a butcher in the field. More seriously, Ewing charged Davis with feigning injury to remain in New York and lobby for the manager's job while the team embarked on a disastrous road trip in early July.

Much of this sounds like sour grapes. A 21-41 record is not produced solely by poor defensive play at third base. Ewing's complaints, however, cannot be dismissed out of hand. It does appear, for example, that Davis began scouting for new playing talent even before his appointment as manager had been announced. And the water on the knee excuse that prevented Davis from accompanying the Giants on their fateful July road trip did not stop him from returning to the lineup the very day that he was appointed the team's new manager.

It should also be said that the Giants play immediately improved under Davis' command. The factionalism that plagued the team under Ewing disappeared. And the maligned Hickman produced a .313 batting average with a late-season 27-game hit streak—perhaps in atonement for his stunning ineptitude in the field: 86 errors and a .842 fielding percentage, abysmal even by turn-of-the-century standards.

Due to injuries, real or contrived, Davis played in only 114 games in 1900. His performance when he was in lineup, however, was stellar. He hit .319, tops for NL shortstops, and he led the league in fielding percentage, chances per game, and double plays by a shortstop.

Under manager Davis, the Giants played 39-37 ball. Late in the season, moreover, the team acquired a promising collegiate pitcher named Christy Mathewson. Following their initial on-field encounter, Davis advised Matty to abandon the jug-handled curve that had befuddled his college opponents—counsel that Mathewson first resented but later thanked Davis for. Mathewson biographer Ray Robinson also credits Davis with coining the term "fadeaway" for Matty's signature pitch. At the outset, however, Mathewson was not effective, going 0-3 in six late season games. Still, Davis and others convinced Freedman to retain the young pitcher on the roster and Freedman agreed, if only to use Mathewson in a stillborn scheme with John T. Brush, the kindred spirit who owned the Cincinnati Reds.

Despite improved play under Davis, the Giants' woeful start had consigned New York to last place in the newly consolidated eight team National League of 1900. Cries for new field leadership were sounded at the season's close and Freedman was sorely put out by a championship banner waving in Brooklyn—a franchise that Freedman wanted evicted from the city. But Freedman remained unexpectedly steadfast regarding his manager and Davis returned to pilot the team in 1901.

The White Sox controversy—The chain of events that would attend the second and more enduring controversy in the career of George Davis followed a dismal 52-85 season. Ignoring, as did a multitude of other contract jumpers, the reserve clause in his 1901 Giants contract, Davis inked a seemingly ironclad contract with the White Sox drawn up by his lawyer and former baseball mentor, John Montgomery Ward. Because Freedman did not want the shortstop back in New York, the move was uncontested at the time and Davis went on to enjoy a solid 1902 season in Chicago.

He batted .299 for his new club with 93 RBIs and 31 stolen bases. He also played well in the field, leading AL shortstops in fielding percentage.

In the winter of 1902, the prayers of Giants fans were answered when Freedman relinquished control of the club. The new owner, none other than John T. Brush, shared many of Freedman's disagreeable attributes, but unlike Freedman, he was a sound baseball man, a point he quickly demonstrated by retaining John McGraw as his manager. McGraw had taken over midway in the 1902 season, too late to keep the team from another last place finish. In the off-season, McGraw immediately set about rebuilding the Giants into a pennant contender. The first place that needed fixing was the hole at shortstop, where the likes of Joe Bean had proved no answer to the problem created by the departure of George Davis.

McGraw's solution was simple: replace Davis with Davis. This McGraw appeared to have accomplished when he succeeded in obtaining Davis' signature on a lucrative two-year contract to play in New York. White Sox owner Charles Comiskey, however, was not about to let Davis go, and threatened legal action based upon the contract that Davis had signed with Chicago. When Davis took his troubles back to Ward, the lawyer was faced with the problem of advising a client who wished to break a contract that Ward himself had drafted. In the end, Ward argued that the reserve clause in Davis' 1901 Giant contract constituted a prior lien on Davis' 1902 services, rendering invalid any White Sox claim to Davis. Davis, according to Ward, was entirely at liberty to rejoin the Giants as per his new contract.

The state and federal judges from whom Comiskey sought relief did not agree, and injunctions restraining Davis from playing for the Giants limited his action to four games during the 1903 season. But even this brief appearance by Davis in a Giants uniform proved momentous, threatening a rupture in the fragile peace agreement that had just been reached between the rival leagues. A full account of the controversy can be found in *July 2, 1903*, Mike Sowell's absorbing 1992 book on the life and death of Davis' fellow contract jumper, Ed Delahanty. For the sake of peace, the Giants eventually backed down. Davis returned to the White Sox for 1904.

It appears that the White Sox bore no animosity toward Davis when he returned. McGraw did not suffer either, securing the capable Bill Dahlen to shortstop a pennant-winning Giant team in 1904. The real loser was Ward. His role in the Davis affair incurred the lasting enmity of AL President Ban Johnson, who a few years later used his influence to scuttle Ward's appointment to the presidency of the National League.

American Leaguer—A first look at his 1904 numbers suggests that advancing age and the year layoff took their toll on Davis. His batting average, for instance, fell to .252. But offensive stats in general had continued the trend downward—the AL batting norm was only .244—and Davis' bat still had pop, producing 43 extra-base hits. His 32 stolen bases, fourth highest in the league, showed that there was still life in Davis' legs and his defensive abilities remained intact. In 1904, he led AL shortstops in putouts, assists, double plays, and chances per game. He was also durable at age 34, playing a then major league record 152 games at the demanding position of shortstop. Perhaps more important, Davis proved a good fit with the White Sox, a team of savvy veterans that relied on excellent pitching and fielding and on intelligent use of meager offensive assets to finish a strong third in 1904.

The White Sox moved up to a close second in 1905, finishing two games behind Philadelphia. Davis did his part, playing in 151 games and batting .278 in a league that had only three .300 hitters. Davis was also once again outstanding on defense, leading AL shortstops in fielding percentage. In 1906, the White Sox won it all. The "Hitless Wonders"—a .230 team batting average with a grand total of seven home runs for the season—parlayed intelligence, exceptional pitching, and sound defense into a pennant winning 93-58 record. Much of the Sox offense consisted of turning a league-leading 453 walks received into runs. Cleanup batter Davis drove in his share. His 80 RBIs led the Sox and ranked third among league leaders. His .277 batting average and 27 stolen bases were also creditable for a 36-year-old shortstop.

Davis' importance to the Sox was amply demonstrated in the 1906 World Series against the heavily favored Cubs of Tinker to Evers to Chance fame. Missing the first three games due to illness, and held hitless in Game 4, Davis sparked the run-scoring outbursts that carried the Sox to decisive victories in the final two games. His four hits included three doubles and produced 6 RBIs, tops for both sides. Davis also stole home in Game 5 and thoroughly outplayed Tinker, notwithstanding the fact that he appeared in only half the series' six games.

The World Championship season of 1906 would prove the final highlight of George Davis' playing career. Although sound in the field to the end, Davis' batting skills quickly deteriorated after 1906. Averages of .238 in 1907 and .217 in 1908 reduced him to part-time status by 1909. Age and injuries limited him to pinch hitting and a handful of games at first base in that final year, and he was released by the Sox at his own request when the 1909 season ended.

The forgotten man—The conclusion of George Davis' twenty year major league career does not end the fascination of his story. Unfortunately, recent efforts to revive interest in him have been frustrated by the enig-

matic nature of Davis' personality and by the paucity of information about his life outside the majors.

Davis is an elusive figure to modern day researchers. Obviously, none of his contemporaries survives to provide firsthand reminiscences about him, and he made little off-the-field impression on the media of his time. Few amusing or informative anecdotes exist about him—which is telling, given the uninhibited nature of the turn of the century sporting press. Davis was evidently poor copy with no aptitude for public self-promotion. Illustrative here is an incident early in the 1900 season, when Davis and two teammates responded to the scene of a tenement fire and saved a number of women and children. In the aftermath, Davis flunked his chance to play the hero in the press, deflecting praise onto Kid Gleason and Mike Grady. The matter quickly became a forgotten one-day story.

Davis' failures as a manager remain perplexing, for he was undeniably an astute baseball man. Working under the Freedman regime was tough for all of the many men who tried it, but there is also evidence that Davis was not much of a disciplinarian. He seems to have had trouble commanding the respect of strong-willed players. Dirty Jack Doyle, a teammate and unsuccessful Giant manager himself, publicly berated skipper Davis throughout the latter part of the 1900 season. Following that season, moreover, Davis was ousted as manager-captain of a Giants-laden squad headed for postseason play in Cuba in what appears to have been a players revolt. And when Doyle found himself on the trading block that winter, he excoriated Davis as an incompetent, and claimed—without ever producing promised written proof—that virtually all the other Giants had little respect for Davis.

Davis' off-the-field life is also a mystery. Research by Schenectady area sportswriter Steve Amedio has unearthed information that Davis lived with his parents in Cohoes during the off-season until he moved to Troy in 1900. Davis was single at that time and it has generally been believed that he remained a bachelor throughout his playing days. Bill James has written that Davis got married in St. Louis around 1918, but Ward's 1909 libel suit against Ban Johnson brought out testimony that Davis' Giants contract for the 1903-04 seasons had been signed by McGraw, Davis, and Davis' wife. In any event, Davis was married to the former Jane Holden at the time of his death in 1940.

Following his release as a player by the White Sox in 1909, Davis was engaged to manage Des Moines of the Western League. The owners were so confident of success that they insured Davis' life for $25,000, but Davis fared no better as a minor league manager than he had in the majors. Going 72-96 with a team that had finished first the previous year, he was released following the 1910 season.

From 1911 to 1913, Davis oversaw the Columbia

Academy, a Manhattan bowling alley, and developed into an excellent bowler himself. A gushing March, 1913, news report announcing Davis' imminent departure from New York to become baseball coach at Amherst College includes a photo of Davis, bowling ball in hand, looking fit at age 43. It is the last known photograph of him.

From 1913 to 1918, Davis coached at Amherst, supplementing his income by scouting for the Yankees (1915) and the Browns (1917). There are also reports that he coached for St. Louis under his old White Sox leader Fielder Jones during the 1917 and 1918 seasons. The last press mention of Davis has him out of baseball and working as an automobile sales agent in St. Louis late in 1918.

Thereafter, George Davis vanished from public view for almost 50 years. In 1968, a dogged search by Hall of Fame historian Lee Allen uncovered Davis' death certificate. It showed that he had died in Philadelphia State Hospital on October 17, 1940.

Davis' hospital records were discarded when Philadelphia State Hospital was razed in 1986. Recent inquiry into the subject, however, revealed that Davis' medical master card survived in the archives of Norristown State Hospital. That document indicates that Davis was admitted to Philadelphia General Hospital on August 25, 1934. Within three weeks he was transferred to the Philadelphia Hospital for Mental Diseases (Philadelphia State Hospital). At the time of his admission, Davis was mentally impaired and suffering generalized paralysis.

He remained at the hospital until his death six years later. The immediate cause of death was paresis, the creeping paralysis and dementia which mark the terminal stage of syphilis. Davis also suffered from arteriosclerosis and cellulitis—an inflammation of the connective tissue—prior to his death.

Although Jane Davis signed her husband's death certificate on the date of death, and arranged for a quick and quiet burial, next to nothing is known of the Davis marriage. A story that Davis and a diamond-draped wife had left Amherst to play professional bridge in New York could not be substantiated by Allen and has been dismissed as apocryphal by James. It does appear, however, that the Davis marriage was childless and that before his hospitalization in 1934, Davis had worked as some type of inspector. During this time, Davis lived with his wife at 3815 Chestnut Street, then an upscale address near the University of Pennsylvania campus in center city Philadelphia.

Jane Davis had her husband buried in a single, unmarked grave in Fernwood Cemetery little more than twenty-four hours after his death. There appears to have been no ceremony at the burial—which cost his widow $41—and Davis' family would not learn of his death until years afterward.

In the final analysis, of course, neither Davis' shortcomings as a manager nor the obscurity of his final years bear on any assessment of his standing as a ballplayer. His numbers are impressive: a .295 career batting average over twenty major league seasons, with 2,660 hits, 1,539 runs scored, 1,437 RBIs, and 616 stolen bases. His fielding statistics, adjusted for time and circumstance, appear even better. According to *Total Baseball*, only five shortstops in 120 years of major league play saved more runs with their glove than Davis (who might rank even higher had he not spent his first seven seasons playing other positions). Melding Davis the hitter with Davis the fielder, the portrait of a truly exceptional player emerges. Underappreciated in his day and now forgotten, George Davis was one of the finest shortstops ever to play major league ball. The longtime neglect of his career is as puzzling as it is undeserved.

Sources

Alexander, Charles, *John McGraw*, Viking Penguin, Inc., 1988.

The American Pocket Medical Dictionary, 17th ed., W.B. Saunders Co., 1942.

The Baseball Encyclopedia, Jos. L. Reichler, ed., 4th ed., Macmillan Pub. Co., Inc., 1979.

The Ballplayers, Mike Shatzkin, ed., Arbor House/Wm. Morrow, 1990.

Honig, Donald, *Baseball America*, Galahad Books, 1985.

Hynd, Noel, *The Giants Of The Polo Grounds*, Doubleday, 1988.

James, Bill, *The Bill James Historical Baseball Abstract*, Villard Books, 1985.

James, Bill, *The Politics Of Glory*, Macmillan Pub. Co., Inc., 1994.

Mathewson, Christy, *Pitching In A Pinch*, University of Nebraska Press reprint, 1994 (originally published in 1912 by Putnam).

Murdock, Eugene C., *Ban Johnson, Czar Of Baseball*, Greenwood Press, 1982.

Nineteenth Century Stars, Robert L. Tiemann and Mark Rucker, eds., SABR, 1989.

The Perfect Game, Mark Alvarez, ed., Taylor Pub. Co., 1993.

Robinson, Ray, *Matty: An American Hero*, Oxford University Press, 1993.

Seymour, Harold, *Baseball, The Early Years*, Oxford University Press, 1960.

Sowell, Mike, *July 2, 1903*, MacMillan Pub. Co., 1992.

Sporting Life

The Sporting News

Total Baseball, John Thorn and Pete Palmer, eds., 3rd ed., Harper Perennial, 1993.

also:

National Baseball Hall of Fame Library and Archive materials including files on George Davis, John Montgomery Ward, Jack Doyle, Buck Ewing, and Ban Johnson, and the Reach Official Baseball Guides, 1891-1910.

Recent articles on George Davis in the *Times Union* (Albany, New York), October 23, 1990, and *Daily Gazette* (Schenectady, New York), April 11, 1993, and article by Judson H. Hamlin on 19th Century Stars in *The Vintage and Classic Baseball Collector*, September, 1995.

Interview, *Daily Gazette* sportswriter Steve Amedio, November 1, 1995.

Alston Takes A Seat

Steve Daly

Salvador Anthony Yvars would certainly be remiss if he didn't take some credit for the success of the Brooklyn Dodgers of the 1950s and, later, the Dodgers in Los Angeles in the early '60s. But you won't find Yvars' name anywhere alongside such Dodger greats as Roy Campanella, Jackie Robinson, Duke Snider, Gil Hodges, Pee Wee Reese, or Don Newcombe.

Yvars' contribution to Dodger glory came nearly a decade before the long-suffering Brooklyn franchise won its first World Series title in 1955, with a four games to three victory over the powerful New York Yankees. Yvars never wore a Dodgers uniform. In fact, he spent almost seven of his eight major-league seasons playing for the rival New York Giants. But it was one play, in his first season of professional ball as a backup catcher for the Manchester, New Hampshire, Giants of the Class B New England League, which would alter the history of Dodger baseball.

Beginning in 1947 Yvars would spend four seasons shuttling between the Polo Grounds and Jersey City of the AAA International League, with a season in Minneapolis in 1949, before reaching the majors to stay in 1951. He made the final out of the Subway Series of 1951 against the New York Yankees, lining to outfielder Hank Bauer with the tying run on second base in a 4-3, series-clinching victory for the Yankees in Game 6.

"Bobby Thomson got us into the World Series," Yvars said in an interview, referring to Thomson's historic homer off Brooklyn's Ralph Branca in the final game of a three-game playoff series that gave the Gi-

ants the National League pennant, "and I got us out."

The 5-foot-10, 187-pound Yvars batted .244 in 211 career games, mostly as a backup to starter Wes Westrum, and finished his career with the St. Louis Cardinals in 1954. His most productive season was 1952, when he hit .245 (37-for-151) and drove in 18 runs (43 percent of his career RBI total) with four homers and three doubles.

Yvars made his major league debut on September 27, 1947, against Philadelphia. Giants manager Mel Ott was so impressed with his work behind the plate that he told Yvars to expect to catch both games of a doubleheader the next day.

"I said to myself, 'Wow. Here I am, after my first game in the majors, and I'm gonna catch a double-header tomorrow,'" Yvars remembered recently. "I was pretty excited."

In the excitement, however, Yvars forgot that he had more pressing plans. Long before he could envision being a September call-up for the Giants, Yvars had made plans to marry that day. And if it weren't for the insistence of a teammate, he might very well have strapped on his catcher's gear and crouched behind the plate.

"I figured I could get married any time," Yvars said. "I wanted to catch a doubleheader. When was I gonna get another chance to do that? But I left and got married."

It was his first big league experience, but it was nearly 16 months after Yvars made what was probably his biggest impact on baseball.

On May 24, 1946, he unwittingly solidified the future of the Dodgers. It could be construed as a virtual act of

---

Steve Daly is: the assistant sports editor at The Telegraph in Nashua, New Hampshire and is working on a history of the New England League.

treason if you were a New York Giants fan.

The New England League— Yvars was struggling to get at-bats with the Manchester Giants back in that '46 season. Charlie Fox, who had appeared in three games as a 21-year-old catcher with the New York Giants in 1942 before being drafted, returned to baseball and found himself as the starter in Manchester. He was seeing the bulk of the action behind the plate and Yvars, who had been optioned down from Jersey City at the start of the season, was growing increasingly frustrated with his lack of opportunity.

Yvars had shown promise with his bat, but because of Fox' presence, when he did find his name on manager Hal Gruber's lineup card he was often playing in the outfield.

On May 24 the Giants pulled into the parking lot of Holman Stadium, the home field of the rival Nashua Dodgers, with a 6-5 record and a one-half game lead over the Dodgers. The teams had split their first two meetings, the Giants winning 11-10 in eleven innings and Nashua taking an 8-1 victory two days later at Holman.

On the road the Dodgers had become a drawing card in New England League cities. Nashua, through the directive of Brooklyn president Branch Rickey, was helping to break down the racial barrier which had barricaded baseball for more than sixty years. Its starting catcher, Roy Campanella, and one of its best young pitchers, Don Newcombe, were making history by being among the first black ballplayers to play for a major league affiliate in the United States since Moses Fleetwood Walker appeared in 42 games with the Toledo Blue Stockings in 1884. Jackie Robinson, their future teammate in Brooklyn, was making his debut with the Montreal Royals in the AAA International League.

George Brown, hoping to pitch Nashua to its third straight win and his second victory of the season, got the call for the Dodgers, while Roy Bridges was on the mound for Manchester, which had lost two of its last

Walter Alston

three games.

It didn't take long for the Dodgers to jump on Bridges. The righthander walked the first three batters he faced before Campanella ripped a single back through the box to score two runs and send him to an early shower. Campanella scored on a single off reliever Ed Carpentier for a 3-0 lead.

Confrontation— Yvars, batting eighth for the Giants and making a rare start behind the plate, drew a walk off Brown in his first at-bat in the third inning, but not before a few pitches sent him sprawling. Trotting down the firstbase line, Yvars began voicing his displeasure to the Dodgers' first baseman, Walter Alston, who also happened to be handling the managerial duties for the team that season.

"What the hell is going on?" Yvars yelled. "Your

pitcher's throwing at my head."

"You got no guts," Yvars claims Alston said to him. "Swing the bat."

Yvars was stewing.

Alston, an easygoing, humble man, had taken a leave of absence from a teaching and coaching position at Lewiston (Ohio) High School to be a player-manager with the Dodgers. He had spent three years as a player-manager in the Middle Atlantic League beginning in 1940, first at Portsmouth, Ohio, where his 59-68 club finished last in the six-team league (although he led the circuit in home runs with 28), and then at Springfield, Ohio, in 1941 (69-57, fourth place) and '42 (59-71, fifth place). Alston was again a more prolific hitter than manager, pacing the league in homers (25), RBI (102), and runs scored (88) in 1941, and homers (12), and RBI (90) in 1942.

Alston, who struck out in his only at-bat in the majors with the St. Louis Cardinals in 1936, played the 1943 season with Rochester, New York, in the Class AAA International League and returned to Rochester for his tenth season of professional baseball in 1944 but was given his unconditional release in mid-season.

Not long after Alston's release, Rickey, who had been with the St. Louis organization before taking over in Brooklyn, offered him a position as a player-manager with Trenton, New Jersey, of the Class B Inter-State League for the remainder of the season. In 49 games in 1944, Alston guided Trenton to a 31-18 record. In 1945 Trenton finished third in the six-team league with a 70-69 mark. Still, Rickey had seen enough of Alston to believe he was the man to take over in Nashua.

Upon his arrival, Alston wasn't harboring any more thoughts of a comeback. But at 34, he was the only experienced first baseman on the Nashua team. He had no choice but to pencil his name onto the lineup card.

Most importantly, however, Alston was the man expected to help ease the potentially turbulent integration of Campanella and Newcombe. Campanella had played the 1945 season with the Baltimore Elite Giants of the Negro National League, with whom he began his professional career as a 16-year-old catcher in 1938. Newcombe was a 19-year-old whose right arm was more powerful than anyone in the Dodgers organization had ever seen. He had played two years with the Negro National League Newark, New Jersey, Eagles.

Alston understood a pitcher's mentality. With Yvars crowding the plate, Brown wanted to establish control of the inside half. Yvars, as any batter might, objected to this strategy. He obviously didn't receive any sympathy from Alston when he reached first base.

Stories differ on what prompted the angry exchange between the two. Yvars has spent much of his life denying that, upset by the way he was being pitched to, he scooped up a handful of dirt and tossed it into Campanella's face. He insists he threw it into Campanella's shin guards. Whatever the location, the stocky Dodger catcher let it be known that it wouldn't be tolerated.

"Try that again and I'll beat you to a pulp," Campanella reportedly said as he tossed his mask aside. For Campanella, who played the game with boyish enthusiasm belying his 24 years, it was one of the few run-ins he would have with other players on the field that summer.

"We hated each other on the field," Yvars remembered, "but after the game, everything was great between the guys."

Nashua and Manchester had a natural rivalry. With the cities just fifteen miles apart, each team's fans could make the short drive for road games. And any competition between teams representing the cities—whether it be CYO basketball or professional baseball—had a great chance of taking on an ugly edge.

Trailing 3-0, Yvars was still upset when he came to the plate for his second at-bat in the fifth inning. Hoping for a big hit to get his team back into the ball game, Yvars swung at Brown's first offering, a fastball on the outside corner, and lofted it down the first-base line. Alston moved under the ball in the basepath and called Campanella off. But before he could catch the ball, Yvars, running fullsteam, leveled him. The ball landed with a thud in the grass beside Alston.

"He was right in the baseline," Yvars recalled. "There was nowhere for me to go and he was in the way."

"He did what any ballplayer probably would have done," said E.J. "Buzzie" Bavasi, the general manager of the Nashua Dodgers at the time. "He just did it a little harder than anybody else might have."

Yvars reached first base and turned around to see where the ball—and Alston—had ended up. But Alston wasn't interested in where the ball was. He was tearing down to first to get a piece of Yvars.

"In all the years I was around Walter Alston," Bavasi said. "I've never seen him so angry. Walter was pretty mild-mannered. You really had to do something that got under his skin before he'd get mad. I think Yvars succeeded in doing that."

By Bavasi's account, and that of a handful of players on that Dodger team, it was a one-sided fight. Despite his easy-going reputation, Alston landed several solid blows before the benches emptied and a handful of Nashua police rushed onto the field to restore order.

Yvars was ruled out for interference and despite the fight, both men remained in the game. Yvars went 1 for 4 and Alston was hitless in three at bats.

After the game, Alston was apologetic.

"The first thing I knew, everything was black," Alston told the Nashua *Telegraph*. "I was sorry I hit the kid, but at the moment I couldn't help myself."

To the dugout for good—During the collision, Alston suffered two displaced discs in his back. He played through the pain for another month or so before taking himself out of the lineup, effectively removing "player" from his player-manager position. A back specialist had told Alston he would be wise to give up on his playing career. Though it may not have seemed that way at the time, it turned out to be a godsend, first for the Nashua Dodgers, and then for the parent club.

"It may sound cruel, but that was the best thing that could have happened for the organization," Bavasi said. "Our shortstop [future major-leaguer Billy DeMars] was taking two steps after catching the ball before throwing it to first. Of course, Alston couldn't see that when he was playing because he was heading for the bag. All of that changed."

In fact the Dodgers, who got off to a 5-5 start before the Yvars-Alston brouhaha, would thrive as Alston became more comfortable in the dugout, concentrating on his role as a full-time manager. (He appeared only two more times—as a pinch hitter the following year with Class A Pueblo, Colorado, of the Western League.) He even began thinking like a manager.

"It's getting so I stay awake nights thinking up nasty things to call the umpires," Alston said.

Oscar "Gus" Galipeau, whose lively bat had helped him make the team as a backup to Campanella, had never played first base in his life but took over for Alston at first and immediately proved he belonged in the lineup.

"Wally said to me, 'Gus, you'll knock in more runs than you'll let get past you,'" said Galipeau, a French-Canadian who played professional hockey in the off-season. "That was all I needed to hear."

The Dodgers had compiled just 17 hits over the four games prior to Alston ending his playing career, but Galipeau, in his first start at first base, went 2-for-3 with a triple and home run. In 84 games for Nashua, Galipeau would bat an even .300. His nine home runs were second only to Campanella's 13, and his 58 RBI were third on the team behind Campanella (96) and third baseman Stan Lipka (60).

Galipeau's entry into the starting lineup coincided with a Dodger resurgence. On June 25 Nashua's record stood at 24-18. Six weeks later, with Alston calling the shots from the dugout, the Dodgers were 19 games over .500 at 56-37, and firmly entrenched in second place in the New England League after winning 32 of 51 games.

Nashua would finish with an 80-41-2 record, second to the Lynn, Massachusetts, Red Sox 82-40 mark. In the best-of-five first round of playoffs, Nashua eliminated Pawtucket, Rhode Island, 3-0, while Lynn took care of the Manchester Giants, also 3-0. Nashua, paced by League manager of the year Walter Alston, defeated Lynn four games to two in the Governor's Cup finals.

By the spring of 1947 Alston was managing Pueblo, where he brought the team home third (70-58), but won the playoff title. In 1948 Alston captured his third straight title in a different league, this time finishing third with St. Paul, Minnesota, of the AAA American Association, and winning the playoffs. He went 179-128 in two years at St. Paul before moving to the Dodgers' top farm club, Montreal, in 1950. There, Alston compiled a 365-245 record in four years (1950-53) before replacing Chuck Dressen as manager in Brooklyn to start the 1954 season. Dressen's Dodgers had gone 105-49 in 1953, but were no match for the Yankees, who won their fifth consecutive World Series. It also made Brooklyn 0-for-7 in World Series appearances.

As the 43-year-old Alston made his major-league managerial debut in 1954, Yvars was beginning his final season in the majors. He appeared in 38 games with the St. Louis Cardinals—ironically, the team that Alston had his only previous major-league experience with. Yvars found himself in a familiar position—as a backup—this time to Bill Sarni, who hit .300 in 123 games.

Alston led the Dodgers to a second-place finish in 1954, but helped end fifty-two years of futility in 1955, when Brooklyn finally won a World Series championship, beating the Yankees four games to three as Johnny Podres' complete-game shutout and Gil Hodges' two RBI powered the Dodgers to a 2-0 victory in Game 7.

By 1958 the Dodgers had left Brooklyn for Los Angeles, but Alston won World Series in 1959, '63, and '65. Alston would make it to two more World Series, but his Dodgers were swept by the Orioles in 1966, and lost to the Oakland Athletics, four games to one in 1974.

In twenty-three years in the majors, Alston compiled a 2,040-1,613 regular-season mark (23-21 in postseason play) before announcing his retirement in 1976 and being replaced by Tommy Lasorda. He was inducted into the Baseball Hall of Fame in 1983, the last manager to be voted in until Earl Weaver was inducted in 1996. Just over a year later, on November 1, 1984, Alston died in Oxford, Ohio.

"We decided Alston would never be a major league player," Rickey told the Associated Press when Alston was named Brooklyn manager in 1954.

And what foresight it was. Alston left behind a managerial legacy—both in wins and longevity with a single team—unlikely to be approached by anyone ever again.

"That s.o.b. should have given me half his money," Sal Yvars said with a laugh. "I made him what he was."

You certainly can argue that he had something to do with it.

Lou Gehrig on the Air

Steve Smart

The year 1939 was a sad and tragic year for Lou Gehrig and baseball. It started for Lou in spring training when he realized his health was keeping him from performing up to his standards and in his heart he knew something was seriously wrong. After eight starts in the regular season, Lou held himself out of a game on May 2, ending his consecutive game streak. He was never to play again.

On June 12 he entered the Hall of Fame on a rule waiver and on July 4 he had his "Day" at Yankee Stadium. During this time Lou was consulting doctors at the Mayo Clinic in Rochester, Minnesota, to diagnose his deteriorating condition. On one of these visits, Lou consented to a radio interview with Dwight Merriam at KROC radio in Rochester. What follows is a transcription of that August 22, 1939, broadcast.

ANNOUNCER: Ladies and gentlemen, we present at this time an interview with Lou Gehrig. Now I'm sure I don't have to explain who Lou Gehrig is because he's a gentleman of whom we have all heard. And because we have all heard about Lou, we know a great deal about him. Our interview today will deal strictly with baseball as a game, rather than Lou as a man.

Lou, is baseball played differently now than when you first started playing?

LOU: Well, that's a difficult question. I think it was played harder and it was made more difficult for the young man of fifteen, twenty years ago when I broke in. He had to go out and fight his way for a job under many adverse conditions. The young man today is sur-

rounded with old-timers' advice and experience. So you can see readily where the difference lies.

ANC: Speaking of up-and-coming ballplayers, you being associated with the Yankees, what do you think of Joe Gordon as a second baseman?

LOU: Why I think Joe Gordon in two years will be one of the real greats and will go down in the class with Eddie Collins and Gehringer, and there is a slight possibility that he will overshadow them defensively.

ANC: He seems to be going that way at the present time.

LOU: Well, there's no question about it.

ANC: Lou, what's your opinion of night baseball?

LOU: Well, night baseball is strictly a show and is strictly advantageous to the owners' pocketbook, but as far as being a true exhibition of baseball, well, I don't think I can say it is and it's very difficult on the ballplayers themselves. Of course, we realize that the men who work in the daytime like to get out at night and really see a spectacle and we do all in our power to give them their money's worth. But after all it's not really baseball. Real baseball should be played in the daytime, in the sunshine.

ANC: You can't see the balls as well at night as you can in the day, is that the trouble? It's hard on the eyes?

LOU: Well, you can't see the what you call the spin on the ball. You see, it looks faster than it really is and your timing's slightly off.

ANC: Is that why some ballplayers can hit very well at night and not so good during the day and vice versa?

LOU: (Laughter) No, I would say there are no ballplayers that hit better at night than they do in the daytime. Now you look at comparative averages at the

Steve Smart *is a former sandlot star from Rochester, Minnesota. He saw his first major league game in 1957: Brooklyn vs. the Braves at Milwaukee County Stadium.*

close of the season and I believe that you will see it's strictly a pitcher's game at night.

ANC: More close, more low-hit games.

LOU: More low-hit games and low scores. Now [Cotton] Pippen beat us a night game in Philadelphia, our first night game, he beat us 3 to 2 and we had pretty fair luck with him in two innings in a daytime game.

ANC: I remember that time. I think that was the first game Philadelphia won from the Yanks in a long time, wasn't it?

LOU: Yes, I believe it is. That particular night game.

ANC: We often hear about ballplayers as ballplayers, Lou. Of course, the fans have their favorites. But ballplayers see things that the fans don't see. For instance, one ballplayer may be very smooth and make plays that the fans wouldn't catch. So who would you say has been the ballplayers' ballplayer?

LOU: Well, there's no question about the three greatest and most outstanding ballplayers in the history of baseball have been Ruth, Cobb and Wagner. Now personally, Ruth was a typical fans' ballplayer and Cobb was a typical individual ballplayer, because I believe he had more enemies on the ball field than any man in the history of baseball because he played it so hard and he thought of nobody, I mean cutting or slashing or anything to gain his end, he went through. And yet I think

Honus Wagner was the typical ballplayers' ballplayer or the managers' ballplayer. Because he was always thinking of winning and doing what he could for the other fellow, for himself, and for his manager and for the fans.

ANC: That's Babe Ruth, Ty Cobb and Honus Wagner.

LOU: That's right.

ANC: Do you think there's a different—of course, this is a question that comes up from time to time—do you think there's really a different brand of baseball played in the National and American Leagues?

LOU: (Laughter) Well, being an American Leaguer I'd be naturally prejudiced, but the difference is not exactly noticeable, I don't believe. Of course, the American League will use the figures in the World Series and All Star games of the last ten or twelve years as proof.

ANC: When you take the star players from both leagues, I imagine each has about as many star players as the other.

LOU: Well, no question about it.

ANC: Do ballplayers read the sport sections as avidly as the fans do, that is, read the sports pages, the line-ups of the day's games and do they resent criticisms of sportswriters and the boos of the fans?

Dwight Merriam interviewing Lou Gehrig on August 22, 1939

LOU: They don't resent the fair criticism and they probably read the sports pages much more closely than the fan does because ballplayers know how to read the box score. They read down below and they read everything very carefully, and they can probably give you more of a resume of a ballgame from not being there. They can tell you more about it. That's how closely they read that box score.

ANC: It's business to them, and fun for the average public.

LOU: Right, we read it every morning as a business, where the fan will only read it at his convenience, you see.

ANC: Are the pitchers able to get an idea of the weakness of the various players from the box scores at all?

LOU: Definitely. We may have trouble with a certain type hitter and we may pitch him high, we may pitch him low, we may switch on him, we may do different things. And yet we see a certain type pitcher that will have success with them continually and we know his type of pitching will be a weakness, so we tend to throw him accordingly.

ANC: I've often wondered, how is it possible for one pitcher to know all about every batter that he pitches against. Is that entirely possible?

LOU: Absolutely is. A lot of major league ballplayers even go so far that they don't depend on their memory at all. They go home at night and jot down the weaknesses of certain hitters and any time they come to that town they take out that notebook and review the notes and they refresh themselves and when they walk out at the ballpark they know the first man hits a high ball. They know the second man, the third man hit low balls. And then they pitch accordingly.

ANC: You've got to have an education of some sort to play baseball?

LOU: No question about it!

ANC: Do you believe the young player should receive thorough seasoning in the minor leagues?

LOU: I don't think there's any question about that. There are very few major league ballplayers in the history of the game that have proven themselves capable of jumping from the sandlot or college into major league baseball, and it usually requires two to four years' seasoning and then another year's seasoning in the major leagues while they are learning. Constant reminding of different things. Which plays they're making wrong or little "pepper-uppers" is what we call them.

ANC: That has often been proved by what we call players who have come up too soon and have had to go back.

LOU: Oh, no doubt about it.

ANC: Do the majority of ballplayers tighten up during a World Series game or do they usually take it as another game?

LOU: That depends entirely on the individual's makeup. Now personally, I was always as tight as a drum before the game, before the World Series game. The constant milling around, the hundreds of photographers, the hundreds of newspapermen, and the thousands of requests for autographs on scorecards and baseballs and things like that. They tend to tense a ballplayer up. But the minute that bell rang and the field was cleared and the first ball was thrown and the first ball hit my glove, then I was just as relaxed and it was just another ballgame after that.

ANC: It sort of reminds me of players on the stage. They're tightened up until they get out on the stage reciting their lines, then they are as free and easy as possible.

LOU: That's quite similar.

ANC: Is it the same before every World Series game or just the first?

LOU: Oh, every game. Every game.

ANC: There's no game like the World Series game?

LOU: Well, the All Star game's just the same.

ANC: Are you in favor of the All Star game?

LOU: Oh, I think it's a great thing. Just great. I'm thrilled to death every time I can attend one and you can imagine the thrill I can get when I was chosen to play in them.

ANC: The receipts from the All Star game go to what?

LOU: They go to a benefit the ballplayers have amongst themselves, an organization that we pay ten dollars a year to, to take care of the old ballplayers in the event of sickness and inability to take care of themselves in their old age.

ANC: Is that fund being disbursed at the present time?

LOU: Oh yes, it's one of the most honest organizations in the country and we get booklets every year telling not the details and not the names, but we know just how much is donated to whom and where. But not publicly.

ANC: Thinking of an organization such as that brings to mind another question. Do you think there will ever be such a thing as a players' union?

LOU: I don't see how it possibly could work. Because at that rate a boy would not be rewarded for his abilities. A ballplayers' union would put everybody in the same class and it would put the inferior ballplayer, the boy who has a tendency to loaf in the same class, as far as salary is concerned, with the fellow who hustles and has great ability and takes advantage of his ability.

ANC: So for that reason, a union would not work as far as you see?

LOU: I can't see it now.

ANC: Would you say ballplayers as a whole play for salary or do you think the majority play for the love of the game?

LOU: I think it's a combination of both. I think every ballplayer is so crazy about the game that he'd go out and play in his spare time if he weren't able to earn a living at it and, of course, we must earn our bread and butter too.

ANC: It's nice to be able to earn money while having fun.

LOU: (Laughter) Oh, exactly right.

ANC: Would you say the young ballplayers now coming up, on average compare with ballplayers of other days?

LOU: I think they're just as good.

ANC: Fine. I'm glad to hear that from a man who should be able to make judgment.

LOU: Absolutely. Men like Connie Mack who've been in baseball for over fifty years still insist baseball today is as good if not superior to baseball of thirty, thirty-five years ago.

ANC: And I can't imagine anybody not knowing, that is, knowing any better than Connie Mack.

LOU: That's the truth.

ANC: What advice would you give, as a baseball player, to boys hoping to become professional baseball players? That is, to keep their health and fitness.

LOU: Well, to be able to play, you have to keep your health. And in order to be able to play, you have to be able to practice and put in a great deal of time. And you have to be a regular fellow or in other words you have to play the game hard and you have to play it to win and you have to play it cleanly. Because if you don't fulfill these qualifications in the major leagues, why the boys just force you to become a lone wolf. They pay no attention to you. That's why you very seldom see a ballplayer who is actually conceited. He might be accused of being conceited because he might feel ill that day or he might have a member of his family, his baby or his wife or somebody, might be ill. And he might be rushing to get home and when he leaves the park there might be five hundred or a thousand youngsters out there requesting his autograph, and often he may rush right on through them in order to get to his car and get home to see his family or whatever might be wrong. And yet a ballplayer under those conditions will be accused of being conceited. I don't think it's quite fair, under those conditions. But in my experience, I don't think I've ever come in contact with any of the boys that we could really call conceited.

ANC: In addition to being a regular fellow they have to keep regular habits.

LOU: Oh, exactly. I've been in the business seven-teen years and I don't think there were a half-dozen nights in the seventeen years that I didn't average my nine or ten hours sleep every night.

ANC: Do baseball teams, professional baseball teams, have hard and fast rules you must keep? That is, in the way of regular hours for sleep? Regular hours for meals?

LOU: They like for their ballplayers to be in the hotel between 11:00 and 12:00 at night. But they don't enforce rigid rules except to those few who absolutely have to have it, who can't govern themselves. But the philosophy in baseball is that a man is making his living at the game and he must be in shape every day when he gets out on that ballfield, and if he's not in shape, why he's transferred down the river. So it's entirely up to himself.

ANC: Who are some of the young players you've seen in action, Lou, that you feel are coming stars?

LOU: Well, I see young [Ted] Williams come out of Minneapolis, he's around this part of the country. And we've got young Joe Gordon with the Yankees. And we've got a young fellow by the name of Charlie Keller, and a young man by the name of [Atley] Donald and there's a couple of young fellas down in St. Louis. A pitcher by the name of [Bob] Harris and pitcher by the name of [Jack] Kramer who looks mighty well, and you've got a young pitcher who was sent back for more experience, had a sore arm, with Boston; a fella by the name of [Woody] Rich. We've got a lot of promising ballplayers coming up this year.

ANC: By the way, what has happened to Donald after he won all those first games then he lost two or three now in a row, hasn't he?

LOU: Well, if we knew that question we'd have rectified it long before now. (Laughter)

ANC: Would you say that baseball is keeping its hold on the fans?

LOU: The attendance figures this year far surpass, I think, those of last year, and I know that last year we drew more people, the Yankees as a whole, than any year that I've been with the team since nineteen-hundred and twenty-three.

ANC: It's good news, isn't it?

LOU: (Laughter)

ANC: Well, for the last quarter hour, ladies and gentlemen, we've brought you a personal interview with Lou Gehrig, for many years a star first baseman for the New York Yankees. Thank you, Lou, for giving us some of your time for this interesting interview. I'm sure all of our listeners join me in wishing you all the luck in the future.

The Curse Of Mickey Haefner

Phil Bergen

Ask many a Red Sox fan and they will tell you that this "Curse of the Bambino" business is a sham, created by a Boston sportswriter as a means of explaining more than seventy years of futility, numerous close calls, and heartbreaking losses that suggest a higher power is watching over the fate of New England's team. To be sure, in my lifetime, Series tragedies in 1967, 1975, and 1986 have all hinged on seventh game defeats. A flare hit caught, a ground ball fielded, an off day by Bob Gibson and the Curse is over. Realistically, in each of these Series the Red Sox were rightful underdogs to superior teams. Gibson's Cardinals, the Big Red Machine, and the Gooden-Hernandez-Carter Mets combined pitching, power, speed and defense in what turned out to be World Championship combinations. While the Sox often rode the bats of righthanded power to the doorway of championship success, lack of pitching depth, a hereditary lack of speed, and often suspect defense kept Tom Yawkey's club from going the final mile. In the case of 1967, Dick Williams can be credited with doing it with mirrors. Generous amounts of luck, career years, and breaks at the right time provided a generation of Sox fans with their happiest season. Like first love, there is always something special about a championship season after two decades of famine.

The Bosox powerhouse—Aah, but 1946. There's the rub. There's where the Sox were a powerhouse, argu-

Phil Bergen *works for the Massachusetts Historical Commission as a National Register consultant, and roots for the Cotuit Ketteleers of the Cape Cod League, his baseball heart having been broken by the Strike of '94.*

ably the strongest club in the majors, with a realistic chance to win it all. With Williams, York, Doerr, Dom DiMaggio, and Pesky at bat; with Ferriss, Hughson, Dobson, Mickey Harris and an adequate bullpen; with a runaway victory in the first postwar American League; with their opponents exhausted from a tense pennant race followed by a unique postseason play-off—here was the chance for a World's Championship to usher in a several-year span of first-rate teams. Perhaps it would have been the Red Sox to finish first with numbing regularity in the 1950s. Remember, at this time the Yankees were coming off two straight also-ran seasons, teams were realigning themselves with returning veterans, newly seasoned rookies, and suddenly productive farm systems filling the gaps. Baseball was in a state of flux, and in the AL, where the influence of black players was much more slowly felt, there was a strong possibility that a non-Yankee team could have gained control.

Then there's Mickey Haefner

The playoff problem—Mickey's role in Red Sox and American League history came about due to a difference in rules between the leagues. Baseball today is seen as a complete entity with few interleague differences, aside from the designated hitter. One difference that had not raised its head until 1946 was the playoff system to be used in the event of a 154-game deadlock. Several seasons had come down to close finishes, but until 1946 the season-long schedule had been enough to differentiate between first and second place. The National League race between the Dodgers and Cardinals has been well documented elsewhere, most recently in

Frederick Turner's *When the Boys Came Back*, a well-researched history of the 1946 season. When the Redbirds and Bums photo-finished (with Cards castoff Mort Cooper beating Brooklyn on the final day), a league mandated best-of-three playoff was required to settle the question of who would face the Red Sox. With an off day and travel day thrown in, the Red Sox were looking at a prolonged stretch of inactivity ahead. National Leaguers said that a best-of-three series allowed for some leeway in picking the better team, that one off day should not be allowed to ruin six month's hard work. Junior circuit supporters, who would have preferred a sudden-death contest, argued that a week's layoff unduly penalized their champion and that baseball's continuing daily rhythm mandated as little down time as possible.

The all star team—Rather than spend the idle time, which threatened to be as long as a week, in practice sessions, Sox general manager Eddie Collins remembered a 1910 postseason series that he participated in with the Philadelphia Athletics. That year the National League season ended a week later than the American League, and the A's played a series of exhibition games against a picked all-star team which included Walter Johnson, Ty Cobb, and Tris Speaker, before beating the Chicago Cubs in five games.

Bob Feller had already rounded up a team to begin a celebrated series of games against Satchel Paige and his Negro League mates, a series which achieved more attention in 1946 than usual with Jackie Robinson destined for Brooklyn the following year. But working on short notice, American League president Will Harridge managed to round up a representative team, not a great one, to face the Sox in a three-game series.

It says a lot about league loyalty in 1946 that ballplayers were willing to spend their first week in the off-season playing meaningless practice games in order to help their champions get ready for the series. One must remember that interleague trading was much less prevalent at that time, and players often played their careers entirely in one league. None of the all-stars had played in the senior circuit by 1946, and there was a strong spirit of cooperation in a joint endeavor against a common enemy, whether it be Brooklyn or St. Louis. It was also more common in those days for major leaguers to barnstorm immediately after the season, while the weather was good, playing exhibition games.

Harridge produced a team with four future Hall of Famers, several above-average players, and a couple of men unknown to fans of today. The team had a Washington slant because the Senators had finished the regular season in Boston and were already on hand. They had finished fourth in '46 after coming in second the year before, and were a respectable if not an outstanding team. Third baseman Cecil Travis had led the AL in hits the year that Ted Williams hit .406 and Joe DiMaggio had his 56-game streak, but he was possibly the charter member of the "he lost it in the war" club. Travis had suffered frozen feet in the Battle of the Bulge, and this had curtailed his speed and range. He batted .251 in '46 and would finish his big league career the following year with a .216 mark.

Outfielder Stan Spence's figures (.292/16/87) represented a career year for him. He would be traded to Boston in 1948 in time to play in the American League's first playoff game.

Backup catcher Jake Early had hit only .201 in 64 games. Appearing on this team could be regarded as a career highlight.

Right fielder Joe Grace was probably the least known of the all-stars, hitting .278 with three homers. 1947 would be his last year; being on hand in Boston probably secured his place on the team.

Of more import was the other outfielder. Joe DiMaggio's appearance undoubtedly was a favor to younger brother Dominic, but having him in center field brought immediate respect to the team.

Another power hitter to test Red Sox pitching was Hank Greenberg, the American League home run and RBI leader. Having Greenberg and DiMaggio batting back-to-back in Fenway Park would provide a solid offensive base for any team. Ironically, this would be Greenberg's final appearance as a Detroit Tiger. He would be traded out of the league to Pittsburgh during the offseason in a deal that would go against the custom of keeping stars in their own league.

Joining Greenberg in the all-star infield was dependable Yankee Snuffy Stirnweiss (.251/0/37), the 1945 batting leader, and Old Aches and Pains Luke Appling, who had hit .309 that year. New Englander Birdie Tebbetts of the Tigers would handle the catching. He was heading home anyway after the season and no doubt impressed the Sox, as he was traded to Boston during the offseason.

The pitching staff had a decided lefthanded look, the result of a request by the Red Sox to Harridge for southpaws. With the possibility of facing Howie Pollet and Harry Brecheen in St.Louis or Vic Lombardi and Joe Hatten in Brooklyn, all lefties, the Sox wanted to look at as much lefthand pitching as possible. Five of the seven pitchers the Sox faced were indeed lefthanded, led by arguably the best leftie in the game, Hal Newhouser. With a league-leading 26-9 mark and a 1.94 ERA Newhouser had silenced critics who claimed he was only a star against diluted wartime hitting.

Newhouser's Tiger teammates Stubby Overmire (5-7, 4.62) and Dizzy Trout (17-13, 2.34) added quality, and White Sox Ed Lopat (13-13, 2.73) was only a few years away from stardom with the Yankees. Joe Page was already with the Yankees. His 9-8 record presaged

Luke Appling, Old Aches and Pains

while Zoldak and Lewis never appeared in a box score. It would have been cruel indeed for the two players to sit on the bench for three games, so undoubtedly they were not present. Greenberg was delayed on business en route to Boston and missed the first game. His place at first was taken by pitcher Lopat (who had hit .253 that year). The team was "managed" by Detroit's Steve O'Neill, who could hardly have

his greater bullpen fame. (He only had three saves in '46 and started in nearly half his appearances.)

The appearance of Philadelphia's Phil Marchildon on the staff was a tribute to one of the amazing stories to come out of World War II. Canadian Marchildon's plane was shot down over Germany in 1944, and he remained in a prisoner of war camp until it was liberated by the British the following spring. Malnourished, he was treated in an English hospital before being discharged. Amazingly, Marchildon pitched for the A's later that summer and recovered sufficiently to win 13 games in 1946.

And then there was Mickey Haefner from the Senators, whose fame to this point was tied to being one of the four knuckleballers who made up Washington's rotation in 1945. His 14-11 record with a 2.85 ERA was creditable, but his lasting influence in Boston would hinge on one pitch.

Newspaper accounts of the team's makeup also included Yankees Billy Johnson and Tommy Henrich, St. Louis Browns pitcher Sam Zoldak and Washington outfielder Buddy Lewis. Johnson and Henrich never showed up for the games (talk about Old Reliable!),

been challenged with nine players for eight positions, and Frank Shellenback served as pitching coach. Umpires already in Boston would work the games. The All-Stars would split the gate receipts, while the Sox continued to draw their regular salaries. Regular season ticket prices would remain in effect.

It sounded like a good idea. Unfortunately, the good intentions would backfire and seriously crimp the Red Sox's plans for victory.

Exhibition fiasco—To begin with, New England's weather refused to cooperate. It was so cold and damp that the Boston Yanks–New York Giants football game was postponed for one night to better attract a crowd at Braves Field. Tebbetts and Trout, driving to Boston from Detroit, reported traveling through snow in the Berkshires. Crowds, if they can be called that, were miniscule and *totaled* just over 6,500 for the three games. Even the lure of their hometown champions going up against DiMaggio, Greenberg, and others was not enough to lure Bostonians out on chilly weekday afternoons, especially as the NL games that really counted were being broadcast on radio.

And these exhibitions were not really taken seriously by the players. In fact, Boston papers reported that they quickly took on the aspect of a practice game. "As it went on, it appeared the idea was to get it over with as soon as possible," reported the Boston *Post*. Every game was played in well under two hours, as the frigid players hurried through the nine innings. The opening game took only eighty-five minutes.

For what it was worth, the Sox took two out of three from the All-Stars, winning the first game, 2-0, dropping the second, 4-2, and rebounding to take the rubber game, 4-1. The All-Stars used two pitchers in each game, the Red Sox three, and the frosty hurlers were ahead of the frozen batters in every contest.

What is remembered today about the series occurred in the opening game. With amazing foresight, *Post* beat writer Jack Malaney had written that morning:

It isn't possible to remind the Sox that they must be careful and not take chances in these games. It is when players start being careful that injuries are suffered…the All-Stars must bear down and play hard baseball. It is a cinch that they would not want to be responsible for an injury that might take a Sox regular out of the Series, but suppose one of them was sliding into second base and accidently cut either Bobby Doerr or Johnny Pesky, who would be making plays instinctively!

By the fifth inning the Red Sox were up, 2-0. Ted Williams had walked and scored in the second and grounded out in the third. Following Dom DiMaggio, who singled, to the plate, Williams studied the left-handed Haefner for a knuckleball:

"When the ball was halfway to me," he told the Boston *Herald*, "I saw that it was spinning so I got set to belt the curve. Then I saw it wasn't going to curve and I sort of tucked in my shoulder and took the pitch on the elbow."

Haefner's pitch had struck

Williams solidly on the elbow joint. The Thumper trotted gingerly to first and was replaced immediately by Leon Culberson. By the time he reached the clubhouse the elbow had swollen up to the size of a tomato. Trainer Win Green and Sox doctor Ralph McCarthy immediately sent Williams for X-rays which came back negative for a fracture.

"Ted Williams, his right arm swollen, is in very bad shape," began Gordon Campbell's column in the afternoon *Traveler* that day, throwing fear into Bostonians on their way home from work. For the moment the game was forgotten—Malaney's prediction had come true. The health of the leading Red Sox hitter had been altered by a pitch in a meaningless game.

Using the rest of their regular lineup throughout, the Sox maintained their 2-0 lead behind the pitching of Tex Hughson, Joe Dobson, and Bill Zuber. Haefner re-

Dizzy Trout

tired after the fateful fifth.

Other Boston baseball news intruded on the game. The up-and-coming Braves pulled off a major trade, sending veteran second baseman Billy Herman to Pittsburgh for Bob Elliott. Herman would become manager of the woeful Bucs, while Elliott's next two seasons would result in an MVP award and a World Series. For the first time in thirty years, the Braves and Sox would both be contenders.

If the first game produced a memorable moment in Sox history through a hit batsman, Games 2 and 3 did not develop into a beanball war. Indeed, the remainder of the series had few remarkable achievements. Irrepressible Dizzy Trout clowned his way through his five-inning stint, throwing eephus pitches to Boston hitters and engaging in a running dialogue with umpire Red Jones, who "played the part of a stooge with his usual good grace," reported the Boston *Herald*. Veteran Sox relief pitcher Mike Ryba, the twenty-fifth man on the roster, pitched two perfect innings, striking out Greenberg and DiMaggio in succession, as Boston emptied its bench. But the lack of true effort was reflected in the fact that manager Cronin missed the final two games to scout the National Leaguers in Brooklyn.

Rudy York homered in Game 3 for the only circuit clout of the series, off Hal Newhouser, who received an ovation after his stint by Boston fans appreciative of his "terrifically fast" pitching. His all-out effort was indicative of the league pride felt by all of the all-stars, a compliment that was returned by the Red Sox. "Those guys deserve a lot of credit for coming to Boston just to help us out," said Williams, whose participation was curtailed after his injury. "We want you to beat the daylights out of those National Leaguers, and if we can help, we're glad to do it," replied Cecil Travis, who could easily have been excused if he had begged off.

The sparse crowds provided a lean payday for the all-stars. Snuffy Stirnweiss lamented, "I wish now I'd made my wife pay to get in." It was reported that Tom Yawkey dug into his own pocket to add to the pot. Journeyman outfielder Tom McBride led all batters by going 5 for 11 in the series; Snuffy Stirnweiss went 4 for 10 and Luke Appling 3 for 12 for the All-Stars. York had the only home run, Appling the lone triple. Some competitive spirit was evident. The all-stars stole four bases. Stan Spence argued long and loud with umpire Bill Summers when his drive down the right field line was ruled foul, and Joe DiMaggio received kudos from the *Herald* as he hustled from first to third on a Stan Spence single to center. But it was evident that the spirit of a regular season game was lacking, and despite the good intentions, much of the benefit provided by the advanced competition was diminished.

Results—The lingering result of the series was Ted Williams' injury. Constant heat treatment, diathermy baths, and inactivity was prescribed in order for Ted to be ready for the series opener. Coupled with a chest cold that affected his stamina, Williams' only World Series appearance was a bust. Five singles, one RBI, and an inability to beat the Cardinals' version of Boudreau's shift began the talk in Boston that the Splinter did not come through in the clutch, and Williams' unproductive series would remain a sore subject with him throughout his career.

Whether a totally healthy Williams might have made a difference is open to conjecture. But a one-run, late-inning loss in a seven-game series always allows for the losers to lament "What if?" That lamentation continues in Boston a half century later. Williams' woes were also compounded by rumors of an impending trade in the offseason that would have sent the Splendid Splinter to either Detroit or New York, depending on the source. Turner, in his book, implies that the rumors were deliberately leaked by Boston sportswriter Dave Egan on the eve of the Series—the worst possible time—but whatever the reason, the fact remained that Williams' physical problems were exacerbated with the threat of future upheaval. Egan's antipathy to Williams was well documented and the rumors could not help but throw Williams off his game.

Five years later the Dodgers and Giants tied for the National League pennant and played a best-of-three series culminating in the most famous home run in major league history. The Yankees, the eventual World Series opponent, had several days to wait.

They rested.

The All-Stars (* Led League)

The Brain Trust:

Steve O'Neill (Det) Manager

Frank Shellenback (Det) Coach

The Players:

Birdie Tebbetts: (Det) C 87 G. .243/1/34—To Sox in '47

Jake Early (Wash) C 64 G .201/4/18

Hank Greenberg (Det) (HoF) 1b .277/44*/127*—To Pit in '47, 1 yr to go

Snuffy Stirnweiss (NY) 2b .251/7/37—'45 Bat Champ

Luke Appling (Chi) (HoF) Ss .309/1/35

Cecil Travis (Wash) 3b .252/1/56—Retired after '47, .216

Joe DiMaggio (NY) (HoF) Of .290/25/95—1st under .300 back from service

Stan Spence (Wash) Of .292/16/87—To Bos in '48

Joe Grace (Wash) Of .278/3/44—Career ends in '47

Pitchers:

Hal Newhouser (Det) (HoF) (L) 26*-9 1.94

Stubby Overmire (Det) (L) 5-7 4.62

Mickey Haefner (Wash) (L) 14-11 2.85

Ed Lopat (Chi) (L) P - 1b 13-13 2.73 .253 BA

Joe Page (NY) (L) 9-8 3.57 3 Sv—Started half the time

Dizzy Trout (Det) (R) 17-13 2.34

Phil Marchildon (Phil) (R) 13-16* 3.49

Umpires:

Bill Summers

Red Jones

Joe Paparella

Forgotten Champions

Greg Beston

The 1946 Boston Red Sox had the chance to become one of the great teams of all time, but because they were given so little competition by the rest of the American League the team floundered over the final third of the season. Boston, which started the season 41-9, had all but wrapped up the American League pennant by the All-Star break, then mysteriously dropped off in production through August and September. The team ended up winning an impressive 104 games, but its sluggish play at the end of the year led to a crushing defeat in the World Series against the St. Louis Cardinals. Everywhere the Red Sox went during the 1946 season, people filled ballparks in record numbers, longing to see the game they had known before World War II. By late May, fans in Boston were spending the night on the sidewalk in order to buy tickets to a Red Sox-Yankees doubleheader.

Before the start of the season, many were unsure how the Red Sox would fare. This would be the first time since 1942 that the Sox would field their true starting nine. There were questions about whether or not Ted Williams, Bobby Doerr, Johnny Pesky, and Tex Hughson had retained their form.

But through the first few months of the season, the Red Sox showed that they were the best in baseball. In one of the greatest stretches any team has ever had, they set records both on the field and at the turnstiles. By June 11, they had already rattled off twelve- and fifteen-game winning streaks, the latter still a club

Greg Beston *has been a SABR member since 1992, and is an avid member of both Retrosheet and the Baseball Records Committee. He recently graduated from Princeton University and will be attending law school in the fall.*

record. Boston's run was a team effort. Through the first half of the season, Red Sox batters were clumped among the leaders in most offensive categories.

Hitting—Returning from three years in the military, Ted Williams had a superb year. He looked to be a shoo-in for the Triple Crown until, like most of his teammates, he slumped over the final third of the season. Still, e finished with a .342 average, 38 homers, and 123 RBIs, second in all three departments. Despite his slump, he was voted MVP for the first time in his career.

In only his second big league season, Johnny Pesky showed why he was the best shortstop in baseball. His early season batting feats included an 11-for-11 hit streak, one short of the all-time record. On May 8 he set an American League record by scoring six runs in a 14-10 victory over the White Sox. He was hitting .430 by early May as the Red Sox cruised to the top of the standings. He too would drop off over the final months of the season, but he would still finish at .335, and lead the league with 208 hits.

Off-season acquisition Rudy York added both veteran influence and a potent bat. He drove in 119 runs, ten of them coming on July 27 in St. Louis, when he socked two grand slams. Dom DiMaggio, Bobby Doerr, and Hal Wagner had All-Star seasons, despite being overshadowed by the slugging of their teammates. Boston's newly acquired veteran players—Wally Moses, Pinky Higgins, and Bob Klinger—blended nicely with the young talent.

Even the obscure players contributed. On April 22 Johnny Pesky was beaned by Washington's Sid

Hudson. He was replaced by Eddie Pellagrini, making his major league debut. When he stepped to the plate in the seventh inning, he homered, joining an elite group who hit home runs in their first at bats.

But it was Williams who continually astounded fans with his batting feats. Questions about whether he had lost his touch were answered on the first pitch of spring training when Ted hit a long home run. In Washington for the season's opener, he hit one of the longest homers ever seen at Griffith Stadium. Even President Harry Truman tipped his hat as Williams trotted by. On June 9 he hit a tremendous blast off Detroit's Fred Hutchinson at Fenway Park. The ball landed thirty-three rows behind the Red Sox bullpen, breaking the straw hat of a man snoozing in the bleachers. Today the seat, nearly 500 feet from home plate, is painted red to signify the blast.

On July 14, in the first game of a doubleheader, Williams knocked three homers out of the park against Cleveland, compelling Indians manager Lou Boudreau

to invent what became known as the Williams Shift. Placing nearly all of his team on the right side of the diamond, Boudreau hoped to cut down on Ted's offensive output. The shift only motivated Williams more, as a week later he hit for the cycle against St. Louis. Williams also had a sharp enough eye at the plate to draw an amazing 156 walks, which helped him score a league-high 142 runs.

Pitching—While the Red Sox were battering opponents left and right, the pitching staff was remarkably solid as well. Boo Ferriss, coming off a rookie season which saw him win 21 games, went 25-6. He put together two winning streaks of ten or more games, matching the feat of the great Walter Johnson. During the team's magical run, Ferriss started the season 10-0, and finished the year with a home record of 13-0. Almost as effective as Ferriss, Tex Hughson went 20-11. Joe Dobson, Mickey Harris, and Jim Bagby rounded out a respectable staff which was overshadowed by the Boston offense.

Team accomplishments—In a fitting touch, the Red Sox hosted the 1946 All-Star game at Fenway Park. With eight Boston players on the squad, the American League cruised to a 12-0 victory. Leading the way was none other than Ted Williams, who went 4-4 with two home runs, the second of which came off a blooper pitch thrown by Pittsburgh's Rip Sewell.

Aside from their individual accomplishments, it is truly astounding what the Red Sox accomplished as a team. They were never swept in any of the twenty-seven doubleheaders they played that year, while they themselves swept fourteen of them, tying an AL record. Against the western clubs at Fenway Park, the Sox started the year 19-0, only to have the streak broken by Cleveland's Bob Feller on June 12. By mid-July, Boston was 28-2 at home against the western teams in the AL In fact, the Red Sox were an amazing 61-16 at home, leading to their first annual attendance of over one million fans.

Late season slump—But almost all of these feats took place during the early portion of the season. When it became evident that Bos-

Tex Hughson

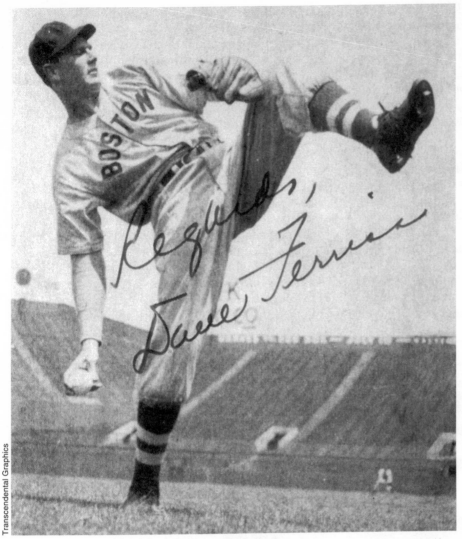

Transcendental Graphics

Dave "Boo" Ferris

an inside-the-park homer because left-fielder Pat Seerey was positioned well toward center. The homer gave the Red Sox a 1-0 victory, clinching the pennant.

While the Cardinals and Dodgers played a three-game playoff series to decide the winner of the National League pennant, it was decided that the Red Sox should stay sharp by playing three exhibition games against all-stars from the American League. In the first game of the series, Washington's Mickey Haefner hit Ted Williams in the elbow with a pitch. Unfortunately, this would hinder his batting throughout the World Series. [See previous article.]

Many Boston fans blamed Williams and Pesky for their team's defeat in the World Series that fall. Pesky is often excoriated, probably unjustly, for "holding the ball" on a relay throw in Game Seven, and Williams was criticized for his poor performance at the plate. But these were the two offensive players who made the biggest contribution during the season. There are many reasons why the 1946 Red Sox lost that fall to the underdog Cardinals, notably St. Louis' strong play and the clutch pitching of Harry Brecheen. But perhaps the biggest reason was the fact that the Red Sox were never seriously challenged during the last half of the 1946 season. They had such an easy time of it that they didn't have to fight their way through their extended late-season slump. While the Cardinals were in a dog fight for the NL title, Boston sat back and sloppily played out the schedule.

Despite their disappointing loss in the series, the Boston Red Sox went 104-50, and gave their fans much to hope for in the remainder of the decade. But it was not to be. The hitters continued to have great success at the plate, but most never again matched their 1946 numbers. The pitching staff fell apart, and Hughson and Ferriss were both out of the majors within five years. The Red Sox came painfully close several times from 1947 to 1950, but they couldn't quite win another pennant. But with one of the greatest starts by any team in history, Boston packed stadiums around the American League, giving fans reassurance that all would be well with the postwar National Pastime.

ton would cakewalk to the pennant, the players began to slump. The day-to-day effects of this drop-off were nearly invisible, as Boston continued to hold a comfortable lead over Detroit and New York. Perhaps if the lead had been smaller, the Sox would have been forced to regroup and refocus. But August and September breezed by with the Red Sox eying the upcoming World Series. Since the team never had a lead of less than ten games after July 15, Cronin would often send his regulars home from road trips a day early, to rest them for the postseason.

Clinching the pennant turned out to be the team's toughest task of the year. Needing just one more victory to wrap up the title, Boston management brought champagne along as the club began the season's final western road trip. The Sox, however, proceeded to go into a prolonged losing streak. With the bubbly on ice, they were swept in Detroit and were beaten in Cleveland. There, finally, Boudreau's shift would come back to haunt the Indians' manager on September 13, when Williams lofted a routine fly to left field that turned into

A Diary of the Negro Leagues

G. Edward White

Afew years ago I made a speech to a group of lawyers and academics on the West Coast. In introducing me, the speaker said that I was planning a book on the history of baseball. After the speech there was a reception and two youngish lawyers from the area came up to me. One was black, a graduate of a California law school. He seemed moderately interested in the subject of my speech, but much more interested in my baseball project. He asked if I were planning a chapter on the Negro Leagues. I said I was if I could find something more to say. There had been a fair number of books, some good ones, I felt, on the subject. The topic belonged in any account of baseball in the early twentieth century, but I felt a certain amount of unease writing about it, especially because I wanted to address the subject of race consciousness, black and white, and I wasn't at all sure I could convey both sides of that consciousness with sufficient richness.

The conversation took place in a crowded room and was confined by that setting. I went on to have additional conversations on widely divergent topics and did not attach any particular significance to my chat about baseball. When I returned to the East, however, I got a phone call from the young black lawyer with whom I had talked. He said he had done some thinking about what we had discussed, and the Negro Leagues. He had a document he was inclined to show me, but he wanted to talk about it first.

The document was a diary that his grandfather, who had played Negro League baseball for many years, had

kept. The young man's grandfather had attended college, had taught high school, and had more education than most of his teammates. The diary was described to me as "just random jottings, about all kinds of things," in the form of entries apparently compiled at the end of a day, perhaps while the ballclub was traveling or after the players had checked into their lodgings. Not much in the diary was about baseball itself. It was more about the life of a Negro Leagues player and his acquaintances.

There was some sensitivity about the diary, the young man explained. His grandfather had kept it for his own amusement, and to show family members. He never had any intention of publishing it, even when he noticed an increased public interest in the Negro Leagues. There were several reasons. First, the grandfather was a proud man, proud of his education and his capacity to write, and he regarded many of the entries, written in haste, as crudely done. Second, his observations had a certain detachment, both about his contemporaries and about his life, and he did not want to offend old teammates or their relatives. Third, he genuinely didn't think that the diary would be interesting to anyone save a handful of persons who had experienced that world. He said to his grandson, in fact, that the young black players in major league baseball today didn't have any idea about the Negro Leagues, and didn't care. He often expressed some contempt and even bitterness about that.

It was the last reason, paradoxically, that had made his grandson think about publishing the diary someday. He felt that his grandfather's instincts were right: today's black players didn't know the history of black

G. Edward White *is University Professor and John B. Minor Professor of Law at the University of Virginia. Among his books is* Creating the National Pastime *(Princeton, 1996).*

baseball. They didn't appreciate what their Negro Leagues predecessors had to endure; they couldn't imagine the world of major league baseball completely closed to them. They bitched about racism and tokenism, and how much harder it was for blacks to make "the show" than whites, but they had things pretty good, and they had no idea what things had been like only sixty years before. Maybe they should be exposed to his grandfather's diary as a kind of lesson. For one thing his grandfather's diary was about being black, and being able to play ball, and appreciating those things.

In thinking things over, the young man said, he'd hit on an idea. He would show me the diary, and I could use it in my book, but he would respect his grandfather's wishes at the same time. If I would agree to a few conditions, he would let me see if I wanted to use it. First, his grandfather could not be identified, and some details would be slightly changed or omitted so that anonymity could be preserved. Second, the diary should be silently edited, removing passages that seemed to give offense or be hastily written. Third, only excerpts from the diary could appear in my book, in case he changed his mind and wanted to publish the entire document at some point.

I agreed that I would respect the conditions, but I pointed out that baseball aficionados were shrewd, persevering, and resourceful. They were likely to ferret out his grandfather's identity, however much I sought to conceal it. I also said that I did not necessarily think it a good idea to delete "offensive" or "crude" passages, since they might convey authenticity, and that crudity or offensiveness, especially in historical documents, was often in the eye of the beholder. I volunteered to change names, places, and dates if I thought references were too pointed, and to rewrite the diary in other respects to deter sleuthing. I agreed to show him my version of the diary when I had completed it, which I have. He has approved this version, and he remains more sanguine than I that we will be successful in concealing the author's identity. I have agreed not to reveal my source.

Friday 12th. Another spring! Of course I don't get the cold weather in the winter like some of the guys do. And I keep my arm as fit as I can. No time to get it back in shape, I got to pitch in games right away. We got to make some money. The boys look mean again this year. I hope we get some good competition. Driving all around on those dusty roads, playing on some cowpasture of a field, staying in fleabag places is harder to take when the team you're playing is a bunch of local stiffs who can't even catch the ball. Still it is fun to doctor up those baseballs and watch them dance.

Tuesday 16th. A funny thing happened to me. We were heading north to start regular barnstorming and stopped in Columbus. One of the cars broke down and we had to stop to fix it so we ended up driving all night and when we got into town it was the morning of the game and it was raining. Mr. Brown don't recognize rainouts, so we were planning to play but the other team says if we wait a couple of hours the weather will stay dry and the field will drain. So I head off from the ballpark into town, thinking maybe I'll get a paper to read. I go into the local drugstore and ask the girl behind the counter where I can find a paper. I got my uniform on, so I guess it looks a bit peculiar, and I can see her looking at me the way white folks do a fair amount, a look that says is he white or black. I'm pretty light-skinned and when I got my cap on you can't tell that my hair's curly. She looks at me like, "You got to be white, boy, 'cause a nigger with a baseball uniform on wouldn't be readin' no paper, couldn't read at all." At the same time she's lookin' like, "You is not so bad lookin', boy, I wonder if I hopes you is white or black."

I see that look so I make sure to speak to her as white as I can, not dropping the ends of my words, not using any colored slang. She directs me to where I can find a paper and I go on out.

Well, next thing I know we are out there playing the game and there she is in the stands with a girl friend, white, of course. In Columbus it's no big deal whites coming to our games, white folks and blacks both do, more whites usually, we charge 50 cents a head. I see her and I tip my cap. Some of the boys see that and they start ragging me, saying where'd you meet that white trash, who's that puss, that kind of thing. By now, of course, she knows if I ain't black I'm the only white guy on the team and we're a pretty dark lot.

I don't know what got into me, usually I'm a pretty straightminded guy, and I don't fool too much with the women, 'cause I've seen some guys pick up clap and that can set you back, and a lot of the women that hang around the club are pretty ugly for my taste. But I guess I wanted to see if the fact that now she knew I was black made any difference to her. I wasn't pitching that day so I coached first. I strutted out to the bag pretty good and I tried to make a good show of myself, chatter up the other guys. I wasn't much for that usually and some of the boys figured me out.

At one point, T. J. Young hit a hard ball down the first base line, fair by a few feet. I yelled, "Yessuh, that baby was *hit*. Yessuh, that's the hardest hit ball I've see this year, or my name ain't _____. Of course, I wanted that girl to know my name case she wanted to look me up later. We were staying the night in Columbus. The boys knew why I did it, too. They knew I never talked up plays like that.

After the game a bunch of us went out to dinner. I didn't expect I'd see any white women there and I didn't. Then we went back to the hotel and I didn't expect to see any there, and I didn't. But sometimes women would find out where you were staying and call you on the phone. I figured if she'd do anything, she'd do that. But nobody called for me. I went to bed, and some of the boys was ribbin' me pretty good about it. "Looks like she found some more money," they said.

The next day we get packed up and are loading the cars and there she is, with her girl friend. She comes up to me and says, "Hi, Mr. _____," calls me by the name I'd called myself, full name. Then she says, "I hope I see you again in Columbus sometime." Well, the boys are just about cracked up, and I can't think of anything to say. So I just say, "Goodbye, then," and she and her girl friend wave.

Now of course I can't usually figure women but I gotta say that whole thing puzzles my mind. I still don't know whether she was glad or sad I was black. Anyway, when we get back to Columbus I'm going to call her bluff.

Thursday 9th. Well, I never thought I'd travel as much as I have in my lifetime. Been all around the country and now we are going to Mexico! Well, I'll go anywhere the money is and I can pitch some ball. We hear things are pretty fine for colored players down there, and the Mexicans are crazy about ball.

Now I do have my doubts about Satchel running this trip. Of course, Satchel is a great pitcher, the finest control I've ever seen. And he's a great showman. He picked that stuff up when he was with the Black Lookouts. He plays the crowd, does stunts, but of course he's careful only to do them against weak hitters. Me, I like my baseball straight. I think Satchel plays up to the white folks, gives them the Stepin Fetchit act. Of course, he don't like whites, he's just in it for the money, he'd sleep with as many white women as he could. But I don't like that clowning stuff.

The main problems that I see with Satchel are two. First, he's just plain unreliable. You never know where he's going to be, how long he's going to stay somewhere. Things are never quite what Satch says. He'll say, "We got a guarantee of ten grand," then it turns out it was one grand for ten games. "We'll pack the house every night," then it turns out there's a carnival booked and we can't play. Second, Satchel is only out for himself. I got to hand it to him, he is great at working the owners and drawing the fans, and he'll always listen to a better offer. So he makes sure he does well. But he don't care about the rest of his teammates. They are just his supporting cast. Satch especially don't want other pitchers doing too well. He don't want you stealing his thunder.

Friday 10th. I'm going to try to write something down every night on this trip because this is sure interesting and who knows when I'll come this way again. I

got to say for Satch, he can put people in the stands. And thus far we've had pretty good ball. Of course, the other team can't speak English and we can't speak Spanish, but that doesn't much matter in baseball games.

I'm pitching tomorrow so today I just rested in the dugout. I've been trying to observe the people on the streets, in the stands, see how they look at us. Some ballplayers say the Mexicans don't look down on colored players. I say they look at us like we're pretty strange. But of course we are to them. Any Americans are strange to them. We have been staying in a nice hotel, better than we'd get back home. Whites are in the hotel too, Mexicans, of course. And so far it looks like we can go in restaurants without anybody making a fuss. But we still get stared at plenty.

Saturday 11th. I pitched and won the game. Andy Porter hit a home run, and Cool Papa drove them crazy on the bases. That man is amazing. I've heard of him being around for fifteen years at least, and if he's slowed down any I'd like to see it. If he hits a single it will be a double if you hesitate. On the bench Cool Papa doesn't say much. I don't think he's had much book learning. But he takes pretty good care of himself and he's dedicated to the game. I plan to do that myself. I plan to play in this game as long as I can. Pretty good money, more than I could make teaching or coaching. And much more fun. When you have a good day on the mound, like I did today, you can just feel those batters in your hand, you just twist them around, change speeds, give them the curves, rub the ball up, make it break. They get so frustrated! They come up, sure they're gonna rap—they'll yell from the bench, "You got a glass arm, you got nothin'." Not down here, of course, you can't understand what they say. Then when you throw them some junk and when it dips under their bat you can see the smoke coming out of their ears. Then you feel like you are a man and you could live forever! Of course, you get shelled sometimes too. Baseball is not a sport that you can get a swelled head over. It comes back to get you, sure enough.

Wednesday 23d. I'll be sorry to leave Mexico. I got a little sick from the food or the water, but they say everybody does, and I'm over that now. We have played before big crowds and won our share. They have made a fuss over us, given us Spanish names. I am "the Black Fox." I guess that's because they think I'm sneaky out on the mound, which I try to be. It might also be because I've picked a couple of guys off first.

The good things about Mexico are 1) the hotels 2) the crowds—they know their baseball down here and if they razz you, you can't understand them—3) the good level of competition 4) no bullshit stuff about sitting in the back or not being served or just being thought of as a no-account nigger. Maybe they think of us that way but we can't tell. The bad things are 1) some of the food is too spicy for my taste 2) my stomach is tender 3) the women aren't really accessible. They look nice but they are definitely off limits except for whores and I ain't messin' with foreign whores. Also Satch has been vague about money as usual and I suspect he's taking stuff off the top but I can't complain much 'cause we've been paid well. Still we got to wind up because we start spring training soon. One thing about Negro baseball is you never are sure who you're playing for until the season starts. It's always a question of money.

Wednesday the 15th. We just had the East-West Classic in Chicago. Man, was it something, as usual. I don't always get to pitch, but it's fun just watching.

We all get new uniforms for the game, even though it is a one-shot affair. Satchel is always one of the pitchers unless he wasn't in the leagues at all, off barning, but several years he was off, so that made more room for the rest of us.

The game is more of a show than a game. Nobody wants to get hurt, so we don't slide hard into people or try to cut them. Tricky baseball is out. The pitchers don't throw at anybody unless a guy tries to show you up and then of course you have to come in on him. The fans are there to see the glamour as well as the players. Today was a beautiful day, not too hot, and the fans started arriving early while we were working out on the field. They were dressed, I tell you. The men had on their Sunday best suits, some guys with zoot suits. The ladies had on big hats and tight dresses and jewelry. Everybody watched everybody else and took turns trying to look finer than their neighbors.

I guess a lot of folks had brought liquor in with them, and a lot had brought food. The All Star game is the only game I know where there is continuous noise in the stands. In the other games there is noise and then quiet, depending on the way the game is going. In the East-West game people come to have a good time. We got enough problems getting people to come out as it is.

Think about it for a minute. The white teams always have their games in the paper, league standings, box scores and all. We don't even get our games, most of the time, in the black papers. Some white papers say we aren't a league at all, just a front for the rackets. The Cardinals are on radio around here. In the towns in which we play games you can stay home and listen to the Cardinals game. The only thing we got going is that we are the only league where you see colored players. If you're black, you ain't gonna see any niggers in the big leagues.

October 27. Flying around with Satch's All Stars makes me think about the old days traveling. Not that we still don't do it, but the Leagues are doing better now, and we got better conditions. In the late twenties, before the new leagues got started, traveling was rough. For one thing, we'd play as much as we could, so right after the game we'd hit the road, drive to the next site, play some more till it was dark. A lot of times we'd drive through the night, taking turns at the wheel. Part of the reason for that was to save money, part was because we couldn't always get a decent hotel, especially in the South.

One time we were driving through Tennessee, kind of around dusk, on this road that was so narrow that the cars had to stride ditches on either side. We had two cars. The first car hits a bump in the road and skids, ending up in the ditch. The guys crawl out, nobody hurt, but one of the wheels is out of line, and the car's pretty beat up. We stop the second car and pull it off the road. Then we sit there scratching our heads. While we're figuring out what to do a car comes along with some white guys in it. They start laughing, say, "Look at those dumb niggers, run their car into a ditch." They don't offer to help, just drive on. A little later a cop shows up. "Hey boys, get that car out of there. Somebody might run into it!" We say we're trying, we got no tools to fix it. He says, "Well, if you don't get it off the road, I'm just going to have to run you in." We don't want to spend the night in a Tennessee jail, so after he leaves we push the car out of the ditch partway down a ravine in the woods. We leave it there, we all climb into the second car, head for the nearest town. We finally find a colored guy with a truck and a rope, and the next day we get the car out and fixed. Meanwhile we don't show up for our game, and of course we lose the gate receipts.

Another time, in Oklahoma, we saw a sign for a place called the Grand Cafe. The sign said they sold "Nigger Chicken." We stopped and took a picture of the sign, and then a little on down the road was the Grand Cafe. We knew, of course, that they wouldn't serve colored, but we decided to have a little fun. Both cars pulled in, and we went into the restaurant. The boys liked me to talk, because I could talk real white when I wanted to. I went up to the counter and said, "We saw your sign up the road, and we'd like to order some of your nigger chicken." The guy behind the counter got flustered, and mumbled that they didn't serve colored. I then said, "Well, how do you know that your chicken really tastes like 'nigger chicken' unless some black folks say so? Seems like we've got some good tasters right here." He didn't think that was funny, of course, and he told me to get out. There were some white guys in the restaurant, and I didn't want to get anything going, so I walked out, and as I did I said to some of the guys in a loud voice, "Boys, I was wrong. Ain't no nigger chicken here. Sign must of been for some other place."

They all murmured stuff like, "Too bad," and "No kidding." Then we got back in the cars, all laughing. You had to laugh at stuff like that.

Saturday the 16th. This was a night to remember. We played today in Memphis and afterwards some of us headed on down to Beale Street. There is a lot of music and action on Beale Street, all the colored folks in Memphis go there, specially on Saturday night. We heard there was some jazz musicians in town, so we went down.

We was sitting around having a few drinks when Turkey Stearnes comes in with a guy who he met in another place. The guy plays clarinet in a jazz band. He says if we'll go along with him he'll introduce us to some more musicians. So we head down the street to this place, really crowded and smokey, where they got some jazz band playing. We go in and there's this table and sitting at the table is Lena Horne! Of course everybody knows who she is and she is one great lookin' woman. It turns out she is in town with a band, playing at some place for white folks, and she had some time between shows so she came on down to Beale Street with some friends.

Now I follow jazz pretty good and I know some of Lena Horne's songs, so I strike up a conversation with her. It turns out that she follows Negro League baseball! You could have knocked my socks off. She knows a lot of the players names, and she's met some. She even has thrown out the first ball at the start of the season. I don't think she really knows much about me but she acts like she does and believe me I'm thinking of anything I can say just to keep her around.

Well, we hang around there and have some more drinks and next thing I know there's an impromptu jazz session at the place and Lena's singing some numbers and they call us to come up on the stage and sing with them. Well, I can follow music but I can't sing a lick and so I just stand up there with this big grin on my face, not singing a word. So she says, "Come on, _____, sing along with me," and I just keep smiling.

You run into a lot of black musicians on the road but that was a real highlight for me.

Lady Base Ballists In Quad
(from the Ottumwa (Iowa) Daily Democrat, *June 11, 1890)*
DANVILLE, ILL, JUNE 9— The "Ladies" Base Ball Club, composed of women from Chicago and Cincinnati, defeated the Danville Browns by a score of 23 to 12 to an attendance of 2,000. Last evening State's Attorney Blackburn swore out a warrant for their arrest for unlawfully disturbing the peace and good order of society. Officer Patterson arrested them as they were leaving town in carriages for Covington, Indiana.

—Ray Schmidt

Lifting the Iron Curtain of Cuban Baseball

Peter C. Bjarkman

For a tradition-minded American baseball fan fed up with ear-piercing Diamond Vision entertainment, cavorting cartoon-style mascots, shopping-mall stadia, luxury-box extravagance, inflated beer and parking prices, plastic-grass fields, and spoiled ballplayers, a trip around the Cuban ballpark circuit in mid-February—during the National Series championships comprising the Cuban postseason—seems a refreshing escape into baseball's pristine past. In Havana and Pinar del Rio and Santiago de Cuba, the diamond action remains pure, the off-field distractions are minimal, and the game continues to thrive at its own beautiful pace and rhythm.

Havana's 55,000-seat Estadio Latinoamericano is a genuine throwback. The park's electronic center field scoreboard features only lighted displays of lineups and line scores, and is entirely void of video displays or between-inning commercials. The ballplayers' uniforms are equally simple, recalling modern-day industrial league or softball uniforms in the States. The fans are focused on the game alone for nine innings (or less, since Cuban baseball features aluminum bats and an Olympic ten-run rule after seven innings) and they commune joyfully about baseball's timeless rhythms. In a nation of severe material shortages and limited personal freedoms, baseball is a welcome panacea.

Of course, there are stark differences from old-time North Amercan baseball, as well. The outfield wall decorations urge spectators to remain loyal to the Castro revolution. A nationwide paper shortage means

no printed scorecards and souvenir stands, and beer vendors are unheard of. Team rosters represent geographical regions, and players are therefore never traded among teams. And a sight entirely foreign to North American ballparks—glowing electric-light foul poles—reminds the visitor that this is not Brooklyn or the Bronx or Philadelphia.

Problems—For Cuban fans, however, the 1997 winter playoffs hardly represented a throwback to past glory days. Cuban baseball has changed drastically in recent seasons and most fans agree that this has been largely for the worse. Many of the nation's top stars have defected to the majors or have, inexplicably, been forced to retire. The defectors—great young pitching prospects like Diamondbacks recruits Larry Rodriguez and Vladimir Nunez, and spectacular Mets shortstop Rey Ordonez—generate little ill-will among the fans and ballplayers left behind. But the forced retirements of perhaps Cuba's best-ever shortstop, German Mesa, and one of its most popular sluggers, outfielder Victor Mesa, have left the fans feeling cheated.

The recent *Series Nacional* season and the following postseason playoffs were often played in half-empty stadiums, especially in Havana. Fans complain that the game is being gutted by the peddling of players to the Japanese Industrial League and to fledgling pro circuits in Italy, Nicaragua, Ecuador and Colombia. Meanwhile officials of the Cuban League maintain their steadfast insistence that the nation's emphasis remains on amateurism in baseball and on preparing for another Olympic triumph in Australia in the year 2000. One rumored cash deal for Omar Linares and Orestes

---

Peter C. Bjarkman *is an award-winning baseball historian who recently traveled throughout Cuba while researching his forthcoming book,* A Pictorial History of Cuban Baseball *(with Mark Rucker).*

Kindelan with the Japanese pro circuit was quickly nixed. Yet veterans like Victor Mesa (reportedly headed to Japan's Industrial League) and 1992 Olympic star hurler Lazaro Valle (bound for Italy) are being retired and sent overseas. Mesa was inexplicably sent packing while only a few homers short of breaking the all-time Cuban career record. German Mesa and exiled hurler Orlando "El Duque" Hernandez—brother of Marlins farmhand Livan Hernandez—were supposedly banned for dealing with a North American agent. (The agent, a Cuban-American with Venezuelan residency, is now serving a twenty-year Cuban prison term for his part in the affair.) Rumors persist that the forced retirements of the two Mesas and others mark an effort to clear space on the national team for young stars like Miguel Caldes, Eduardo Paret, and Jose Estrada, who might otherwise also consider the option of big-league defection.

Isle of Youth	31-34	.477	19.0	Ciego Avila	20-45	.308	17.5
Group B				**Group D**			
Industriales	33-30	.524	—	Santiago	49-16	.754	—
Havana	30-35	.462	4.0	Holguin	34-31	.523	15.0
Cienfuegos	25-40	.385	9.0	Granma	28-37	.431	21.0
Sancti Spiritus	16-49	.246	18.0	Guantanamo	23-41	.359	25.5

Batting Leaders			Pitching Leaders		
BA	Jose Estrada (Matanzas)	.391	W	Jose Contreras (Pinar)	14
2B	Oscar Valdes (Metro)	23	IP	Jose Ibar (Havana)	132.2
3B	Enrique Diaz (Metro)	9	S	Raidel Cordero (Pinar)	9
HR	Julio Fernandez (Matanzas)	15	SO	Jose Contreras (Pinar)	135
R	Jose Estrada (Matanzas)	60	BB	Alfredo Fonseca (Granma)	58
RBI	Julio Fernandez (Matanzas)	60	G	Jorge Fumero (Industriales)	28
SB	Eduardo Paret (Villa)	43	CG	Omari Romero (Santiago)	12

The crisis has in part been brought on by changes in the economic structure of baseball abroad. Pro ball in the U.S. with its mega-level salaries is now a far greater lure than ever before for low-paid "amateurs" toiling with major league skills in the talent-rich Cuban League. And Japan is becoming a magnet as well. The unconfirmed story about Linares and Kindelan and top Cuban pitcher Pedro Lazo reportedly involved a $10 million offer from the Japanese.

The Mesa messes—At the top of the list of retirees and suspensions stand German Mesa and Victor Mesa, unrelated stars of the past half decade who are two of the finest players in recent Cuban history. The popular and muscular Victor Mesa, who toiled with Villa Clara during the past decade, is a lifetime .313 hitter and extraordinary basestealer, who also stands well up on the career homer list. German Mesa was the starting shortstop on the Cuban national team for six seasons before being dropped from the Olympic squad in favor of hot prospect Eduardo Paret. While Paret flashed his defensive brilliance for two weeks in Atlanta, and Rey Ordonez is already drawing legitimate big league comparisons with Aparicio and Concepcion in New York, Cuban fans still swear that Mesa is the island's best-ever shortstop.

Most recent defectors have been pitchers. Failures to dominate in the majors as they did in Cuba by Rene Arocha (an arm injury sidetracked his career after 11 wins for the Cardinals in 1993), Livan Hernandez (he labored at AAA Charlotte last season), and Oswaldo Fernandez (7-13 with the Giants in 1996), have raised questions about the true level of Cuban talent. Indeed, the aluminum bats used in the Cuban League spawn throwers, not pitchers. Cuban hurlers are also consistently overused at home as both starters and relievers.

Several new defectors may soon resurrect the Cuban reputation. Ariel Prieto is a top pitching prospect with Oakland despite his slow start in 1996 (6-7, 4.15 ERA). Larry Rodriguez may be even better than Prieto, and

Victor Mesa

Final Standings in 1996-97 Cuban National Series							
Western Zone				**Eastern Zone**			
Group A				**Group C**			
Pinar del Rio	50-15	.769	—	Villa Clara	37-27	.548	—
Metropolitanos	42-23	.646	8.0	Camaguey	33-32	.508	4.5
Matanzas	39-26	.600	11.0	Las Tunas	28-37	.431	9.5

Transcendental Graphics

was given a $1.25 million signing bonus by Arizona. And Ordonez has caused a storm of excitement in only one season with the Mets. Ordonez is a useful yardstick, since he was far from the best Cuban shortstop at the time of his defection. The future Mets star had been buried behind German Mesa and Paret, who is the best all-around shortstop I have seen since Luis Aparicio. He runs with abandon (swiping 43 bases in this year's short 65-game Cuban season), hits with power, and tracks down aluminum-bat liners with flawless precision. And Abdel Quintana, a hot 17-year-old prospect with the playoff-bound Industriales team, was recently rushed into the starting lineup in Havana and may soon be even better than either Mesa or Paret.

The old days—If the talent pool is thinning, this, like much else in Cuba these days, is a sharp departure from the heady years during the '60s, '70s, and early '80s. For three decades, the Cubans maintained the world's greatest showcase of amateur baseball talent. The ballparks in Havana, Holguin, Mantanzas and other cities were home to some of the greatest diamond stars that U.S. fans never saw. Heroes of this era included Wilfredo "El Hombre Hit" Sanchez, Luis Casanova, Fidel Linares (Omar's father), Antonio Munoz, Manuel Alacron, Augustin Marquetti, and Braudilio Vinent. Lefty-swinging Wil Sanchez was one of the greatest hitters in Cuban history, winning no fewer than five batting titles, including the first back-to-back pair in 1969 and 1970. Today, his lifetime mark of .332 trails only those of Linares (.373), the league's first-ever .400 hitter, and Alexander Ramos (.337), the latest Cuban to reach the 1,000-hit plateau. In the '80s the heavy hitting of Wilfredo Sanchez was replaced by that of Antonio Munoz (370 career homers), Lazaro Junco (the all-time home run leader), and finally Omar Linares. Linares has dominated the hitting of the '90s (with three .400- plus seasons), along with slugger Orestes Kindelan (now only three short of Junco on the homer list with 402), fleet-footed leadoff specialist Luis Ulacia (last year's batting champion), and a group of young stars paced by Jose Estrada and Miguel Caldas.

The pitching of the '70s and '80s was largely dominated by popular flamethrowing righthander Vinent, considered the greatest Cuban hurler of the Castro era. Most of the lifetime pitching marks are still held by this superb hurler who won (221) and lost (167), more games than any Cuban moundsman, and in 1986 also became the first island hurler to reach the 2,000 career strikeout mark. He also still holds the marks for complete games and games started.

Cuba's rich baseball history stretches back long before Castro and the 1959 revolution. The game was first played there two years before the birth of the National League. Cuban Steve Bellan became the first-ever Latin big leaguer, when he appeared with the National Association Troy Haymakers in 1871. Cubans also appeared in the National League before the First World War (Rafael Almeida and Armando Marsans with Cincinnati in 1911), and Dolf Luque was a legitimate star (27-8 with Cincinnati in 1923) long before major league integration. But it was the post-World War II period that saw a full-scale Cuban invasion of the majors—first with a handful of Washington Senators journeymen, then with flashy '50s stars like Minnie Minoso, Camilo Pascual and Pete Ramos, and finally with Zoilo Versailles, Luis Tiant, Tony Oliva, and Tony Perez, who made their marks in the '60s and '70s.

Back home in Havana, the Cubans had been hosting top-flight winter league play between black and white Cubans and North Americans since the mid-'20s. They were also dominating the world amateur scene throughout the '30s and '40s, and the winter professional Caribbean World Series during its first phase from 1949 through 1960. Cuba won the first title in Havana in 1949 and seven of the first dozen competitions.

A top pro league in the '40s and '50s featured legendary teams representing Club Havana, Almendares, Cienfuegos and Marianao, and showcased a mixture of Cuban stars and major leaguers in the sparkling new El Cerro Stadium (today's revamped and renamed Estadio Latinoamericano).

All-Time Individual Career Leaders in Castro's Cuba
Based on Select Series and National Series (1962-1995)

	Batting Records			Pitching Records
G	Antonio Munoz (1,945)		G	Braudilio Vinent (447)
In	Antonio Munoz (16,345.2)		GS	Braudilio Vinent (400)
AB	Fernando Sanchez (6,956)		CG	Braudilio Vinent (265)
R	Antonio Munoz (1,281)		RG	Euclides Rojas (279)
H	Wilfredo Sanchez (2,174)		W	Braudilio Vinent (221)
BA	Omar Linares (.369)		L	Braudilio Vinent (167)
2B	Antonio Munoz (355)		Pct.	Lazaro Valle (.784)
3B	Wilfredo Sanchez (69)		SO	Braudilio Vinent (63)
HR	Lazaro Junco (405)		S	Euclides Rojas (60)
TB	Antonio Munoz (3,569)		IP	Braudilio Vinent (3,259.2)
SA	Omar Linares (.640)		SO	Rogelio Garcia (2,499)
SB	Victor Mesa (507)		BB	Rogelio Garcia (1,077)
RBI	Antonio Munoz (1,407)		ERA	Jose Huelga (1.50)
SacB	Giraldo Gonzalez (118)		R	Braudilio Vinent (1,122)
SacF	Pedro Rodriguez (69)		WP	Braudilio Vinent (178)

The Cuban Structure—After Castro's takeover, the powers of Organized Baseball pulled the plug on the International League Havana Sugar Kings. (For interested readers the details of Cuban baseball history are laid out in my book *Baseball with a Latin Beat* published in 1994.) Castro's reaction was to mandate a strictly amateur league and a yearly national series between regional teams that consisted of two short

Omar Linares

Santiago, Holguin, Cienfuegos, and several smaller cities. What gives Cuban baseball its distinctive appearance within this lavish system of amateur competition is the use of aluminum bats and a total absence of any peripheral commercialism. The one lends a strange feeling of college baseball to games staged in professional venues. The other means that no outfield or scoreboard advertisements or ear-splitting between-innings video ad campaigns contaminate pristine Cuban ballparks.

How good *are* these guys?—What is the status of the Cuban league and its mysterious cache of potential big league talent? Are the Cubans really as good as their Olympic and international records suggest? Is a recent claim on the cover of a leading U.S. baseball weekly that Omar Linares is the "best third baseman on the planet" a case of overhype or a bold measure of reality? Stripped of their aluminum bats would the Cuban sluggers who dominated in Atlanta succeed against big league hurling? Does Cuba really contain a deep untapped talent pool for big league clubs?

seasons and a championship playoff round. It is from this internal season that national teams have long been selected to represent Cuba in Olympic, World Cup, Pan American, and other international competitions. The result in recent decades has been a series of powerhouse Cuban teams that have posted an 80-1 international record between the 1987 Panamerican Games in Indianapolis and the 1996 Olympics in Atlanta, captured fifteen of eighteen world amateur titles since 1969, won both Olympic baseball tournaments, and taken every Pan Am gold medal (and all but one game) since 1963.

The organization of the Cuban League and the Cuban playoff system has undergone several overhauls over the decades. It now consists of a season of 65 games featuring sixteen teams in fourteen cities (Havana has three teams), which are divided into four divisions (two groups in the West and two in the East). A second Selected Series season with eight teams and 63 games has long been a staple of summer-season play. A February four-team postseason culminates the *Series Nacional* and corresponds to a stateside LCS playoff.

The showcase ballpark is still the 55,000-seat El Cerro. Impressive 25,000-plus capacity parks of AAA quality are also situated in Pinar del Rio, Matanzas,

Team and Batting Champions in Castro-Era Cuban Baseball Leagues

Abbreviations:

Occid.	Occidentales		Indust.	Industriales
Orient.	Orientales		Hab.	Habana
Azuc.	Azucareros		Heneq.	Henequeneros
Agric.	Agricultores		Ganad.	Ganaderos
Citr.	Citricultores		SS	Sancti Spiritus
VC	Villa Clara		PR	Pinar del Rio
Veg.	Vegueros		Sant.	Santiago

Yr	Team (W-L)	Mgr	BA Leader	HR Leader
1962	Occid. (18-9)	F. Guerra	E. Walter (.367)	R. Valdes (3)
1963	Indust. (16-14)	R. Carneado	R. Gonzalez (.348)	R. Valdes (5)
1964	Indust. (22-13)	R. Carneado	P. Chavez (.333)	J. Trigoura (3)
1965	Indust. (25-14)	R. Carneado	U. Gonzalez (.359)	M. Cuevas (5)
1966	Indust. (40-25)	R. Carneado	M. Cuevas (.325)	L. Betancourt (9)
1967	Orient. (36-29)	R. Ledo	P. Chaves (.318)	E. Walter (7)
1968	Hab. (74-25)	J. Gomez	J. Perez (.328)	F. Sarduy (13)
1969	Azuc. (69-39)	S. Borges	W. Sanchez (.354)	A. Marquetti (19)
1970	Heneq. (50-16)	M. Dominguez	W. Sanchez (.351)	R. Reyes (10)
1971	Azuc. (49-14)	S. Borges	R. Resique (.352)	M. Cuevas (10)
1972	Azuc. (52-14)	S. Borges	E. Mancebe (.327)	A. Marquetti (11)
1973	Indust. (53-25)	P. Chavez	E. Cruz (.341)	A. Capiro (22)
1974	Hab. (52-26)	J. Trigoura	R. Resique (.347)	A. Munoz (19)
1975	Agric. (24-15)	O. Leroux	F. Laffita (.396)	F. Sanchez (6)

1976	Ganad. (29-9)	C. Gomez	W. Sanchez (.365)	A. Munoz (13)
1977	Citr. (26-12)	D. Lorenzo	F. Osorio (.359)	P. Rodriguez (9)
1978	Veg. (36-14)	J. Pineda	F. Sanchez (.394)	P. Rodriguez (13)
1979	SS (39-12)	C. Andrade	W. Sanchez (.377)	P. Rodriguez (19)
1980	Sant. (35-16)	M. Miyar	R. Puente (.394)	L. Casanova (18)
1981	Veg. (36-15)	J. Pineda	A. Zamora (.394)	A. Lescaille (15)
1982	Veg. (36-15)	J. Fuentes	F. Hernandez (.376)	L. Junco (17)
1983	VC (41-8)	E. Martin	J. Hernandez (.367)	L. Junco (15)
1984	Citr. (52-23)	T. Soto	W. Sanchez (.385)	L. Junco (20)
1985	Veg. (57-18)	J. Fuentes	O. Linares (.409)	L. Junco (24)
1986	Indust. (6-0)*	P. Chavez	O. Linares (.426)	R. Fernandez (18)
1987	Veg. (5-1)*	J. Fuentes	J. Mendez (.408)	O. Kindelan (17)
1988	Veg. (5-1)*	J. Fuentes	P. Rodriguez (.446)	L. Junco (25)
1989	Sant. (5-1)*	H. Velez	J. Bravo (.414)	O. Kindelan (24)
1990	Heneq. (4-2)*	G. Junco	O. Linares (.442)	E. Urratia (20)
1991	Heneq. (4-1)*	G. Junco	L. Madera (.400)	L. Junco (17)
1992	Indust. (5-1)*	J. Trigoura	O. Linares (.442)	R. Martinez (19)
1993	VC (4-2)*	P. Jova	O. Linares (.446)	L. Junco (27)
1994	VC (4-3)*	P. Jova	L. Gurriel (.395)	L. Junco (21)
1995	VC (4-2)*	P. Jova	A. Zamora (.395)	M. Caldes (20)
1996	VC (48-17) (Regular season record)			
		P. Jova	L. Ulacia (.421)	A. Benavides (25)
1997	PR (50-15) (Regular season record)			
		J. Fuentes	J. Estrada (.391)	J. Fernandez (15)

*Playoffs between Western and Eastern Division champions used to determine winner starting with 1985-86 season.

Wilfredo "El Hombre Hit" Sanchez, the Cuban League's first back-to-back batting champion, 1969-70.

Atlanta provided a clue for American fans privileged to see the Cubans' best players firsthand. Even allowing for aluminum bats, Kindelan and Linares are awesome long ball hitters. Kindelan strokes blasts that remind one of K-brothers Killebrew and Kingman. Paret is as talented at shortstop as any major leaguer of the past several generations, flashier than Ordonez and more potent at the plate (completing this year's National Series with a .290 BA).

There are several others with major league potential. Miguel Caldes is an impressive outfielder some tout as the next great Cuban star. Luis Ulacia is a leadoff hitter with major league tools, and rifle-armed Juan Manrique is potentially a solid big-league receiver. Pedro Luis Laso (11-2 with Pinar del Rio this season) demonstrated in the recent national playoffs that he has a genuine big league arm, professional savvy, and an overpowering delivery effective even against aluminum rocket launchers.

The rest of the Cuban pitchers are not especially impressive. Jose Contreras (14-1 with Pinar del Rio) throws hard but is undisciplined and features only two pitches. Lazaro Valle is now gone from the scene, and southpaw Omar Ajete (a 1992 Olympic mainstay) is far past his best years. The best up-and-coming young arms—Rodriquez and Nunez—have already defected.

So Cuban talent is a mixed bag. Pitching is thin, but Cuban fielding and hitting is still impressive. Linares stands head and shoulders above the pack. At twenty-

eight the slugging third sacker seemed this past winter season to be losing interest. Cuban fans complain that he has put on weight and rarely hustles. But I believe Linares is the best ballplayer this island has ever produced—including Perez, Canseco, Oliva, and perhaps even 1930s-era Negro League wonder Martin Dihigo. He has been described as Brooks Robinson grafted onto Albert Belle. My impression is more along the lines of a mid-career Aaron, Mathews or Mays. Omar Linares is as good—and as exciting—as anyone I have ever seen, with the possible exceptions of Clemente and Mantle.

The best assessment of Cuban baseball is that the talent is there but the product is waning. The same claim, of course, can be made of the majors. The crisis in Cuban baseball will only be resolved when the sport's top leadership decides to go in one direction or the other—strict amateurism or free-market professionalism. In the meantime Cuba still harbors elements of what appears to an outsider as the last vestiges of the game we all once knew and loved—the game joyfully played more for prideful victory than for bulging bankrolls.

A Monument For Harry Wright

Jerrold Casway

Today's baseball fan would be hard pressed to identify Harry Wright, let alone appreciate why he deserved a monument. Wright had to wait until 1953 for the Old-Timers Committee to select him to the Hall of Fame. He was overlooked in sixteen ballots, covering a span of seventeen years before he got his recognition. In Philadelphia where he served as the Phillies longest tenured manager, second in wins to Gene Mauch (636 to 646), he is not even on the Philadelphia Hall of Fame wall at Veterans Stadium. This ignorance and its accompanying oversights would have astonished Wright's contemporaries. They thought so much of Harry they erected a monument to him as a unique testimony to his humanity and contributions to the national game.

Wright's record puts him in select baseball company. Only Connie Mack, John McGraw, and Bucky Harris managed more than Harry Wright's twenty-five years in the major leagues. He managed 2,145 games, winning 1,225 for a .581 percentage. Historically, Harry Wright has his own page in baseball history. Henry Chadwick, often called the "father of baseball," always referred to Wright in those terms. The Cincinnati *Enquirer* called Wright the "Edison of baseball" because more than anyone else he invented the professional game and the way it's played.

Wright's most famous accomplishment was his role as the organizer and manager of the first fully professional baseball team. That ball club, the Red Stockings of Cincinnati, in 1869 had a record of 60 and 0. His

great Boston teams in the National Association and National League (1871-1881) won six championships, four of them in a row. Only a technicality in 1871 kept Boston from five straight pennants. His 1875 ball club posted a 71–8 record. During these years he coached and brought along such stars as his brother George Wright, Jim "the Orator" O'Rourke, Tommy Bond, "Old Hoss" Radbourne, "Deacon" White, and Al Spalding.

In 1884 Harry Wright was drawn to Philadelphia by Al Reach, the sporting goods magnate and owner-president of the year-old Phillies. Within a few seasons Wright assembled talented and competitive teams, but he never finished better than second place, despite developing some of the franchise's greatest players— Charlie Ferguson, John Clements, Art Irwin, Jimmy Fogarty, Sam Thompson, Ed Delahanty, Billy Hamilton, Charlie Buffington, and "Kid" Gleason.

But Harry Wright's managerial accomplishments are only part of his importance to the game, which he changed fundamentally. He suggested moving first and third bases into fair territory, instituted shifting defenses, had pitchers back up bases, moved infielders off their bases, made outfielders throw ahead of runners, and used hand signals from catchers. He also introduced pregame batting practice, off-season conditioning programs, and spring training in the south. He also was the first to introduce gloves in 1870 and catcher's masks in 1875. His Cincinnati Red Stockings were also the first team to wear knickers.

Wright's contributions carried over into the image of the sport. He preached teamwork, fair play, and game strategy. It was said that Harry Wright saw a baseball game as an evolving set of moves and circumstances.

Jerrold Casway *teaches history at Howard Community College in Columbia, Maryland. He is currently working on a biography of Ed Delahanty.*

For him there was a science and rhythm to a baseball game. Hall of Fame player and manager Hugh Jennings said Wright "could look further into a ball game than any man I ever met…before the game started, he had every inning figured out and expected the play to go precisely along the lines he had planned." A great teacher and psychologist, Harry Wright preached personal modesty, temperance, and honesty. He often said, "We must make the game worth witnessing."

Born in 1835 in Sheffield, England, William Henry "Harry" Wright made his initial mark playing cricket in New York. Baseball for him was a challenging sidelight to which he devoted three decades of his life. But by the early 1890s some people in Philadelphia believed the game of baseball had eclipsed their pioneering manager. The Phillies appeared to be locked into fourth place, and Colonel John Rogers, Reach's partner and team treasurer, grew impatient for a championship. Rogers never considered the team's ill fortune—the untimely deaths of Charlie Ferguson and Jimmy Fogarty—union and labor strife, and his own poor front-office decisions. The plight of the Phillies also mirrored Harry Wright's own misfortunes. Recently widowed, he was suffering from failing eyesight and poor health. At the end of the 1893 season, the impetuous and impatient Rogers released Harry Wright as the Phillies manager.

People were taken aback by Wright's treatment and a debate arose about his future role in baseball. The sporting press was dismayed that the owners had no plans for "old Harry." Hurt and disappointed by his dismissal, Wright never spoke his mind. It was only under mounting pressure from the press that the magnates rewarded Wright's silence by setting up a

The late SABR stalwart Ed "Dutch" Doyle at the Harry Wright monument in Philadelphia's West Laurel Hill Cemetery.

new position for him as the chief of the National League umpires. Unfortunately, Harry had no executive power and his opinions and proposals often disturbed the owners. Wright continued making recommendations and carried out his functions with dignity and integrity until, in the late summer of 1895, he fell ill and contracted catarrhal pneumonia. On October 3, 1895, after surgery to drain his chest, Wright died at the age of sixty in a sanitarium in Atlantic City, New Jersey.

Accolades and testimonies to his character and career were immediate and eloquent. Even the Phillies board of directors, led by Reach and Rogers, issued a statement proclaiming that Harry "had no enemies. His friends were legion and we—among his closest—mourn him as a brother…. [his] name and fame were treasured household words of emulation." The day of the funeral, the Scorer's Association of Philadelphia appointed a committee, headed by Wright's close friend, Frank Hough, the sports editor of the Philadelphia *Press*, to look into the possiblity of establishing a fund for the erection of a Harry Wright monument.

Wreaths of flowers and floral arrangements decorated the Episcopal Church of the Advocate as more than 1,000 people paid their last respects to "Old Harry." The Phillies sent a wreath that read "Safe at Home" and the league sent a broken ladder of roses. Phillies manager Art Irwin and club secretary Bill Shettsline were pallbearers, and Rogers and Reach served as honoraries. Wright was laid to rest overlooking the Schuylkill River at the West Laurel Hill Cemetary.

His interment did not proceed without embarrassments for the Phillies. It was reported that Ed Delahanty and team captain Jack Boyle attended the funeral, but newspapers asked how that was possible if the Phillies were playing a Sunday afternoon exhibition game in Paterson, New Jersey. The Phillies front office replied that Delahanty and Boyle had gone that morning to Hough's home to pay their last respects to their late manager. The players delivered a beautiful casket pillow. After the viewing the players joined their teammates and left for the ballgame. These actions were seen as being disrepectful to Wright's family and memory. Harry was opposed to Sunday baseball and many felt that the Phillies should not have gone through with this meaningless exhibition game. Reach and Rogers astonished everyone when they said the game was arranged by the players and was out of their control. This thoughtless act and alibi tarnished the franchise's image.

As for Harry Wright's monument, the editor of the Philadelphia-based *Sporting Life* reminded the magnates about their debt to Harry Wright. The paper called on the owners to do something to commemorate the man who gave so much to the national pastime. The Boston *Globe* editorialized: "Past services count for little with the people [owners] who endeavor to get out of base ball all there is in it for themselves." When the magnates finally responded, they set up a committee consisting of John Brush of Cincinnati, J.A. Hart of Chicago, and John Rogers of Philadelphia to arrange a day in the spring to be called "Harry Wright Day." On that designated afternoon exhibition games would be played with the revenue going toward Wright's monument. The selected date, April 13, 1896, was not well received. It was criticized because it was thought that the weather and scheduling conflicts from spring training sites would curtail attendance. Many newspapers worried how upsetting it would be if the plans for Harry's day were not successful. *Sporting Life* suggested that it would be best if each team picked its own date to honor the late manager. The National League was also censured when the owners refused to put up $100 apiece for the monument fund. The Philadelphia *Inquirer* said that Wright's beloved Phillies had a special responsibility and should take the lead in the memorial effort. They suggested that every employee at the ball park should volunteer his services and all concessions and receipts be donated to the fund. The Phillies ultimately succumbed to the pressure and the Chestnut Street Trust and Savings Fund Company was designated to act as the custodian of the money.

Once the Phillies became active, local amateur ball clubs were mobilized in support of the campaign. Tickets for the grand pavilion were priced at $1, lower pavilion seats cost 50 cents, and general admission remained at a quarter. A large number of sites around the city were set up to sell tickets for the game. Four thousand people showed up to honor the "noblest Roman of them all." The Phillies beat the American Association Athletics, 9–2. Receipts were announced at $1,400. Other games were played in Rockford, Illinois, Baltimore, Indianapolis, Washington, Wilmington, New York, and Louisville. With revenue totaling over $3,300, the Memorial Association met and commissioned Edmund Quinn, a former student of the famed artist Thomas Eakins to sculpture and cast a bronze statute of "Uncle Harry."

Initially, the Association hoped that the monument would be set in a place like Fairmount Park, a site where playing children could be reminded of Harry Wright's ideals. Public pressure and newspaper editorials exerted whatever influence they could mobilize to lobby the Philadelphia Park Commission. Their efforts were in vain, and the Association decided to erect the monument over Harry Wright's grave in the West Laurel Hill Cemetery.

On the rainy afternoon of Sunday, June 20, 1897, a crowd numbering about 1,500 admirers assembled for the unveiling. The bronze statue, slightly more than life size, stood on a 7-foot 6-inch granite pedestal. Chiseled on the pedestal's base were the words, "Father of Baseball." Below it were two crossed bats and a ball. Harry's effigy conveyed the dignity and grace for which he was remembered. In his hands he held his trademark top hat.

Colonel Rogers gave the dedication tribute. In his typical long-winded fashion, Rogers identified Harry Wright with the engraved epitaph on the pedestal's right side. From Shakespeare's *Julius Caesar*, it read, "His life was gentle, the elements so mixed in him that nature might stand up and say to all the world 'This was a man.'" This testimony, Rogers declared, was given "nearer fidelity to the absolute truth." To baseball fans, he said, gray-haired men will remember Harry from his youth because like all generations they can never fail to honor the man for his contributions and style of living. The assembled guests nodded their heads in unison when Rogers reminded the gathering that everything Wright did "refined and ennobled" the great national pastime.

The monument remains at the cemetery site for all to see. When you are in Philadelphia, honor Harry Wright's memory. It is situated on the right side across from the main steps of the cemetery's administration building. Your visit would make up for his neglected memory. We owe him that much for the game he gave us.

The Rochester Hop Bitters

Tim Wolter

At some point in their careers most baseball players have had to don a uniform emblazoned with the name or product of their team's sponsor. Generally this occurs at the lower amateur levels, where generations of Little Leaguers have cheerfully become walking billboards for local used-car dealerships and septic services. But this practice occasionally extended into the professional ranks, most notably in the nineteenth century, where the roots of many of baseball's odd quirks can be found slumbering. An interesting case in point are the Hop Bitters baseball teams of 1879 and 1880, squads that are among the oddest in baseball history.

In the spring of 1879 you could scarcely speak of organized baseball without judicious placement of quotation marks around "organized." The National League was only a couple of seasons old, and it competed with numerous minor leagues of varied quality. Schedules were flexible, and it was not thought unusual for a minor league team to play a League team—and perhaps even to win. Of course, there were doubts about the honesty of many games of this era.

Rochester, New York's 1878 team had in fact disbanded after a disappointing season during which rumors of malfeasance abounded. The prospect of their city being unrepresented by a team caused a modest stir in the spring of '79. Finally in mid-April a team was launched with the financial backing of local magnate Asa T. Soule, who had made a fortune selling an alcohol-based patent medicine known as Hop Bit-

ters, the Invalid's Friend. Although Soule publicly said that the team was "...purely to furnish innocent entertainment...and not as an advertisement..." he outfitted it in uniforms with HOP BITTERS stitched across the front in large scarlet letters. He also outfitted several amateur teams around the area in variations on the Hop Bitters theme. The local ball field was renamed Hop Bitters Grounds, and it was announced that the players would each receive a tablespoon of Hop Bitters before games to spur them on to victory.

Initial public opinion was restrained. The *Union and Advertiser* opined that, "If it is a necessity for the existence of Rochester that we have a ball club, it should be taken hold of in the right manner...." It also implied that if the new manager Joe Simmons could not assure victories over traditional rival Buffalo that he had best "...retire to some favored locality where base ball nines and bumming players are unknown."

Due to the team's late entry to the field there were some difficulties obtaining quality players. It finally proved necessary to purchase the hapless and recently disbanded Capitol City Club of Albany. But Soule was still able to assemble a fair team with some experienced players. Manager Simmons had played for several teams in the old National Association, predecessor to the National League. Another player, "Dick" Higham, was also an Association veteran, but he carried an unsavory reputation. His career had always been under a cloud because of his perceived fondness for strong drink and the company of gamblers.

The Hops, as they were sometimes called, were entered into the new National Association, a nine-team league of New York and New England clubs. At first all

Tim Wolter *practices medicine and coaches Little League in Chippewa Falls, Minnesota. He has sons named after Harmon Killebrew and longtime Twins broadcaster Halsey Hall.*

went well, with an opening-game victory on May 15 over the major leaguers of Troy. A series of victories over Association opponents and the hated Buffalo team followed, and there was hope that "...the present nine is the best Rochester ever had." But trouble was brewing. The Hops faltered in early June, struggling to stay in eighth place. Soule doubled the pregame dose of Bitters, to no avail. Considering its alcoholic content this should not have been surprising.

Reorganization—It transpired that first baseman Alex McKinnon had earlier signed a contract with a National League team, and the NL was refusing to release him from his commitment, threatening to suspend League-Association play if he stayed with Rochester.

McKinnon departed the scene in mid-June, having been "...stricken with paralysis of the left side." This illness was likely feigned, as his doctor was quoted as saying he would probably recover in a few days. Without their star the Hops losses mounted and interest in them was said to be fast dying out.

By early June the "demoralized Hop Bitters nine..." was disbanded and reorganized. The New Hop Bitters were to be a wildcat team, independent of any league affiliation. New players were assembled from the recently disbanded Manchester, New Hampshire, nine along with about half of the old team led by captain Higham. As an independent team the Hop Bitters were free to play whomever they chose. They handily dispatched lesser opponents such as the Deaf Mute nine of Columbus, Ohio and the Haverly Minstrels, a multitalented club that serenaded the crowd between innings and burst into harmony when they turned a double play. They enjoyed mixed success against League teams, besting Buffalo twice more, but faring less well against Boston, Providence, and Syracuse.

By early August the Hops appear to have exhausted the available local opposition and departed on an ambitious road trip. Their odyssey took them from Pennsylvania to Baltimore, across the Midwest to Iowa, then through Utah to California and back. They compiled a 20-7 record on their journey, encountering difficulties only with the League clubs of Chicago and Cincinnati, and with a pesky semipro team in Dubuque, Iowa, that featured a young Charles Comiskey at second base.

In general, Soule should have been pleased with the performance of his Hops, who in their new incarnation had become regarded as the premier barnstorming team in the nation. They had, after all, acquitted themselves well on the field and put the name Hop Bitters before the public from coast to coast. But Soule's son referred to the team as "...a hard gang to get along with...a great deal of annoyance." He was in fact quite candid in his opinion that the only way for a team to succeed was to be "...owned by some firm for advertis-

ing purposes...we have had enough."

A new, new team—But only a few weeks later another Hop Bitters team was organized. This crew had none of the previous Hops, and was composed of major leaguers from the Worcester and Boston clubs. They set sail for Cuba in December of 1879 and spent the better part of that month trouncing all comers in Havana and elsewhere. Their next port of call was New Orleans, where they arrived in early January. Local New Orleans lore has it that the Hop Bitters played a two-month long series of games there that were so popular that a special ball park was constructed for their stay. But contemporary records suggest that an initial 21-1 defeat of the amateur Eckfords persuaded all concerned that the local clubs were no match for the Hops. In the rematch the Hops traded pitchers and catchers with their opponents and still won handily. Later contests with clubs such as the R.E. Lees and Wrights featured various Hops players farmed out to these clubs, but not playing as a unit.

Yet another life—These further successes notwithstanding, there was little interest in reviving the Hop Bitters for the 1880 campaign. Indeed it was not until mid-May before the *Union and Advertiser* sourly noted "...the agony has at last commenced, and Rochester is again destined to have a base ball nine. As the season is so far advanced, and without any previous talk in relation to a ball club, it was fondly hoped that Buffalo would be granted an exclusive patent on the business for this section of the state. But these hopes are shattered...."

The 1880 Hop Bitters started out as a makeshift squad with no holdovers from previous teams except for Joe Simmons, pressed into service as an infielder. But they soon added players that should have made them both competitive and interesting to watch. By mid-June the Hops had the services of two future Hall of Famers, Buck Ewing and Big Dan Brouthers, and a one-armed pitcher, Hugh Daily, known as "the One Armed Wonder." Daily could not only pitch, he batted a respectable .250 and got at least one extra base hit. Although the team struggled it was able to muster another three wins against their hated rivals from Buffalo, now demoted to minor league status.

But the 1880 Hop Bitters were very much less than the sum of their parts. They had rejoined the National Association, but it was a weakened league of only four teams. And Asa Soule's support of the team was diminished as well. He was said to be tired of having the newspapers of rival cities refer to him as "the medicated sportsman," and to his team variously as the Liverpads, Curacoffs, or the Gambler's Friend. Midway through the season he even retired the old uniforms replacing them with new ones marked simply

ROCHESTER.

Public interest in the Hops dwindled as they ran up a series of losses. In fact, of the dozen games they are said to have played I can find scores for only seven. Their only wins of the regular season seem to have been those over Buffalo.

With reporting on their activities so sketchy it is difficult to tell just how the team finally collapsed. But something seems to have happened on a trip to New York in August. Soule had wired money to cover expenses and salary. Simmons, the long-suffering manager of the club, is said to have taken it, gone on a monumental drunk and then vanished. This was too much for Soule, and he severed all connections with the team.

For the last few weeks of their existence the Hop Bitters were a "tramp club," with no sponsor and only infrequent opportunities to play. They were included in a three-team tournament in Brooklyn in late August, playing creditably against a strong Washington team and a hastily assembled Brooklyn squad. In exchange they were expected to play a series of games with Washington at home. What followed was what the Washington paper described as "...an exhibition that completely disgusted the public, and the final disbanding of the club."

It seems that in their first game the Hops took exception to the umpiring and walked off the field. Only with difficulty were "the One Armed Wonder" and his battery mate induced to return. Interest in the next day's game was much reduced by this display, and the crowd was sparse. Daily kept them waiting a good forty-five minutes, and a complete game could not be played due to darkness. By now it was apparent that the gate receipts were going to be slim, and for the third game the Washington club tried to renege on their financial commitment to the Hops. The Rochester men refused to play and were told that their services would no longer be wanted. The Hop Bitters passed from existence with little fanfare, described by one publication with the enigmatic but doubtless derogatory term "nine kickers."

Loose ends—Asa T. Soule had other adventures. Concurrent with his baseball enterprise he promoted a single-shell rowing race that was so ripe with the aroma of corrupt betting that this once popular sport has to this day not recovered. He also invested heavily in real estate in Kansas, creating a town called Ingalls. When an election invested a rival community with the status of county seat, Soule hired a gang of armed thugs to hijack the county records. They succeeded, after a gunfight in which one man was killed. But the railroad went elsewhere and the town of Ingalls became a ghost. Soule suffered a severe financial reverse, but returned to Rochester to live out his days, still a wealthy man.

When Joe Simmons disappeared with the team payroll Soule put detectives on his trail. They seem to have had no greater luck finding him than I had over a century later.

Dick Higham, the former captain of the Hop Bitters, went on to a career as a major league umpire. His honesty was called into question and detectives were also put on his trail. They found evidence that he was indeed fixing games. Higham was banished from baseball, the only major league umpire ever to be so dishonored. I have found an undated news item that finds him being "horsewhipped" in Kansas City for spreading gossip regarding a saloon keeper's wife. Perhaps his presence in Kansas means that he was still working for Soule. In any case, his character can be gauged by the notation on his 1905 death certificate that lists the cause of his demise as cirrhosis of the liver, and his occupation as "agent."

Dan Brouthers and Buck Ewing left the team before the final collapse, and both went on to illustrious careers that are enshrined at Cooperstown. Surprisingly, at least three other players from the woeful 1880 Hops went on to play in the majors, including one Michael Kennedy who got his nickname "Doc" when a heckler suggested that he would be unable to send a dose of Hop Bitters as far as the outfield fence. Supposedly he responded with a home run.

As to Hop Bitters, the concoction that started it all, it dwindled in popularity in the late nineteenth century, and was presumably done in along with most of the rest of the vigorous patent medicine industry by a series of shattering investigative reports that became public in 1905. The reporter was a man named Samuel Hopkins Adams, who as a young lad growing up in Rochester had once been on a team of ten-year-olds who refused the offer of Asa T. Soule to outfit them in spanking new uniforms emblazoned BABY HOP BITTERS.

The Baseball World Of Frank O'Rourke

Darryl Brock

As a boy I read them all: Duane Decker, Ed Fitzgerald, Dick Friendlich, John R. Tunis and many more—a galaxy of sports-fiction writers. Frank O'Rourke[1] stood out from the rest. His characters possessed quirky depths and seemed to inhabit larger, grittier worlds. They included pressure-plagued managers pacing their hotel rooms at night, end-of-the-road veterans fleecing rookies in high-stakes card games, scouts perching on splintery bleachers and eating greasy food in hash joints. O'Rourke's ballgames typically were warlike affairs—strategy-driven conflicts waged in smoke-grimed ballparks. Moreover, his fictional players faced "real" stars—Maglie, Musial, Robinson—in situations echoing actual pennant races of the time.

Frank O'Rourke's realism derived from two sources: his playing experience and his intimacy with the major leaguers he portrayed. During the 1940s he and his wife Edith spent their winters in Florida, and in the fall of 1948 rented a house on the beach in Clearwater, site of the Philadelphia Phillies training camp. The following spring, through an accord between Phils' management and *The Saturday Evening Post*,[2] O'Rourke worked out with the pros each day until the club went north—the first writer ever allowed such an opportunity.

"Frank was in very good shape," Edith remembers, "Better than some of the players. At six feet two he was physically imposing, with an athlete's body." A short-stop on the sun-baked rural Nebraska diamonds of his youth, O'Rourke described himself years later in a let-

ter to Jack Knarr, a newspaper columnist, as "the corn-field Babe Ruth in my neck of the woods."

> I played with my hometown team, and hired out to other towns for special games (that was in the '30s, the time of depression and drouth; the only thing people had was baseball, and the big games during the fairs and holidays were the best of all because both towns spiked up with hired players.) I usually got ten bucks and expenses to play a game. Got to know all the good players in three states. Many were former American Association and Western League pitchers [and] others were college boys, like myself....

A decade later, in the late 1940s, he still played and managed small-town summer ball in Minnesota. Although he hit over .500 each of those years (once over .600), he readily acknowledged his inability to cope with big-league curve balls. Still, did he secretly aspire to making the Phillies squad? "Good God, no!" he said, decades afterward. "I was there to be part of a long-established routine of major league baseball. I [had my] own locker in the clubhouse, and absolute entry anywhere...I worked out with the team, got to know everybody, and most important, gained their confidence."

"He ran track," Edith recalls. "Played pepper games, caught [coach Benny] Bengough's fly balls....The idea was to suit up, do the workout, not interfere with the actual play, shower with them, sit in the dugout. This made him part of the club in a way that simply circulat-

---

Darryl Brock *is the author of* If I Never Get Back.

ing among them as a sportswriter would not have."

The extent to which he was accepted is symbolized by the special copy of his novel *The Team*, autographed by players and coaches, and inscribed, "TO FRANK O'ROURKE, THE FATHER OF THE TEAM, FROM HIS KIDS, THE FIGHTING PHILLIES." The club's management gave him the red-trimmed wool Phillies uniform he worked out in. Notes made with Jim Konstanty for a book on pitching, never completed, currently reside with other O'Rourke papers in the Special Collections of the Marriott Library at the University of Utah.

"It's been thirty-five years or more now, and those men are still my friends," O'Rourke said in a 1985 *Contemporary Authors* interview. "I used them as my fictional team. I called them the Quakers and I changed the names phonetically." The majority of his baseball books[3] involve those Quakers, and in them the Whiz Kid Phillies are easily recognized: Richie Ashburn is "Robbie Ashton," (who even claims Ashburn's hometown of Tilden, Nebraska); Robin Roberts is "Robbins" or "Ramsay," Waitkus is "Watkins," Seminick "Semik," Hamner "Hammett," and so on.

Mirroring the postwar era as they do, the stories and novels take on a marvelous time-capsule quality when they're read now. "I'm tighter than a dollar watch," one character exclaims. "I've unloaded on everything but income tax and President Truman." Players bunk in swaying Pullmans on road trips and toss their gloves on the grass when they come in to bat. Fans tune in Mel Allen and Red Barber on the radio at World Series time, and we see Joe DiMaggio again, with "that easy look, that ambling stride...seeming never to reach a ball until the last moment," and hear Yogi Berra "shouting in his funny, froggy voice, throwing around the horn to Johnson, to Rizzuto, to Coleman, to Hopp...." The bonus baby phenomenon has appeared and "reached the height of foolish speculation with Pettit;[4] now every kid with a fast ball wanted fifty thousand and a yellow convertible."

Juxtaposed with such contemporary flourishes, O'Rourke's narrators, usually old-time players or sportswriters, frequently harken back to earlier times. A prospect isn't merely promising, but "the hottest pitcher since Chief Bender and Bullet Joe Bush came out of the jackpines to make history in a bygone day." Another delivers fastballs down the middle "the way old Dizzy used to pull himself from holes." A skipper contemplating using an untested rookie hurler in the World Series can't avoid ruminating back two decades on "the most daring, magnificent gamble a manager ever took," Connie Mack's choice of washed-up Howard Ehmke to open the '29 fall classic.

Mack himself, whom the O'Rourkes met at a St. Petersburg luncheon, makes a cameo appearance in *Bonus Rookie*. Edith remembers him as a tall, slender, alert man wearing an elegant pinstriped suit, vest and starched white shirt, "no longer his high collar but it made you *think* it was," whose courtly manners and reserve set him apart. Her husband sketches this ballpark portrait:

> ...wearing the dark suit and high white collar and string tie that were throwbacks to another age...the Old Gentleman seemed touched with the lasting ivory yellow of eternal youth. He had known the greatest victories and the worst defeats; he was the living bridge between the present and a forgotten generation of ball players, a relic of time in one sense, yet conqueror of all time. He sat unmoving in the dugout shadow, holding great moments of ten thousand past games in his mind, watching the young men and thinking....

There is abundant time in the stories for such sidelights, for referencing the past, as when we revisit Grove vs. Ruth in a climactic 1928 confrontation, or learn Paul Waner's technique for suckering pitchers, or see how a 1950s catcher's stance differs from that of old-timers like Cy Perkins.

The most haunting among O'Rourke's historical figures appears in *Flashing Spikes*, an aging shortstop on a barnstorming team that challenges local nines at county fairs.

> ...he moved with great deliberation, fielding easy ground balls and tossing them carelessly to first. But his face made me look time after time; it was browned and seamed and filled with some old, old knowledge.... It was a tired and resigned look as if he didn't care who won the game or how he played. He had a big nose and a wide mouth and I could tell that his fingers had been broken and were bent and gnarled like an old-time catcher's.

The young shortstop opposite him (essentially O'Rourke himself) eventually recognizes the notorious "Dane Bjorland, of the old Black Socks." In the novel Bjorland becomes an important mentor figure, and also appears, in altered form, in *Never Come Back*, which deals sympathetically with an alcoholic player's struggle to return to the top. Of the latter's composite nature, O'Rourke wrote, "There's a little of a right-handed pitcher who came up with the Cubs back in 1932, had a helluva half season, came back the next year and set the league on fire, and was out of baseball by 1935 already a complete drunk,[5] [and also] a little of a shortstop who was banned from baseball, pushing forty, looking fifty, and unforgettable."

Unforgettable indeed: a transparency of Swede Risberg.

In his most whimsical creation, *The Heavenly World Series*, O'Rourke expands his historical scope to otherworldly dimensions. God, besieged by John McGraw [Muggsy in Paradise?], reluctantly allows an all-star contest to settle the issue of which league, National or American, is superior. The respective squads are managed by McGraw and Miller Huggins; starting pitchers are Christy Mathewson and Walter Johnson. Judge Landis is on hand, Bill Klem umps at home plate, and all of baseball's immortals—literally—up to that time (1952) are eager to play. Studying the lineups, God Himself, obviously a fan, remarks, "It seems the Americans have a preponderance of hitting power." Nonetheless the contest is tied after 26 innings, when it has to be called due to recurring uncelestial behavior by the opponents.

"Frank had a baseball aficionado do some research for him," Edith recalls, "and one player he suggested was Big Ed Walsh. After the story came out in *Esquire*, a friend of [Walsh] wrote Frank to say that Big Ed was still very much alive and delighted to know that he would be a star in the afterlife, too."[6]

But it is in his evocation of *this* baseball realm that O'Rourke is most impressive. Through his free-ranging pages we visit dressing rooms from Florida training camps to Yankee Stadium, taking in their sounds and scents ("hot and sweaty and slightly moldy in a faint tropical way, not so much from body odors and rubbing solutions and sulphur water, as from the smells of ambition and hope and pride and age"), and are ushered through old-fashioned grandstands with their steel pillars and wooden seats, up to smoke-palled pressboxes where typewriters clatter.

And of course we are on the diamond. O'Rourke's flowing use of detail renders his action passages gripping yet free of cliches so characteristic of this genre. A squeeze bunt, for example:

> I saw the Dodger catcher, Campanella, as if in slow motion, begin his charge from behind the plate, hold up suddenly as realization struck him, then cover the plate and, voice completely lost in the crowd roar, shout desperately for the ball; I saw Hammett round first base as the Dodger third sacker reached the ball, now dead on the grass just inside the foul line and halfway between home and third; I saw the third baseman make his desperation one-handed stab and magnificent underhanded toss to the plate, going head-over-heels with the force of his movement and lying sprawled out on the baseline as ball and runner came together; I saw Robbie, running faster than man has a right to move under any condition, go headlong to the right of the plate, diving in a streak of twisted, blurred features and dust

and spikes gleaming in the slanting sun, left hand stabbing out and slapping the white rubber as Campanella caught the chest-high throw and lunged for him with the ball; I saw the umpire standing over the plate, big and crouched low, arms at a strange tight angle along his thighs; and then Robbie and Campanella were rolling together in a mad ball of arms, legs, and faces, covered with the swirling dust as the umpire was sheared from his own feet and rolled with them, all three stopping and lying completely still for one last breathless moment.

> I thought, 'If it is my time to die, please God, let it be now,' and waited.

The spring training experience yielded a cornucopia of closeup detail, and O'Rourke's early novels are virtually love songs to the Phillie organization—not only the players, coaches, and manager, but also groundskeepers, scouts, traveling secretary, publicity director, and office staff. Marshaling exhaustive minutia, he describes the inner workings of a big league club: 17 trunks crammed with uniforms, equipment, towels and soap; 110 dozen balls for spring training (300 dozen more for the regular season); a dozen bats for each regular; $70,000 total training-camp costs. We are given the precise dimensions of the vintage Clearwater ballpark, and learn that a new underground watering system has been installed. We see the trainer at work with his infrared and sine and diathermy machines, and are favored with an item-by-item inventory of the 60-odd medicines and supplies on his shelves. O'Rourke even provides sample days from a two-week travel itinerary as the club breaks camp and heads north.

In *The Team* (1949), Phils owner Robert Carpenter is "Bob Chambers," a young man "with a sincere love for baseball, topped by a shrewd mind and the ability to understand [that] there was no easy shortcut to a pennant.

"He told all of us that he did not expect the impossible; we had set fourth place as our goal for that season and if our young men came through we might do a little better...."

The Phillies did indeed do better in 1949. So did the fictional Quakers—and O'Rourke's reputation as a crystal-ball gazer was launched.[7] Their exploits written six months before the actual outcome, he has his youthful players spurt to a third-place finish, 87-67, two games behind the Boston Braves, one behind the Dodgers. In real life the Phils, too, rode a late-summer surge to end in third, albeit sixteen behind winner Brooklyn. O'Rourke's Quakers top their league in fielding (the Phils were sixth) and he projects some of their final batting averages: Ashton .345 (Ashburn actually would log a modest .284); Hammett .287 (Hamner .263); Del Anderson .310 (Ennis .302); Semik .262 (Seminick .243). In one instance he hits it on the nose, Quaker first baseman "Watkins" duplicating Eddie Waitkus's .306.

O'Rourke's powers of prognostication reached an amazing zenith the following season, with pre-publication serialization of *Bonus Rookie*. Beginning July 29, 1950, it ran for three weeks in *The Saturday Evening Post* and provoked enormous reaction—over 50,000 letters, the magazine's record to that time. Even the Phillies, who happened to move into first place that very week, took note. "On Wednesday," claimed O'Rourke, "the day the *Post* hit the stands, they were all there after breakfast to grab their copies and read, and find out what they were supposed to do that week!" Some of the Whiz Kids took to kidding each other, the *Post* later boasted, with their fictional names, "Sipler" for Sisler, etc.

Here is the closing scenario of *Bonus Rookie*, which, as the actual season drew to an end, appeared to form an uncanny script: The Quaker City club, with catcher Semik sidelined by an injury to his right ankle from a collision with a Giants player at the Polo Grounds in the final week, cling to a two-game lead over the Dodgers with two games remaining. As fate and the schedule mandate, they meet Brooklyn head-on to decide matters. The Dodgers nail down a victory in the first game with three runs in the eighth inning. Facing Don Newcombe in next day's finale, his other pitchers exhausted, the Quaker manager goes with young bonus hurler Ramsay.[8] The game is tied after eight, both starters going the distance. Brooklyn loads the bases in the ninth, but Ramsay whiffs Hodges to end the threat. The Quakers score dramatically and win the pennant.

On the final Saturday of the '50 season, O'Rourke was sitting in the dugout box at Ebbets Field beside Robert Carpenter, thinking, he said later, "about the hundreds of letters Dodger fans had written...saying that if O'Rourke was in their ball park those last two days, they'd kill him."

Perhaps the Brooklynites had cause. Except for minor variations (it was Seminick's *left* ankle he sprained against the Giants on September 27 and played on anyway, learning later that he had a bone separation; Hodges *flew out* in the ninth against Roberts with the bases jammed) all the things capsulized above occurred as O'Rourke had projected, and the Phillies captured their first flag in 35 years.

A pinnacle, in fiction and reality. Afterward came a different story. In 1951 the "Fizz Kids" sank to fifth, finishing 25 games out. Seminick was traded in December. Third baseman Jones was fined $200 the following spring for "conduct detrimental to the club," and Hamner was relieved of his team captaincy. Man-

ager Eddie Sawyer was fired 63 games into the '52 season, his club in sixth, the timing of it ironic, for earlier that day Curt Simmons had blanked the Giants on three hits.

Sawyer, who remembers Frank O'Rourke as "a wonderful man," when asked in a recent phone interview why he was let go after the shutout victory, replied, with a hint of testiness, "Ask them." However, *Dell Baseball Annual 1953* quotes Sawyer as saying, "They got fat-headed on me...they knew everything. I just had to get tough." The Dell reporter offered this summation:

A kindly, gentle, wise, understanding and fatherly man by nature, Eddie had stepped out of character by his crackdown and his Whiz Kids could not forgive him for it. They got worse and worse....Finally Carpenter read [them] the riot act in an unprecedented meeting. It failed to nudge them. Regretfully and reluctantly, he fired Sawyer.

O'Rourke's final baseball books look backward instead of ahead, a significant shift. They also feature a new fictional team, the Blues, rather than the Quakers, and the players no longer so closely resemble the Phillies. Certain parallels are obvious, however, and O'Rourke's outlook has evolved from his earlier uncritical enthusiasm. In *Nine Good Men* (1952), a manager tries to control swell-headed players by clamping down on them, and although in the end he gains the support of the front office, he entertains these wary thoughts about his boss:

Hell, he's like any owner. He starts out in the game telling himself there'll be none of this hiring and firing every year. No, sir. He'll get a good manager and stick with that man through thick and thin, rain and shine. But he won't. They can't lick the system....

O'Rourke's last baseball creations, two companion novellas, *The Catcher and the Manager* (1953), explore the anomalies of this "system." For one thing, the players have changed, softened. As his narrator says:

I've watched ball players who gave everything for their team, men who went out on the field with injuries an ordinary man could not bear. They played ball in that way long ago, but it doesn't happen often today. DiMaggio had it, and a few others, but today they scratch a finger on the beer-bottle opener and yell for the trainer and a doctor.

It becomes clear that this is due in part to

management's failure to reward loyalty and endurance. The old-style catcher in the story, traded by his team and come back to face them in a crucial contest, is portrayed as thinking, "You ran, and fought, and gave everything for your team; and last year, nursing the bad ankle, you wanted more than ever to help them come back, for you loved that team. And they traded you for that!"

As for O'Rourke's hard-pressed manager, he nods to his Giants counterpart before what proves to be his final game, and reflects:

> He—Art Cassidy—was wrong because he'd come up the old way, then...tried to play this new kind of baseball that everyone said was so necessary, what with the different players and so forth. But Durochur [sic] hadn't changed, not a bit, no matter what the papers said about softening up. Durochur came up the hard, rough, no-quarter way, playing every game for keeps, trusting no man and fighting every man....He'd wrecked one team, getting his kind of club, and now he had it and that team was playing ball....What [Cassidy] should have done was pass among his prima donnas with a pisselm club and a blacksnake whip, and instill a little pride and guts in their hides. And go to the front office, take that general manager by the wattles, and let it be known that one man ran this team, and he was that man.

But the system, with its pampered players and front-office politics, defeats him. Cassidy is fired that day, his team mired in sixth place, after his Blues shut out the Giants, 4-0. "The first law in baseball," he postulates ruefully, is "watch your own skin."

While O'Rourke's old-timers deplore certain contemporary trends, it is clear that modern players, too, are victimized. "He felt that players never shared fairly in profits," Edith says. "He saw that baseball had become a business, inevitably so." O'Rourke himself later wrote, "I felt strongly about the way baseball players were treated in those years just before and after World War II, the way they were forced to fit into and stomach a system in which they became chattels."

Ultimately, he concluded, "I simply stopped writing about baseball. I had gotten too far inside. I had become involved much too intimately and knowingly with too many players who were, first of all to me, human beings...."

Yet even in the relatively bittersweet final stories, the game itself retains its powerful grip on those hu-

man beings. Strapping on his protective gear, his worldly-wise catcher thinks, for the thousandth time,

> Each day you went out in the sun and felt the strain on your legs, all the old scars and cuts and sprains and broken bones, and you knew that just once more you were good for one more time....The game would run its course, and you with it, for no matter where you played, the game was everything.

Baseball, then, as a metaphorical tide sweeping its practitioners along with it. As it did Frank O'Rourke in the years after World War II, when it provided so vivid a focus for his artistry.

Notes:

[1] No relation to the major league infielder of the teens and twenties.

[2] The *Post* published O'Rourke's early stories and serialized his novels. In 1949, age 33, he already enjoyed a huge readership, and went on to a prolific writing career that lasted until his death in 1989. Besides sports titles, his nearly seventy books include contemporary and historical novels, Westerns, mysteries, satires, and children's stories; a number received critical acclaim and several became feature films.

[3] Published by A.S. Barnes between 1948 and 1953, they are, in chronological order: *Flashing Spikes; The Team; Bonus Rookie; The Greatest Victory; Never Come Back; Nine Good Men; The Heavenly World Series; The Catcher and the Manager.*

[4] In January, 1950, the Pirates signed high school pitcher Paul Pettit for a record $100,000, the same amount Joe DiMaggio had received the previous March on signing baseball's first six-figure contract.

[5] An apparent reference to Lyle "Bud" Tinning, a 26-year-old Cub rookie who appeared in the '32 World Series, went 13-6 in '33, 4-6 in '34, and pitched only seven innings for St. Louis in '35, his final year.

[6] Walsh actually fared poorly in the ethereal contest, yielding solid hits to the only batters he faced, Ross Youngs and Frank Chance. Walsh died in 1959, age 78.

[7] Two minor characterizations jump out at a reader today. O'Rourke renamed Phils coach Dusty Cooke "Dusty Baker" and in *Nine Good Men* (1952), he created a lefthanded pitcher named "Herb Score," who is struck by a line drive, his season abruptly ended. Three years later, in 1955, a 22-year-old rookie of that name would break in with the Indians; in 1957, Gil McDougald's liner would effectively end his career.

[8] O'Rourke in a 1988 letter: "Roberts was the bonus rookie, with a few of Curt Simmons' little characteristics, but mostly Roberts. He had so much natural talent, such good control, and dear god! what a fast ball....But he refused to learn to throw a good curve ball. Konstanty warned him, [manager Eddie] Sawyer warned him, Bengough warned him, everybody hinted one way or another, [but he] did not have the sense, or the self-discipline, to learn, and you know what it cost him. He lost the hop on the fast ball in '56, and it took him several years to perfect a good curve ball and pitch with his head."

The Haddie Gill Story

Dick Thompson

Harold "Haddie" Gill

During the summer of 1977, I made the acquaintance of an elderly resident of the Brockton, Massachusetts, Veterans Administration Hospital named Charlie Gill. Charlie was a Harvard man, class of 1917. One Saturday afternoon Charlie and I were watching a Dodgers game on television. Actually, I was watching the game and Charlie was asleep in the chair next to me. Several innings into the game, Charlie woke up and said, "My brother Haddie used to pitch for the Dodgers." I had my doubts but Charlie was adamant. Later that night I checked my Macmillan encyclopedia and found an entry for Harold Gill. The major league Gill was born in Brockton in 1899 and died there in 1932. His nickname was Haddie and his major league career consisted of one inning for the Cincinnati Reds, not the Dodgers, in 1923. I tried to pump Charlie for more information, but all he would say was that his brother had died a long time ago.

I started my file on Haddie Gill that summer and over the years I added bits and pieces when I found them. In the mid-1980s I located a Gill nephew who let me borrow Haddie's scrapbook.

Gill's diamond prowess showed early. He pitched for Brockton High School and Phillips Exeter Academy before matriculating at Holy Cross in the class of 1923. Playing baseball for Holy Cross between the world wars was the college equivalent of playing for the New York Yankees at the height of their dynasty. College baseball in New England in the 1920's had a special aura. While the Red Sox and Braves fielded some mis-

erable teams in those years, Holy Cross did not. From 1917 through 1922, the Holy Cross baseball team was a combined 141-19. Haddie's mark from 1920 through 1922 was 18-1 despite a sore arm that prevented him from pitching during his senior year. Haddie's senior year also coincided with the arrival of Owen Carroll. While Christy Mathewson and Tom Seaver were the greatest major leaguer pitchers who attended college, Carroll, based on his Holy Cross record of 49-2 (or, depending on the source, 50-2), was the greatest college pitcher of all time. But that's a story in itself.

On April 22, 1922, Holy Cross played Boston University at Holy Cross's Fitton Field. Besides Gill, three other Holy Cross players from that game—Chick Gagnon, Freddie Maguire and Doc Gautreau—were future major leaguers. The Holy Cross right and left fielders, twins Len and Leo Dugan, were Jumping Joe's younger brothers, and both later played professionally. Boston University's leadoff man and left fielder, Mickey Cochrane, opened the game with a base hit. After being sacrificed to second, he tried to score on a single to right but was thrown out at the plate by Leo Dugan. Those were the only two hits Gill allowed in recording one of his five Holy Cross shutouts.

On June 24, 1923, Gill pitched a game against the Boston Red Sox in Thompsonville, Connecticut. Gill was playing for the All-Collegians, an independent touring team made up mostly of Holy Cross players. Gill

Dick Thompson *would like to thank SABR members Bob Kane and William Ruiz for assistance with this article.*

pitched into the seventh inning and then, after being relieved with the score 2-2, went to the outfield. The Red Sox had the game won, 4-2, with two outs in the ninth before Gill started a bases-empty rally with his second hit of the day off Boston pitcher Lefty O'Doul. The college boys won the game, 5-4, in ten innings.

Three days later the All-Collegians met the New York Yankees at Haverhill Stadium in Haverhill, Massachusetts. The Yankees were expected to field their regular, predominantly lefthanded hitting lineup, and Gill, a lefty, was expected to oppose them. Instead, Gill split the game between right and center fields. The game was a corker. The Yankees scored eight runs in the last two innings to overcome the All-Collegians' 9-4 lead. Babe Ruth had three singles and a double in five at-bats. He played the first six innings at first base and then pitched the final three frames. Haddie came to the plate four times. He doubled off Pipgras in the second, reached on a fielder's choice in the fifth, and then took a Ruth offering in the seventh, best described by the Haverhill *Gazette*, "towards the gridiron bleachers but Witt ran nearly to the steps and jumping into the air hauled the ball down backhanded with his glove, a sensational stab." Ruth walked him in the eighth.

The historical significance of that game came in the top of the seventh when Lou Gehrig hit a towering home run over Haddie's head into the center field stands. This appears to be the first home run Gehrig hit as a Yankee. He signed with the Yankees on June 11. Between then and the end of July, when he was sent to Hartford in the Eastern League, Gehrig appeared in seven offical American League games, four as a defensive replacement for Wally Pipp and three as a pinchhitter. His lone big league hit during that time period was a single. From June 11 through the June 27 game in Haverhill, the Yankees played two other exhibition games, one in Albany, New York, on June 21, a 9-4 loss to the Brooklyn Dodgers for which no known boxscore exists, and one in New Haven, Connecticut, on June 24 in which Gehrig did not play.

On June 28 Gill joined the Cincinnati Reds after accepting, as reported in *The Sporting News* issue of July 5 and the Boston *Globe* edition of July 9, a signing bonus of more than $15,000. The Reds, relying on a strong pitching staff that boasted three 20-game winners, finished second to the Giants that summer. Gill pitched batting practice and exhibition games. His lone major league appearance came closing out a 7-1 loss to New York on August 16. In addition to his regular season salary and his signing bonus, Gill was voted a full share of the Reds second place money, an additional $1,076. For his one major league inning, Haddie pocketed close to $20,000, a huge sum for the time, especially when contrasted to the eight White Sox players who threw the 1919 World Series for individual gains of just one quarter to one half that amount.

Cincinnati planned to farm Gill out to Springfield in the Eastern League in 1924, but the minors held no interest for Haddie. By the time the 1924 World Series ended Gill was in Egypt, where he joined his two older brothers, the previously mentioned Charlie, and Henry, also a 1917 Harvard graduate.

Henry Gill's Harvard 25th Anniversary Report stated that he was with the Military Intelligence Division of the United States War Department during World War I. In June of 1918, he went to Europe, going to England, France, and Italy, before finally landing in Egypt, where he served as assistant to the United States military attaché until September, 1919.

Henry Gill formed several business firms in Egypt and lived there until 1933. He traveled throughout Europe and the Near East, crossing the Atlantic sixteen times. While in Egypt he lived in Alexandria, where he and his brothers ran an import-export business.

Less is known about Haddie's life in Egypt ,but it appears that he lived there from 1924-1927. On his trips home the Brockton *Times* would write about his Egyptian wanderings, and his name could usually be found in box scores of local baseball games. By the end of the '20s, Haddie was home to stay. His health was failing and he died in 1932 from complications following surgery for appendicitis. His death certificate stated that he had suffered from tuberculosis since 1918.

Henry Gill returned home the year after his brother's death. He practiced law in Brockton until his own death in 1974.

In May of 1941, in one of the stranger events of World War II, Rudolf Hess, third deputy Fuehrer of Nazi Germany, parachuted from a plane into Scotland. He eventually was sentenced to life imprisonment at the Nuremberg war trials and remained incarcerated until his death in 1987.

Hess was born in Alexandria, Egypt, in 1894. His grandfather founded an import-export business there in 1865. Hess's father ran that business at least until the start of World War I. The Gill brothers started their business there shortly after that time. What exactly the Gill's connection to Rudolf Hess is remains unclear, but Henry Gill knew Hess. Gill stated in his Harvard 25th Anniversary Report that, "Last summer the Boston *Globe* carried my picture on the front page as an old friend of Rudolf Hess, and some people have ever since viewed me with suspicion."

Unfortunately, despite reviewing microfilm of the Boston *Globe* from May to August of 1941, I was unable to locate the Gill-Hess story. Was the import-export business in Egypt the link between the two or did Henry Gill know or meet Hess in some other capacity? Did Haddie Gill also know Hess? It doesn't really matter as Haddie's death came long before the horrors of the Second World War. But for a cup-of-coffee ball player, Haddie Gill sure got around.

Nick Whips Blackwell

Eddie Gold

My favorite baseball game? If I had to select one from the thousands I witnessed during my misspent youth, I'd have to go with the Cubs 2-1 victory over the Cincinnati Reds on August 8, 1947, at Wrigley Field. That tense contest had everything—tight pitching, a triple play, and a game-winning homer by Bill Nicholson in extra innings.

Ewell Blackwell and Johnny Schmitz were on the mound and I was in the bleachers. Seated alongside me was an Archie Bunker type, who was busy heaping abuse on Nicholson, the Cubs' right fielder.

It was an overcast day and the temperature was quite mild. And yet Archie sat there, stripped to the waist, sweating profusely, and flagging every beer vendor.

When Nicholson strolled to his position, Archie yelled: "Hey, where were you during the war, ya color-blind draft dodger." Big Nick, an amiable sort, waved to the Ladies' Day crowd and ignored Archie.

Blackwell, the Reds' starter, was long and lean and resembled a fly rod with ears. And when he delivered his buggy whip sidearm he looked like a man falling from a tree.

However, Ewell the Whip was baseball's premier pitcher that season. He had already won 16 in a row, including a no-hitter, and was en route to a 22-win season. Schmitz, a lean southpaw, was the Cubs' stopper.

The Cubs struck first in the second inning when Nicholson lifted a fly ball to left center that was dropped by the Reds' Bert Haas for a two-base error.

"Dat's da only way you can get on base, ya bum,"

Eddie Gold *is a Chicago sportswriter whose boyhood idol was Bill Nicholson.*

yelled Archie.

Nicholson took third on a ground out and scampered home with the game's first run when Len Merullo beat out a slow roller. The Reds tied the score in the fifth inning on singles by Grady Hatton and Haas, a walk to Babe Young, and a force out.

In the seventh inning, Hatton opened with a single and Haas beat out a bunt which Schmitz neglected to pick up. And then it happened!

Young swung and hit a liner over short and both runners were off and flying. Merullo leaped and speared the ball, stepped on second, and fired to first base to Eddie Waitkus for a triple play. It was over in a split second—and there was no instant replay.

Schmitz then matched Blackwell pitch for pitch and the game went into extra innings. When Nicholson strode to the plate with one out in the bottom of the eleventh inning, Archie sat in stoney silence. He was, perhaps, a bit more stoned than silent.

Swish picked up a couple of bats, swung them around until his favorite warclub was chosen. He tapped his shoetops with the bat, hitched his belt, and awaited the pitch with his mouth full of tobacco.

Blackwell peered at Ray Lamanno, his catcher, and whipped across a sidearm strike. The following delivery was wide for a ball. Nicholson then offered at the next pitch and popped it up near the Cubs' dugout. Lamanno waved third baseman Hatton away, but the ball eluded his outstretched mitt.

Blackwell then pumped and delivered—and Nicholson connected. The ball was hit high and deep and landed on the right field catwalk for a game-winning homer. The Cubs had whipped the mighty

Blackwell, 2-1, and Nicholson had done it.

I then turned to Archie, who was grinning from ear to ear. "Boy, dat was some clout," said Archie. "I always liked dat Nicholson."

That evening, in a sandlot game, I picked up a couple of bats, swung them around and selected the heavier one. I tapped my shoetops with the bat, hitched my belt, and stuck a wad of chewing gum in my mouth. I struck out.

Ewell Blackwell, about to whip one on the sidelines.

Rochester, 1928

Brian A. Bennett

The spring of 1995 finally saw the last hurdles removed for the construction of a new ballpark for Rochester's longtime International League franchise, solidifying the team's future in upstate New York. As the Red Wings enjoy new Frontier Field, they can harken back some 69 seasons, when the promise of another new stadium saved local baseball.

The new ballpark will continue Rochester's proud tradition as the International League's flagship franchise, and supporters hope it will spur the team to a run of four consecutive pennants, as did the opening of Red Wing Stadium in 1928. For Rochester fans, however, Frontier Field can never replace in their hearts the ballpark on Norton Street (renamed Silver Stadium in 1968) as the "home of the Red Wings."

In 1927, as in the early 1990s, the future of the franchise was clouded. That season's edition of the Rochester Tribe finished in sixth place at 81-86, 30 games from the top. Of greater worry, however, was the unstable front office situation. During the previous off-season John Hicks and William Gilbert had become the eighth owners since 1921. There had been talk of a new ballpark—a private corporation to plan and finance the project had even been established—but the shaky ownership situation and lack of capital put the plans on hold.

Professional baseball in Rochester dated back exactly a half-century. In 1877 a team represented the city in what was the first league established outside of the self-proclaimed "major league." It was not until 1885, though, that Rochester began its uninterrupted presence in what would become the International League. There had been pennants in 1899, 1901, and 1909–1911, yet in spite of that tradition of success, by 1927 the continued existence of professional baseball in Rochester was unsure.

There was some optimism in late August, when rumors surfaced of interested buyers. Four days after the end of the season hearsay became fact. A group of investors, headed by golf star and city native Walter Hagen and former Rochester manager John Ganzel, had agreed to purchase the team. Ganzel, who had led the Rochester team to those three consecutive pennants in his five-year stint with the club, was also tabbed as manager.

But a hint of difficulties surfaced on December 15, when the would-be owners, $60,000 short of the purchase price, were given an extra week to consummate the sale. League president John Conway Toole made a special trip to Rochester to confer with civic leaders. Impressed with their resolve, Toole stated that the financial details could be "left for a later date."

There was little additional news until January 5, when another bombshell dropped: the Hagen offer fell through. Hicks and Gilbert were given less than two weeks to place the team on firm financial ground or the league would forfeit the franchise. An eager group of Jersey City investors stood ready to purchase and move the team. Hicks and Gilbert were anxious to get out of baseball ownership, "but rather than let the club go to outside interests," set about to meet the league's

Brian A. Bennett *is the author of the recently published* On A Silver Diamond: The Story of Rochester Community Baseball from 1956–1996. *He has also written two books dealing with the Civil War, and several articles for Civil War magazines. He is Director of Publications at the State University of New York College at Genesco.*

requirements.

The Cardinals fly to the rescue—Hicks and Gilbert guaranteed baseball in Rochester if a stadium were built, and they pledged to sign an initial ten-year lease, with all operating expenses to be paid by the ballclub. They set about securing financing. Talk soon centered around a mystery third party said to be involved. One guess centered on the St. Louis Cardinals. That rumor was apparently made moot on January 11, five days before the deadline, when Hicks and Gilbert announced they would put $55,000 into the team.

With the situation seemingly stabilized, it was no doubt unsettling when the rumors concerning the Cardinals gained new life. On January 15 a Rochester newspaper reported that Warren Giles, the president of the Syracuse Stars, the Cardinal-owned International League club, was in the city and involved in "secret conferences" with Hicks and Gilbert. The next day Cardinal executive Branch Rickey was said to have joined the discussions.

Banner front-page headlines on January 17, 1928 trumpeted the announcement: "St. Louis Cardinals Will Operate Rochester Baseball Club." International League owners quickly approved the transaction, which called for the personnel of the 1927 Syracuse Stars to be transferred to Rochester, while the Syracuse franchise would be moved to Jersey City and stocked with the previous year's Rochester players. Less than a week later the official terms of sale were ironed out: $120,000, with $30,000 as a down payment. Warren Giles was named president and Stars manager and former Cardinal Billy Southworth, 34, was retained as the field boss of the Rochester club.

With ownership finally resolved, other concerns were brought off the back burner. The first, of course, was the stadium issue. The proposed 16,000-seat stadium was estimated to cost close to $275,000. It was still hoped that the facility would be operated by a separate local corporation with the team as the principal tenant. The Cardinals expressed no interest in contributing financially, but would guarantee its rental.

Another issue was the selection of a new team nickname and a contest was held to select a replacement for "Tribe." Close to 1,700 entries were received and on February 28 President Giles announced that the club would officially be known as the Red Wings. Giles explained that the selection met three criteria: no team in organized baseball at that time was using the name (nor, incidentally, was Detroit's professional hockey club—it adopted the name in 1932); the name had Indian connotations "typical of the territory which the Rochester club will represent"; and was applicable as "a unit or wing of the Cardinal organization, that bird having red wings."

Finally attention was turned to the team itself and

this was perhaps the cause for the greatest excitement. The Red Wings were at that time one of seven minor league clubs owned by the Cardinals. In the early '20s, frustrated by the prevailing system of having to purchase players from the minors, Cards owner Sam Breadon allowed Rickey to establish a "farm system" of minor league clubs in which the Cardinals could develop their own players. In 1927 the Syracuse Stars had finished second (102-66), and those players would form the nucleus of the 1928 Red Wings.

As opposed to recent Rochester clubs, the new team would consist of young prospects. The league grapevine predicted the closest pennant race in a decade. The Red Wings (or the "Reds" as the local media quickly shortened the nickname) opened the season, ironically, in Jersey City. The Black Cats consisted primarily of Rochester's 1927 squad. The visitors captured a 3-1 extra-inning tilt, with manager Southworth (expected to play at least part-time in the outfield) tripling home the lead run in the 12th.

The home opener matched the same two teams. The many changes sparked new-found interest and the game was played in front of 16,556 fans at Baseball Park. The overflow crowd (the grandstand could seat 9,500) was herded into the spacious outfield behind ropes. It was not an artistic opening, notwithstanding the 7-6 outcome, or the handsome new uniforms which sported a red-winged baseball on the left breast. Football markings were still discernible on the field and the crowd was unruly.

The club hovered around .500 as Southworth and Giles continued to tinker with the roster. By late June the Reds had climbed into a first place tie with Toronto with the Maple Leafs coming to town. In front of the "noisiest crowd" of the season the Red Wings won the opener, 9-2. However the Leafs captured five of the next six between the clubs and dropped Rochester to fourth.

Pennant race—Toronto continued as the front runner and the Reds found themselves contesting with Baltimore, Montreal and Reading for second. A shot at first was seemingly ended in early August. Before and during a doubleheader loss in Montreal, seven Rochester players were injured, including two hurt in a taxi accident on the way to the ballpark. The injuries forced pitcher Tony Kaufmann into the outfield, as Southworth could pencil only two regulars into his starting lineup.

The Reds were second at the time of the debacle, but the resulting seven-game losing streak dropped the crippled squad off the pace. Mid-August found the club floundering in sixth place, a game above .500. But Toronto slumped and as the regulars returned the Reds started their climb back.

The International League pennant race became what

probably still stands as the closest race in league history. During the last week of August, five different teams—Baltimore, Toronto, Reading, Rochester and a resurgent Buffalo squad—held first place. The advent of September found the Red Wings back at the summit, percentage points ahead of the Bisons. The climax of Rochester's incredible run came the next day, when, in front of 17,884 fans (with an additional 3,500 turned away), the Reds swept Buffalo, 12-9 and 5-2. Southworth's squad had won 16 of 19 games, including six doubleheader sweeps.

New hurler Larry Irvin and former hurler Kaufmann were primary reasons for the reversal. Irvin won his first six decisions after being called up. Kaufmann, permanently installed in right field due to his sore pitching arm and Southworth's lame leg, put together a 20-game hit streak and was hitting .443. But Buffalo would not relinquish its crown without a fight, nor would Toronto gently fade away. The three teams continued to swap the top spot, the margins measured in terms of mere percentage points. Rochester reclaimed first place for a day on September 15 with a ninth-inning home win over Montreal. The Reds won another game in similarly dramatic fashion less than a week later. Shortstop Charlie Gelbert led off the bottom of the 10th with an inside-the-park home run for a 3-2 win over the Leafs, realistically ending Toronto's pennant hopes.

Tied with Buffalo, Rochester began its final series with Montreal, but the opener was suspended by darkness with the teams tied at seven. It would have to be replayed in its entirety, meaning the Wings' final six games would be played in three consecutive doubleheaders with the Royals.

Irvin won the first game, 8-0, and Southworth put him back on the hill for the nightcap. The lefty was hit hard, ace Herm Bell could do no better, and the resulting 9-3 loss put the Reds a full game behind Buffalo. With his two hottest pitchers used up, things looked grim for the Rochester skipper.

Southworth had little choice but to turn to recently-promoted rookie Eddie Clough, who responded with a 9-3 victory in what would be his only appearance of the season. Workhorse Art Decatur notched his 16th win, 3-2, in the darkness-shortened second game. However, Buffalo captured its single game, and a victory by the Bisons on the final day would leave Rochester needing a sweep to capture the title.

Southworth went with the exhausted Bell in the first game. The Red Wings trailed 2-0 in the sixth when Kaufmann erased the deficit with a bases-loaded triple. Bell finished off the 5-2 victory (his 20th of the season), and after changing his sweatshirt, returned to the hill for Game Two.

The Reds showed little taste for drama, sending nine men to the plate and scoring four runs in the top of the first. They cruised to a 5-0 pennant-clinching victory behind Bell's seven-inning complete game. The sweep, despite the victory by Buffalo, gave the pennant to the Red Wings by .001 percentage points: .549 to .548. Rochester's final day leapfrog over Buffalo constituted the fifteenth change at the top since August. Rochester played four fewer games than Buffalo, which resulted in the razor-thin margin.

The new ballpark—Despite a subsequent loss in the Little World Series against the Indianapolis Indians, champions of the American Association, it was altogether a fine season. Southworth's pennant-winning squad ignited what one newspaper called a "revival of the sport" in the city. The parent Cardinals went one better, capturing the NL pennant and World Series, and their success kept the Red Wing nucleus together for the entire season.

The first Rochester pennant since 1911 was not the only positive development. The proposed new ballpark became reality in mid-August, when the Cardinals announced plans to build a stadium in the city's northeast side. In a reversal of their earlier position, the Cards expected to do their own financing, and construction was to start immediately. The new ballpark was modeled after Buff Stadium in Houston, home to St. Louis's Double-A farm club.

Work continued through the winter and in mid-December it was reported that the foundation had been poured and "steel [was] mounting at a rapid rate." By late January the small office building in front of the park was completed, along with half of the roof structure. In early March the club offices were moved to the new stadium, the main grandstand was about completed, steel for the bleachers went up, and grass was sprouting in the outfield. The target date for completion was April 15.

The spring of 1929 was unusually moist, and as the Wings opened the IL season in Reading on April 17 the stadium was not yet complete. Fortunately the league weighted the early schedule toward the southern cities and the Wings were not due to open at home until May 2. As the date approached, demand for Opening Day tickets increased to such a point that the Red Wings added 2,000 more grandstand seats to reserved status, making a total of 7,000 booked seats. Excitement was heightened by the fact that the Wings were coming north in first place.

May 1 was an offday, but noteworthy as the $400,000 stadium was turned over to Red Wing management. The players practiced on their new field, watched by 300 curious spectators. Those fans were "unanimous in deciding that the club had spared no expense in putting up a baseball monument for Rochester." The park featured 12,702 grandstand seats and 3,360 bleacher seats, for a total seating capacity of 16,062, almost double the Bay Street Park. By installing bleachers in the outfield and roping off the field, Red Wing management estimated it could handle 23,000 (although it was noted that there would be no carriages or motor cars allowed in the outfield as was prmitted in the old ballpark). The field could also be laid out for football and accommodate 28,000.

Those who previewed the stadium that day were most complimentary about the "color scheme, grandstand pitch, small amount of screen, and condition of field." The structure's steel work was painted cream with maroon trimmings. Not only attractive, the support system aided accessibility and comfort as well, as the construction superintendent stated that the "most unique and yet the finest part about the job is the steel work under the grandstand…, designed…[so] that people will not be forced to dodge [head-high] beams."

On the field, the outfield configuration was smaller than at the Bay Street Park, and it was predicted that left handed hitters would have a decided advantage, as the right field foul pole was a mere 315 feet from home plate. The bleachers, which began beyond third base, extended behind the left field wall, so that home runs hit down the line would carry into the stands. The outfield fence sported just one ad, which extended around each side of the immense scoreboard in left center field. The rest of the barrier was painted green.

The players' dressing rooms and a huge concession stand were located under the stands. The building which fronted Norton Street would serve as the club's offices, and house ticket windows and turnstiles. Access to the park was also improved, as the Norton Street site was easily reached by street cars.

The morning of May 2 dawned cold and damp, and throughout the day the newspaper offices fielded calls questioning whether or not the game would be played. The gates of the park opened at 10 AM for the three o'clock start and the 14,885 in attendance saw a disappointing 3-0 loss to the Reading Keys. The turnout was short of the expected 20,000, but reaction to the new park was universally positive. Rochester was held to only two hits on the dreary afternoon, during which a band in attendance played "Jingle Bells" as a wry comment on the weather conditions.

Solid baseball—The new stadium and the powerhouse teams (the Cardinal-supplied squads went on to win league pennants in the next three years), solidified the future of baseball in the Flower City. Season attendance for the inaugural season was 298,802, and the next season the turnstiles spun at a rate of 328,424, a record that would stand for almost twenty years. A record crowd of 19,006 was present on Opening Day in 1931, a mark which has yet to be surpassed.

A member of the International League since 1885, Rochester has captured at least one championship in every decade since the 1890s. The franchise survived the lean years of the Depression, World War II, and the departure of the St. Louis Cardinals in 1956, to become the model minor league franchise in the 1970s. Renamed Silver Stadium, in honor of Morrie Silver, who helped local interests purchase the franchise and stadium from the Cardinals, the park saw changes in dimensions, seating capacity, and its surrounding neighborhood, but remained a remarkable constant for Rochester fans who traveled to 500 North Street to watch their beloved Red Wings play.

Would you call losing your marbles a bad bounce?

Marty McManus, third baseman of the Boston Red Sox, is now insisting that his five year old boy give up baseball or marbles. On the morning of May 10, young Marty Joe requested Daddy Marty to play ball with him, so they went out to Fenway Park. The youngster took a bag of marbles with him and there the two played catch and marbles. The boy lost his favorite flint and neither father nor son could find it.

In the afternoon, Marty, Sr., found it in Detroit's half of the eight inning. Davis put down a bunt toward Marty at third and had it beat to first, but the ball was rolling foul, until it hit an obstruction and bounded fair.

And that is when Daddy Marty found his youngster's marble. The ball had struck the half-buried marble and rolled fair, out of McManus's reach. (From The Sporting News, *May 19, 1932.)*

—*Dick Thompson*

Uncle Albert

Alan Schwarz

The story begins sometime in March 1995. I was reading *The New Yorker*. (I've always wanted to write that, but I must confess—I was in a doctor's waiting room with few other options.) After taking in most of the cartoons, I flipped to the feature on Bill Bradley. I had written a piece on his Princeton basketball days while in college, and thought I'd check in on him.

While discussing politics, a subject in which I have little interest regardless of whether the speaker can dunk, Bradley mentioned his 1975 book, *Life on the Run*, an account of his pro basketball career. I had read John McPhee's book about Bradley called *A Sense of Where You Are* to research my college story on him, and decided to give *Life on the Run* a try. I found it in my local bookstore.

Churning through tales of Knicks road trips and locker-room ankle-tapings, I discovered this startling passage on page 121:

> The very agency which first makes the celebrity in the long run inevitably destroys him...The newspapers make him and they unmake him—not by murder but by suffocation or starvation...There is not even any tragedy in the celebrity's fall, for he is a man returned to his proper anonymous station...a commonplace man who has been fitted back into his proper commonplaceness not by any fault of his own, but by time itself.

The passage above, Bradley wrote, came from a book called *The Image*, by the historian Daniel Boorstin, which Bradley had inhaled while at Princeton in the early '60s. Boorstin's ideas intrigued me, so I called my bookstore, ordered his book, and found it in my mailbox two weeks later.

The Image, subtitled "A Guide to Pseudo-Events in America," was a revolutionary look at, among other things, how the media was increasingly distorting the values of America by creating events rather than reporting them. Fascinating, groundbreaking stuff. It had nothing remotely to do with baseball, until Boorstin on page 210 described a man as "an advertising master of the twentieth century." His name was Albert Lasker.

Lasker? There are Laskers in my family. In fact, one of them, my great-uncle Morris, was a United States federal judge in Manhattan from 1968 to 1994 and now sits on the federal bench in Cambridge, Massachusetts. He presided at the trial of inside-trader Ivan Boesky and was on the cover of a 1992 issue of *New York* magazine with the headline, "The Brilliance of New York." Having one relative that famous was enough for me, but I called my father just in case.

"Dad, I just came across this name in a book. Are we related to a man named Albert Lasker?"

"Oh, yes," he said. "Let's see. He's your...(long pause while climbing the family tree)...your grandmother's uncle. He would be your great-great uncle."

My dad told me that John Gunther had written a biography of Albert Lasker in 1960, called *Taken at the Flood*. It has been out of print for decades. I searched

Alan Schwarz *is a columnist for* Baseball America *and a frequent contributor to* Inside Sports. *He lives in Manhattan.*

unsuccesfully for the volume at used bookstores, and ultimately forgot about it. But while rummaging through the stacks at the Strand bookstore in Greenwich Village, I found it—misshelved—in the journalism section. Eight bucks. Sold.

The book began by describing all that Albert Lasker was known for: being "the father of American advertising" while running the Lord & Thomas ad agency in Chicago, developing trademarks and slogans for Lucky Strike, Pepsodent, Kleenex, Palmolive, Studebaker, RCA, Frigidaire, and others; making an indelible impact on politics, shipping, and show business, and donating millions upon millions of dollars to charity. "One of the most phenomenal Americans of his time," Gunther gushed.

Since I figured I already would have been aware of being related to Moses, I became rather skeptical, and ultimately quite bored. I was ready to put the book away, inter it forever on my shelves, but instead flipped to the Table of Contents for one last moment of inspiration.

Chapter 8 stood out:

BASEBALL

"Father loved baseball," says Edward Lasker, Albert's son, who now is 85 and lives in Los Angeles. But Albert Lasker did more than love the game. He changed the course of the sport at its most tenuous moment, when the Black Sox scandal threatened the very existence of the major leagues.

Lasker became a baseball fan as a young boy while watching the Chicago Cubs hold their spring training in his Galveston, Texas, hometown. He picked up odd dollars by telegraphing news of the games up to Chicago. He later moved to that city, amassed both fortune and prominent status at Lord & Thomas, and bought the controlling interest in the Cubs in 1916 as a diversion from his advertising work. (He brought in as a new board member a man named William Wrigley who at the time, Lasker claimed, had no interest in baseball at all and didn't even know three strikes made an out. Lasker later changed the name of the team's stadium from Cub Park to Wrigley Field because, he told Wrigley, "This will do your chewing-gum business a lot of good.") But Lasker kept his own baseball profile low. Years later he told a friend, "You never heard of a *respectable* citizen being owner of a baseball team, did you?"

Baseball lost most of its respectability when eight members of the 1919 White Sox threw that year's World Series to the Reds. This is where Lasker ultimately left his mark on the game. It was he who devised the remedy to regain the public's trust: an all-powerful commissioner—someone from outside the industry—to rule over the game. He went on to suggest a man to fill the role: a judge acquaintance of his

named Kenesaw Mountain Landis.

J. G. Taylor Spink noted Lasker's idea in his biography, *Judge Landis and 25 Years of Baseball*:

The Lasker plan, in short, recommended doing away entirely with the old three-man National Commission of baseball men and substituting in its stead a three-man board made up of "men of unquestionable reputation and standing in fields other than baseball," and in "no way connected with baseball...The mere presence of such men on the Board," said the plan, "would assure the public that public interests would first be served, and that therefore, as a natural sequence, all existing evils would disappear." Lasker proposed that this Commission of three would have sole and unreviewable power...It would have provided for the most powerful and absolute tribunal ever thought up to protect and govern a sport in the history of mankind, without the baseball people having the slightest check on the men selected to be the overlords of their sport and business.

The Lasker plan, which later was modified to call for a single czar in place of a threesome, was met with immediate favor by the eight National League clubs. But the American League president, Ban Johnson, feared losing his status as the most powerful man in baseball. He also disagreed that an outside person, no matter how respected and erudite, could understand and govern this complex industry. Five American League franchises, all but those from New York, Chicago, and Boston, joined his staunch opposition to the idea. Thus began a battle that makes the modern infighting between major league owners seem like a playground tussle.

"To enforce their demands on Johnson and the clubs loyal to him," Spink wrote, "the Lasker plan devotees issued an ultimatum that if the five other American League clubs would not come in line by November 1 (1920), the Yankees, White Sox, and Red Sox would secede from the American League, and, with the addition of a twelfth club, join the National League in forming a new 12-club circuit."

The Yankees and Red Sox in the National League? It almost happened. It wasn't a bluff. After not receiving support from the five American League clubs, the eleven teams in favor of the plan convened on November 8.

"At the meeting," Spink wrote, "the old National League was formally disbanded, and its eight clubs and the Yankees, White Sox, and Red Sox organized a new circuit, called the National-American League. The twelfth franchise was awarded to Detroit."

The Chicago *Tribune* wrote, "The five American League club owners who sided with President Ban Johnson in the controversy over the Lasker scheme began to put into operation plans, which have been underway for several months, to locate new clubs in Chicago, New York, and Boston. They intend to fight…to a finish."

The National-American League lived for forty-eight hours. Johnson and his allies finally relented and agreed to the commissioner plan. Landis, who had been sounded out as a candidate through Alfred Austrian, the lawyer for both Lasker and White Sox owner Charles Comiskey, accepted the position on November 12. For trivia buffs, Landis first was hired as "director-general of Baseball," but the judge, saying "that sounds too high-falutin'," chose the title of "Commissioner." He issued a statement to the American public: "The only thing in anybody's mind right now is to make and keep baseball what the millions of fans throughout the United States want it to be."

Lasker, disillusioned by the fight he later called "the bitterest, most complex, and most fatiguing struggle" of his life, sold his interest in the Cubs to William Wrigley in 1925. But his concept of an outside person coming in to rule the game with unfettered control was hailed as brilliant; it later was adopted by the motion picture and garment industries, among others.

"When the Black Sox scandal was announced, father was absolutely shattered," Edward Lasker remembers. "When he sold his share, he never looked back. He never went to more than a couple of World Series games the rest of his life." But, thanks largely to Lasker's ideas and leadership, the public's confidence in his favorite sport never again teetered as it did in 1920—that is, until his commissioner position was eliminated with the owners' firing of Fay Vincent.

Albert Lasker died in 1952 at the age of 72. His niece,

*The author's "Uncle Albert,"
Albert D. Lasker.*

Louise Lasker, married a man named Erwin Schwarz, who today has a grandson named Alan. Alan wrote his eighth-grade term paper in 1982 on the Black Sox scandal, but had completely forgotten about it until, well, he began writing the end of this story.

Though Albert Lasker is mentioned twice in Eliot Asinof's *Eight Men Out*—from which I recall shamelessly plagiarizing in junior high—I don't remember ever hearing the name until it appeared at the end of that absurdly random New Yorker–Bill Bradley–Daniel Boorstin–John Gunther–J.G.T. Spink trail last year. I wonder if I ever would have found it otherwise. And, after nodding that I probably wouldn't, I wonder what I'll stumble across the next time I go to the doctor.

Pre-1900 NL Franchise Movement

Ray Miller

Few subjects seem to confuse even dedicated baseball people more than franchise shifts. There has been no attempt to reach a consensus on, say, whether the A's constitute one club that has happened to play out of three different cities at various times, or three separate and distinct teams. For instance, glancing at Duke Snider's record in the *Baseball Encyclopedia*, you would think he was traded between 1957 and 1958, from Bkn N to LA N. There is no way of telling that he stayed with the Dodgers as they moved from coast to coast. *The Encyclopedia of Major League Teams* even makes such distinctions a point of principle ("Anyone who contends that the Brooklyn Dodgers-Los Angeles Dodgers…constitute the same franchise has not talked to a native of Brooklyn…"). On the other hand, I and many other people would agree with Al Yellon, who, in his article "Team All-Time Records" in *The National Pastime* No. 14, insists on the essential continuity in a team's history despite cross-country moves. To me, it's enough to ask how else are we to account for the fact that the old ballpark in Washington, D.C. bore the name of the owner of the Minnesota Twins?

Since people have such a hard time making sense out of moves that took place twenty-five to forty-five years ago, it's little wonder that the franchise chaos that reigned in the National League for most of the nineteenth century has left them utterly confused. Depending on how you count, as many as thirty different NL clubs took the field between 1876 and 1899. As we know, only eight survived into this century. What hap-

pened to the other twenty-odd?

Many works, especially those written for the casual reader, create confusion because they are not careful with nineteenth-century facts. For example, in *The History of National League Baseball Since 1876* by Glenn Dickey (introduction by that noted baseball historian, Pete Rose), the author treats the nineteenth-century Philadelphia A's and the Phillies as one and the same team going under different names, even though he correctly states elsewhere that the Athletics were expelled from the league after the 1876 season. His treatment of the St. Louis Brown Stockings and Cardinals is similarly muddled, and he doesn't even mention the Maroons of 1885-86.

In many instances, different sources treat the same facts differently. Let's take the Phillies again. Bill James, in his *Historical Baseball Abstract*, says that the earliest franchise shift he's aware of is the Worcester Brown Stockings moving to Philadelphia in 1883 and becoming the Phillies. An earlier version of *The Baseball Encyclopedia* listed this in its section on franchise shifts. On the other hand, Harold Seymour writes in his work *Baseball: The Early Years*, of NL magnates giving Worcester "a gentle bounce out of the membership and moving into Philadelphia…."

A different structure—One reason why it is so hard to grasp the fate of these old teams is that baseball clubs were constituted much differently back then. As James wrote, "A 'franchise', as we know it now—a collection of contracts with players, stadium, and fans—did not exist." For the most part, clubs were locally organized outfits. Even if they might go out and

---

Ray Miller *teaches at Bowdoin College in Maine, and plays second base for the Gardiner Knights of the local men's Senior Baseball League. He has written on baseball history for various publications.*

recruit talent from other places—see Albert Spalding's account in *America's National Game* of his move from Rockford to Chicago early in his career—they had a life of their own in their town, apart from whatever this or that league could give them. Both the NA and the NL started out as voluntary associations of otherwise independent local clubs.

We also must remember that the early National League was hardly the bedrock institution it is today. All but one or two teams lost money until well into the '80s, and club turnover was constant. The NL didn't field the same set of teams two years in a row until 1881-82, and the first time the same unit held for more than two years was the awkward twelve-team lineup of 1892-99. The league was so unstable, Seymour reports, that when A. G. Mills became president in 1882 he refused to list the club names on his letterhead.

Teams could be expelled from the NL for a variety of reasons, or even leave of their own volition. For example, according to *The Encyclopedia of Major League Teams* and *Total Baseball*, the owner of the original St. Louis Browns pulled them out of the league after the 1877 season in the wake of the Louisville gambling scandal. They were theoretically free to join another league or continue to play independently, although this was probably not a financially viable option by the early 1880s. But as James says, "There was no concept of [moving and] doing business somewhere else."

By the same token, holes in the NL roster would be filled, not by freshly created "expansion franchises" as we know them, but by already existing clubs. These might be independents, such as Worcester in 1880, or successful "minor" league teams, like Buffalo, Troy, and Syracuse, who signed on in 1879 out of the International Association. They might even come over from other "major" leagues (the St. Louis Maroons from the United Association in 1885; the Pittsburgh Pirates from the American Association in 1887; a total of seven other AA teams between 1889 and 1892). It is interesting to note that the Providence Grays seem to have been the first club consciously built from scratch specifically to play in the NL (1878).

But still, even if franchise shifts as we know them today were rare, simply dropping out—or being dropped—also came to happen less and less frequently as time went on, and thus we are confronted with a whole series of hybrid transactions that can be baffling to the unsuspecting modern researcher.

Let's take a look at all the different fates that could befall a National League club in the last century. Only two of the cases discussed below will look familiar to twentieth-century fans, although we could argue that some of the others actually represent "franchise shifts" as well.

Team expelled or voluntarily withdraws—This is what normally happened in the 1870s. Teams were also dropped in the '80s and '90s, although by then it had more to do with increasing the profit margins of the other owners than with specific aesthetic or financial shortcomings. Whereas the 1878 Indianapolis Blues were forced to leave the NL because of their total failure on the field and at the gate, the 1889 Indianapolis Hoosiers were given the boot (along with the Washington Statesmen) to make room for successful AA franchises which could better bolster NL fortunes in the coming "players' war." Not that the Hoosiers or Statesmen were wildly successful clubs—far from it—but neither was there any serious thought of expelling them until Brooklyn and Cincinnati expressed their desire to change leagues. Similarly, the Cleveland Spiders, Washington Senators, Louisville Colonels, and Baltimore Orioles were summarily kicked out of the NL after the 1899 season in order to get down to a more manageable eight-team circuit. (More on this below.)

Owner moves team to different city—Think of Walter O'Malley moving the Dodgers to LA from Brooklyn, or Cal Griffith taking the Washington Senators to Minnesota. Only once in the last century did a team owner simply pull up stakes and set up shop in another town. Ironically, even though this is the one nineteenth-century transaction most like those of our day, it is the one most frequently misconstrued by our sources.

The Hartford Dark Blues were a charter member of the NL, coming over from the NA. Although they finished a respectable third in 1876, they lost so much money that owner Morgan Bulkeley felt forced to abandon central Connecticut. Since the expulsion of the New York Mutuals at the end of the '76 season left the lucrative Gotham market suddenly open, Buckeley decided to move his team to the famous Union Grounds in Brooklyn for the 1877 season, where they played for one season before disbanding.

However, almost all sources persist in listing the team as "Hartford" in the 1877 league standings. James doesn't even mention the move in his brief discussion of early franchise shifts. *Total Baseball* mentions the team's move at the end of its paragraph on the Hartford Dark Blues, while *The Encyclopedia of Major League Teams* alone is consistent in acknowledging Buckeley's move: it has separate entries for the "Hartford Dark Blues" (1876) and the "Brooklyn Hartfords" (1877).

Owner sells team to out-of-town interests—This is another familiar twentieth-century maneuver that occurred only once in the last century. Henry Lucas sold his St. Louis Maroons to Indianapolis businessmen, who moved the team to Indiana and renamed them the

Hoosiers for the 1887 season. The deal wasn't consummated until 24 days before opening day.

The other types of franchise movement we see in the nineteenth century could not happen today. They are connected with the rapacious business practices of the time, which make even our carnivorous era seem tame by comparison. They also bespeak a lack of central control and foresight, as well as a dearth of concern for "small-market" teams, all of which might seem a bit more familiar.

One team buys out a competitor—Try to picture the Milwaukee Brewers going bankrupt, and George Steinbrenner buying the team from Bud Selig, lock, stock, and barrel, while remaining boss of the Yankees. This happened twice in the mid-1880s. In November, 1885, NL powerhouse Boston snatched up the proud but insolvent Providence Grays for $6,600, plucked a couple of star players off the roster, and released the rest.

In a much better known transaction from earlier the same year, the Detroit Wolverines bought the entire Buffalo Bisons roster for $7,000 in order to acquire the so-called "Big Four"—Hardy Richardson, Dan Brouthers, Jack Rowe, and Deacon Jim White. While the sale of the Grays to the Beaneaters seemed to have caused hardly a ripple, this deal raised howls of protest from the rest of the league, for many teams had been coveting the four star Bisons. Although the league president intervened, in the end it was all the same: the Big Four played in Michigan in 1886, the rest of the Bisons scattered around the NL, and Buffalo did not field a team.

One team merges with another—Here we have the notorious "syndicate ball" of the late '90s. Certain owners held controlling stock in two teams, and used the financially less viable one as a kind of glorified farm team of the other, while in the meantime both teams were technically competing against one another for the championship.

This dubious practice effectively killed two of the decade's strongest teams, as well as an annual doormat that was about to make its move. The Baltimore Orioles had won three straight pennants between 1894 and 1896, but by 1899, they found themselves owned by Charlie Ebbets and his partners, and all their best players headed for Brooklyn. The Louisville Colonels had been the laughing stock of the league. (Seymour relates that Cap Anson was able to get a laugh in his 1890s stage play "The Runaway Colt" by threatening to expel a player from the league, or "worse, I'll send you to Louisville!") By 1899, though, the club had a stable of impressive talent, including Fred Clarke, Deacon Phillippe, Rube Waddell, and a young Honus Wagner. Owner Barney Dreyfuss, though, bought the Pitts-

burgh Pirates, and engineered a "blockbuster" trade that brought all the star Colonels to western Pennsylvania.

The ugliest example of syndicate ownership involved the hardnosed Cleveland Spiders, a club that was a first-division fixture in the '90s, and once even bested the vaunted Orioles in the Temple Cup series. Despite the team's success, its owners, the Robison brothers, were dissatisfied with attendance in Cleveland, and frustrated in their attempts to find a local buyer. The league had already thwarted their attempt to sell out to Detroit interests—Detroit was a small city in those pre-auto days, and not an attractive major league venue—when the opportunity came to buy the St. Louis Browns, probably the worst NL team of the 1890s. Frank Robison deemed St. Louis better baseball territory than Cleveland, and promptly dispatched the best of the Spiders west (including star pitcher Cy Young). Northern Ohio was left with the dregs of both teams, and finished 1899 with the worst record ever for a major league club. The Spiders, a tough, colorful squad, deserved a better fate, although it is true that the move saved the St. Louis Cardinals for posterity. (William Mead, in his great book on wartime baseball *Even the Browns*, repeats the legend that the Spiders were indirectly responsible for the Cardinal's nickname. According to this story, Robison gave the Spiders' uniforms to the St. Louis team, then known as the Perfectos, and sportswriters started calling them the "Cardinals" because of the red trim.)

The three victims of syndicate ownership, plus the hapless original Washington Senators, were the teams dropped when the NL cut back from twelve to eight teams. All the cities thus deprived except for Louisville were to return to major league baseball in the upstart American League in 1901.

New owner purchases the literal franchise, with or without players—When we hear the word "franchise" in conjunction with sports today, we immediately think of a "team." Popularly, at least, "franchise" has become synonymous with "team" or "club." But look up "franchise" in the *American College Dictionary*, and you find that all the meanings listed have to do with some kind of "right," or "privilege," or "permission to do something." "Franchise," therefore, when referring to a sports association like the National League, really means something like: "permission to play in the league; a privilege granted to certain clubs to perform in association with other clubs under the league aegis," and, by extension: "the slot in the league roster your club occupies; one's space in the league setup."

This dictionary work is necessary if we are to make sense of the last type of club transaction encountered in the nineteenth century. In the 1880s, owners sometimes sold out to out-of-town buyers, but what they were selling was their privilege to operate in the NL, their slot in the eight-team lineup—in other words, the NL franchise. These are "franchise shifts" in the literal sense of the word. The franchise transfers from owners in one city to owners in another, who now have the right to field a team in place of the now-defunct one.

Does this mean we can talk of a *club* moving from one city to another? Well, yes and no. We see clear examples of both answers, plus a few cases that could be interpreted either way. On the one hand, for instance, we have Frank Robison's Cleveland Spiders, an AA team that wanted to join the NL after the demise of the Detroit Wolverines in 1888. After most of the roster had been sold off, *The Encyclopedia of Major League Teams* tells us that Robison purchased "four lesser lights and the franchise itself." Obviously, it wouldn't be right to talk of the Wolverines "moving to Cleveland," even though there is some continuity between the rosters. They expired, and the already-existing Spiders came over from the AA and filled their now-vacated slot after purchasing the right to do so.

At the other extreme, we have the entrance into the NL of the team that would come to be called the New York Giants. At the 1882 NL owners' meeting, it was resolved to expel micromarket clubs Worcester and Troy in favor of new teams in Philadelphia and New York. John Day and Jim Mutrie were asked to put together the New York outfit. What they did, in fact, was purchase the Troy Trojan franchise *and* player contracts, and shift the operation downriver to the Big Apple. Half of the Trojans went to the new NL Gothams (to be rechristened the Giants within two or three years), and the other half went to the American Association New York Metropolitans, another Day/Mutrie enterprise. Although a deal like this would never be allowed in this century, I think it is fair to say that the Troy Trojans indeed moved to New York City, where they eventually became the Giants (and from which they were to move to San Francisco seventy-five years later).

Now we have come full circle, for one of the two problematic "literal" franchise transfers we need to deal with is the nettlesome Worcester-Philadelphia connection with which we opened this article. Just as Day and Mutrie were approached in New York about setting up an NL club there, league president A. G. Mills asked Al Reach, a Philadelphia sporting goods magnate, to put together a team in the City of Brotherly Love for the '83 campaign. And just as the New Yorkers bought Troy's franchise rights, so did Reach's group purchase Worcester's, but *without* the players' contracts.

Similarly, when Henry Lucas brought his St. Louis

Maroons into the NL in 1885 (after winning the first and only United Association pennant the year before), he did so over the collective dead body of the Cleveland Blues. The Blues (or "Forest Cities") had entered the league in 1879 and enjoyed fitful success, but the struggle with the UA (founded and run by Lucas himself) effectively killed them. Lucas purchased Cleveland's franchise rights, and expected the players' contracts to be part of the deal, so that he could merge the cream of the Blues' roster with the best of the Maroons'. But, alas for him, they weren't. Brooklyn, still in the AA at this time, underhandedly siphoned all the players off before the deal could be consummated.

Thinking about the moves—So how should researchers regard all this? I would say the following represent the move of a team from one city to another, although the specific transactions involved are sometimes quite different from the twentieth-century practice:

- Hartford Dark Blues to Brooklyn, 1877
- Troy Trojans to New York, 1883
- St. Louis Maroons to Indianapolis, 1887

The mergers and buyouts were just that—deals between two businesses, one of which survives and the other of which doesn't. The Bisons and Grays expired, and their remains were bought up by Detroit and Boston, respectively. The Orioles, Spiders, and Colonels disappeared through mergers with economically more viable clubs that still exist.

I suppose, if you wanted to, you could say that the old Orioles live on in Los Angeles, the Spiders in St. Louis, and the Colonels in Pittsburgh, although I'm not sure what you would gain by doing so. Perhaps it's best to view this type of transaction as a variation on the buy-out: Team A collapses, what's left is absorbed by Team B.

The expulsion of various teams is straightforward enough, as is the voluntary withdrawal of the original St. Louis Browns, and the Wolverines' franchise passing over to the Cleveland Spiders. That leaves Cleveland-St. Louis (1885) and Worcester-Philadelphia (1883). It was Henry Lucas' intent to move the Blues to St. Louis, but although he got the franchise, he never got the players. The Worcester roster didn't move to Philadelphia, either. Under those circumstances, I think it is wrong-headed to consider the Maroons a continuation of the Bluess or the Phillies as the one-time Brown Stockings.

In conclusion, let me express the hope that good sense and fair play prevail, and we aren't soon left with a whole new spate of franchise shifts to misconstrue. I don't think I'm ready for the Washington Astros or the Charlotte Brewers!

Sources

The Baseball Encyclopedia. 9th ed. New York: Macmillan, 1995.

Dewey, Donald & Nicholas Acocella. The Encyclopedia of Major League Teams. New York: Harper Collins, 1993.

Dickey, Glenn. The History of National League Baseball Since 1876. New York: Stein & Day, 1979.

James, Bill. The Bill James Historical Baseball Abstract. New York: Villard Books, 1986.

McConnell, Bob & David Vincent, ed. SABR: The Home Run Encyclopedia. New York: Macmillan, 1996.

Mead, William B. Even the Browns. Chicago: Contemporary Books, 1978.

Seymour, Harold. Baseball: The Early Years. New York & Oxford: Oxford University Press, 1960.

Spalding, A. G. America's National Game. Rpt. Lincoln, Nebraska: U. of Nebraska Press, 1992 (1911).

Thorn, John & Pete Palmer, Ed. Total Baseball. 3rd ed. New York: Harper Perennial, 1993.

Yellon, Al, "Team All-Time Records," National Pastime 14 (1994), pp. 31-33.

Defunct National League Teams of the Ninetenth Century

Club	In NL	How and Why Left League
NY Mutuals	1876	Expelled for failing to complete schedule.
Philadelphia A's	1876	Expelled for failing to complete schedule.
Louisville Grays	1876-77	Dropped from NL in wake of gambling scandal involving 4 players.
St. Louis Browns	1876-77	Withdrew. Forbidden to keep expelled Louisville players.
Hartford Dark Blues	1876-77	To Brooklyn, 1877. Disband for financial reasons.
Indianapolis Blues	1878	Dropped for financial reasons.
Milwaukee Grays	1878	Dropped for financial reasons.
Syracuse Stars	1878	Disbanded for financial reasons. Did not finish season.
Cincinnati Reds	1876-80	Expelled for scheduling Sunday games and serving liquor at park.
Troy Trojans	1879-83	Dropped from league. Bought and moved to NY.
Worcester Browns	1880-83	Dropped from league. Franchise bought by Philadelphia Phillies.
Cleveland Blues	1879-84	Fold after battle with UA. Franchise bought by St. Louis Maroons.
Providence Grays	1878-85	Bankrupt. Purchased by Boston.
Buffalo Bisons	1879-85	Bankrupt. Purchased by Detroit.
St. Louis Maroons	1885-86	Sold and moved to Indianapolis.
Kansas City Cowboys	1886	Dropped for financial & logistical reasons; too far for eastern clubs.
Detroit Wolverines	1881-88	Bankrupt. Franchise purchased by Cleveland Spiders.
Washington Statesmen	1886-89	Dropped to make room for AA clubs Brooklyn & Cincinnati.
Indianapolis Hoosiers	1887-89	Dropped (with Washington, above) to make room for AA clubs.
Cleveland Spiders	1889-99	Merged with St. Louis Cardinals.
Baltimore Orioles	1892-99	Merged with Brooklyn Dodgers.
Louisville Colonels	1892-99	Merged with Pittsburgh Pirates.
Washington Senators	1892-99	Dropped with above 3 teams to get down to 8-team league.

Schoolboy Rowe and the 1934 Tigers

Herbert S. Hofmann

It all happened more than sixty years ago. In 1934 the Detroit Tigers won the American League pennant for the first time in twenty-five years. The last Motor City entry to capture the flag, in 1909, had ended a three-year reign. This group began a two year run. Throughout the time when the circuits each had only eight clubs Detroit was the only AL western entry to ever repeat as champion.

Yet when great teams are selected, the 1934-35 Tigers are always bypassed. Perhaps this is because they had the misfortune to compete in the era of the fine New York Yankee teams of the 1930s, winners in 1932 and 1936-39. Maybe it is because they were beaten in a seven-game World Series by the colorful St. Louis Cardinal "Gashouse Gang"—a defeat made more one-sided than it really was by an 11-0 blowout in the final game.

Still, these Detroiters with the 101-53 record, the best winning percentage ever by a Tiger team, were seven games ahead of a good Yankee nine, outscored every other team in the majors by over 100 runs, finished a close second in AL fielding, and were second in ERA. Despite hitting only 74 home runs, the club still scored 958 runs—over six per game. Four players reached 100 RBIs and another had 96. The Tigers led the majors with a .300 team average, and with 124 stolen bases, the second best figure for the 1930s, and 55 more than the "Gashouse Gang" swiped. Five Tigers were in double figures for thefts. Six regulars hit over .300—the others were at .296 and .285. Two much-used

substitutes averaged .300 and .293. Another won a game on September 16 by scoring from second base on an infield out in the last of the ninth. Oh, they could beat you in so many ways!

Despite such imposing team statistics, Detroit's individual players were boxed out for leadership in both batting and pitching honors. Here the Yankees prevailed. The great Lou Gehrig won the Triple Crown, with an average of .363, 49 home runs, and 165 RBIs. The fine lefthander, Vernon "Lefty" Gomez, swept the board of key pitching honors. In his finest season he led in wins (26), complete games (25), innings worked (282), strikeouts (158), winning pct (.839), and ERA (2.33). He tied for the lead in shutouts (6).

The players—Still, if great players make up great teams, then the 1934 (and 1935) Tigers have been unfairly ignored. Four of them—Hank Greenberg, Charlie Gehringer, Mickey Cochrane, and Goose Goslin—are Hall of Famers. Many others were solid players with distinguished careers. Outfielder Ervin "Pete" Fox hit .298 in thirteen seasons, including five years over .300. Another picketman, Gerald "Gee" Walker, went .294 for fifteen years, with six .300 efforts. A third flychaser, Joyner "Jo-Jo" White, picked 1934 as his career best, a .313 mark while leading the team with 28 steals. Third baseman Marvin Owen also had his only .300 shot, at .317 with 96 RBIs. Shortstop Billy Rogell also hit his peaks, at .296 and 100 RBIs. He also led the league at his position with 518 assists.

Rogell and Owen were part of an infield that accomplished a feat not seen before, since, or likely in the future. Along with Gehringer at second, each started

Herbert S. "Shan" Hofmann is retired from teaching at Muskegon, Michigan, Community College and the U.S. Army. He is working on a book about the great pitchers.

every game of the season. And Greenberg missed only one start, because of a religious holiday, at first base.

Of the Hall of Fame group, however, none had the finest season of his career. Greenberg, a Tiger for all but his last season, hit .339, but bettered that once. An imposing 139 RBI figure was good enough for only third place in the AL that season, when four first basemen knocked in 130 or more. Hank topped that four times in later seasons. In another offensive department, however, he had 63 doubles, the best in the circuit, and the third highest in baseball history.

Next to him in the infield was Gehringer, a Michigan native who would wear nothing but Bengal flannels for nineteen years. Recently *Baseball Digest* named him as the best second baseman in the game's history. In 1934 he led the league with 134 runs scored and 214 hits, neither of which were career highs. His 127 RBIs were his best, however. His .356 BA placed him second to Gehrig, but would be less than his league-leading .371 in 1937. Likewise his 50 doubles—second to Greenberg, were short of his AL-best 60 in 1936. "The Mechanical Man" also had double figures in both home runs and stolen bases, and with 99 walks, he reached base more than twice per game. Defensively, he led the league's second basemen in assists and tied for the best fielding average.

Goslin's decent .305 BA and 100 RBIs, were both below his usual high standards. Cochrane hit .320, matching his lifetime average. None of his other numbers were nearly his best. If the offense was the game's best, the defense didn't hurt, either. The Tigers' 159 errors were second fewest in the league. No position constituted a glaring weakness.

Pitching—Cochrane inherited a better staff of hurlers than many imagined. In 1933 Detroit had finished third in team ERA with 3.96 against a league 4.28. Partly because of Cochrane's own catching and leadership, the Tiger pitching really picked up in 1934. Their collective ERA rose to 4.06, second to the Yankees, but the league rose to 4.50.

Working at both ends of the game, Fred Marberry delivered a solid 15-5 mark and decisioned all other teams in the league.

Tommy Bridges, the fine curveballer, whose pitching has been described as "when he was good, he was very, very good, and when he was bad he was horrid," had fewer "horrid" stints to mar his work, pitched the most innings on the staff, and led the league with 35 starts. Behind better hitting, he won eight times more than in 1933 to go 22-11. He whipped everyone including New York for the first time in his career on May 17.

Rather unexpectedly, Elden Auker did good work finishing and, as the season wore on, starting. At 15-7, he had the team's best ERA at 3.42. The Tigers also added Alvin "General" Crowder, erstwhile Senator ace, to

their staff from a waiver deal on August 4. He responded with a 5-1 record, including two vital wins over the Bronx bombers.

None of these feats would have mattered, however, had not Lynwood "Schoolboy" Rowe come on with his career season, one which gave excitement aplenty, and would have been even brighter had not Dizzy Dean and Lefty Gomez picked 1934 for their Academy Award scenes as well. Dizzy went 7-0 with two saves in September to move to a magic 30-7, and pitched the Cards to the pennant. With the same 23 wins by the end of August, Gomez also threatened the 30-mark, but was just 3-2 in September. Schoolboy wound up at 24-8 for the Tigers, and was at least as important to his team as were the other two stars to theirs.

A special part of Rowe's season, however, was his 16-game winning streak from June 15 through August 25. Indeed, had he not lost a well-pitched game in Detroit to Chicago on June 10 by a 3-1 count, he would have notched 20 straight scalps. Still he joined some very select company, having tied Walter Johnson (Washington, 1912), Joe Wood (Boston, 1912) and Lefty Grove (Philadelphia, 1931) for the AL record, which still stands.

The impact of such consistent pitching, of having a "stopper" became obvious in better Tiger fortunes. During Rowe's streak the team was 49-21 and had no losing string longer than two games. Almost immune to a slump all summer long, the 1934 Tigers lost four games in a row only once, in early May, before Rowe's heroics; and three straight also just one time, in September, when his run was over.

As for the race itself, Cleveland led at the end of May, but the Yankees took over through June and up to the All Star break in July, closely chased by the Tigers during the period. While the Detroiters moved into the top spot by taking three of four from the Gotham crew in a series in Detroit from July 12-15, the end of the month found New York back in the lead by a few points. However, in the nightcap of a doubleheader on July 31 in Cleveland, Cochrane's nine began a 14-game winning streak which propelled them into the lead to stay. Their great surge was climaxed by winning a twinbill in Yankee Stadium before 77,000 on August 14, beginning a long five-game series. From there they never looked back, being 18-10 in September and even 7-2 after the race was over.

A career year for the Schoolboy—As for Rowe, although this was his career year, it was also one in which he almost found himself back in the minors. He had two starts in April, lost one on the record, and was smashed hard in both. So, just a bit more than two weeks into the season we find these comments from Sam Green in the Detroit *News* on May 3, 1934:

Rowe's position on the staff had been somewhat precarious ... Detroit is still carrying an extra pitcher and Rowe may be the next to go. But he has earned another chance and temporarily, at least, staved off the return to the Texas League. His future depends on his showing in the East.

In what might have been, in retrospect, the most important inning of the season for the Tigers, Rowe kept himself around with a perfect ninth inning in a losing cause to St. Louis on May 2, getting one hitter on a popup and blowing down two more on strikes. On the Eastern trip he performed adequately. However, by May 23 he was still on 1-3 and not really going anywhere.

On May 27 Rowe's fortune began to turn. A solid 9-2 complete win over the Red Sox began five straight route jobs through June 15, all well-pitched, with four wins. Although the June 15 win in Boston started his long streak, for the rest of the month Rowe didn't really scare anyone. He reached 6-4 at month's end.

Now came the dog days of July, Rowe

Hank Greenberg, left, and Lynwood "Schoolboy" Rowe.

Transcendental Graphics

made his move, and forced the baseball world to take notice of another star on the horizon. Splitting his eight wins evenly between starts and relief appearances, he roared on, a vital part of the titanic wrestling match between the Tigers and Yankees. This effort put his team in a position to break the race open in that long winning run in early August. The Bengals were 20-11 in July.

Rowe's blitzkrieg pace slackened only a bit in August, now almost solely as a starter. He added six more wins before falling to the Athletics on August 29. Though his streak was over the team was 23-6 that month.

As the Motor City juggernaut rolled on in September, Rowe continued a major role, winning four more route starts, the last two back-to-back shutouts. He ended the season on the downside by dropping his last two starts, but the race was over by then.

A close examination of Rowe's game-by-game record for 1934 reveals just how valuable he was to Tiger fortunes. Against the second-place Yankees he was 5-0, with two 2-0 whitewashes. Yielding only 30 hits in 46 innings against New York, he also recorded 44 strikeouts. In two different games he fanned 11, his only double-figure results that year. Even these figures do not include the timely importance of his efforts. In a vital series in Detroit in mid-July he won the first and last games, the latter on two days rest to give the Tigers the series. He showed his courage July 12, battling illness in the sixth inning and being wobbly through the seventh, but gamely rebounding to set the Yankees down in order the last two frames. In mid-August an encore in New York followed. First he defeated Red Ruffing, 7-3, in the last of a twin-bill. For his second appearance in that series, on August 17, he worked the nightcap of another double dipper before 46,500 fans. The teams split the first four games and Lefty Gomez won the opener, 5-0. Rowe's response was a brilliant 3-hit blanking with 11 whiffs. He met the major enemy threat by fanning Bill Dickey in the sixth inning with the bases loaded. Even Gehrig went 0 for 3. In Detroit on September 18 Rowe threw another 2-0 whitewash, before 30,000 happy fans. He gave just six hits, with seven strikeouts and no walks. Tiger runs came on a Greenberg homer in the fourth and Rowe's single in the fifth inning, off Red Ruffing. The game was also the second straight blanking by the Bengal staff over the Yanks, as Alvin "General" Crowder had beaten Gomez 3-0 on the previous afternoon.

Tiger batters slumped in September. They scored three runs or less fourteen times. In an eleven-game stretch from September 2 through 13 they had only 29 counters. No tailspin occurred, though, because the Bengal pitching staff won seven of those eleven games.

The fact that Rowe was a part in the Tiger offense on September 18 was no surprise. He played Frank Merriwell with his bat a number of times that season. On May 7 in Boston and July 29 in Chicago he settled contests with home runs. In Detroit he ended an extra-inning affair against Cleveland with a sacrifice fly. On August 25 in Washington he singled in the deciding runs in the ninth. For the season he batted .303, with eleven extra-base hits and 22 RBIs in 109 AB. Indeed, he proved to be a solid hitter throughout his career. In 1935 he hit .312, with three homers and 28 RBIs. In 1943, as a member of the Philadelphia Phillies, he led the league in both pinch hits and appearances, going 15 for 49, while batting .300 for the season. His lifetime average was .263. He also led AL pitchers in 1934 with a perfect fielding record in 55 chances.

How did Rowe compare to Gomez in 1934? Gomez was 4-1 against the Tigers, with two shutouts, but started two other key Detroit games that the Yankees lost. In both cases he blew large leads but was not involved in the decision. He had an ERA of 2.77 in 52 innings against the Tigers. Rowe's ERA against New York was 1.76 in 46 innings. Gomez and Rowe never pitched against each other that season. Player-manager Cochrane wrote in his book, *Baseball: The Fan's Game*, reprinted by SABR in 1992, that he did not believe in pitching his ace against the other team's best hurler.

Rowe remained an outstanding pitcher against the Yankees. He followed in 1935 with a 4-3 mark, including three shutouts, and was 5-2 in 1936, over a great Bronx Bomber nine which lost only 51 games all season. In the three years 1934-36 he was a terrific 14-5 against New York, for almost 23 percent of his wins during that time. And when he made an unexpected comeback in 1940, his 16-3 helped Detroit to a surprise flag. That included a 3-1 card over the third place Yankees, who were only two games behind at the end. Overall, Rowe was 20-12 against the era's greatest team.

Rowe also handled other first division teams with aplomb. In 1934 he was 3-0 over Cleveland and 5-1 over Boston, for a 13-1 record against the first division. No major league pitcher in either league did that well during the 1930s. Grove had been 13-2 off his 31-4 record in 1931. Gomez was 14-3 in 1934. Bill Lee of the Chicago Cubs would be 14-3 in his 22-9 season of 1938.

In other cases, Dean was only 8-4 off his 30-7 in 1934 and 8-9 on a 28-12 record in 1935. Carl Hubbell's best was 13-4 off 26-6 in 1936. Bucky Walters was 13-8 off 27-11 in 1939, and Bob Feller 11-6 from 24-9 that same year. Rowe tops them all. He continued pounding the first division in his other good seasons, going 11-4 in 1935, 9-2 in 1936, and 7-1 in 1940. That comes to 40-8 in his good AL seasons, or 51 percent of his triumphs.

Judgment—With most of the same cast in 1935, the Tigers repeated in the AL and won the World Series against the Chicago Cubs, who had won five more games, scored forty-eight more runs, and had a better team ERA (.43) than the 1934 Gashouse Gang.

Greenberg was AL MVP in '35, but the team as a whole was not quite as sharp as it had been the year before. Detroit won eight fewer contests, and hit ten percentage points lower. In the Series, Greenberg missed the last four games with a broken wrist, but Detroit pitching held the line to give the Motor City its first title, four games to two. Five members of these two Detroit teams (Rowe, Bridges, Greenberg, Gehringer, and Fox) were still around in 1940 for another pennant and a close Series loss to Cincinnati.

Schoolboy Rowe was not a Hall of Fame pitcher, but he was an exciting surprise, a vital cog in a machine that ground down the best of the American League and came closer to victory in the 1934 Series than the final game's rout indicates. During the season, Detroit had much better competition than either the 1968 or 1984 World Champion editions. For regular season play, the 1934 Tigers were the best outfit ever to wear Detroit uniforms.

Lynwood "Schoolboy" Rowe, 1934

Date	Opp	IP	H	SO	BB	W	L	Score	CG
Apr. 19	aChi	2.1	7	1	2	Ch		9-8	
Apr. 30	hStL	3	4	1	2		*	7-2	
May 2	hStL	1	0	2	0	StL		5-2	R
May 5	aNY	4	3	4	0	NY		10-6	R
May 7	aBos	5	2	4	0	*		8-6	R
May 10	Phil	8	7	1	4		*	5-3	R
May 20	hWash	2.2	6	2	3		*	4-1	
May 23	hPhil	3	4	0	1	Ph		11-5	R
May 27	hBos	9	11	5	3	*		9-2	*
Jun 1	aChi	9	6	8	1	*		3-1	*
Jun 6	hClev	9	6	7	0	*		2-1	*
Jun 10	hChi	9	6	7	3		*	3-1	*
Jun 15	aBost	9	9	4	5	*		11-4	*
Jun 20	aWash	5.2	9	3	2	Det		13-10	
Jun 21	aWash	1	0	0	0	W		8-6	R
Jun 24	aPhil	9	12	4	0	*		8-4	*
Jun 28	hChi	1.1	0	1	1	Det		8-7	R
Jul 1	aStL	9	13	4	0	*		12-3	*
Jul 4	hClev	5.2	4	1	1	*		5-2	R
Jul 8	hStL	3	2	1	1	*		5-4	R
Jul 12	hNY	9	6	11	4	*		4-2	*
Jul 15	hNY	6	8	6	3	*		8-3	
Jul 20	hPhil	6	7	1	4	Ph		5-4	
Jul 22	hPhil	1	1	1	2	Ph		1-0	R
Jul 22	hPhil	6.2	6	2	0	*		17-8	R
Jul 25	hBost	1	1	0	0	B		9-7	R
Jul 28	aChi	9	3	6	5	*		11-1	*
Jul 29	aChi	1.2	0	1	0	*		16-15	R
Aug 1	aClev	0.2	0	2	0	Det		10-7	R[s]
Aug 3	aChi	7	1	1	3	*		14-0	
Aug 7	hStL	0	1	0	0	Det		12-8	
Aug 10	hClev	11	13	7	3	*		6-5	*
Aug 14	aNY	9	4	5	1	*		7-3	*
Aug 17	aNY	9	3	11	5	*		2-0	*
Aug 21	aBost	9	9	5	3	*		8-4	*
Aug 25	aWash	9	9	3	0	*		4-2	*
Aug 29	aPhil	6.2	12	3	2		*	13-5	
Sep 5	hPhil	9	11	1	0	*		4-2	*
Sep 9	hBost	10	11	5	5	*		5-4	*
Sep 11	hBost	3.2	4	2	3		*	4-3	R
Sep 13	hWash	9	7	5	3	*		2-0	*
Sep 18	hNY	9	6	7	0	*		2-0	*
Sep 23	aStL	8	11	2	2		*	4-3	*
Sep 27	hChi	4	8	1	4		*	11-0	
Sep 30	hStL	3	6	1	0	Det		10-6	R
45 G (30 sts)		**266**	**259**	**149**	**81**	**24-8**			**20**

13-5 home, 11-3 away, 18-3 in complete games, 5-2 in one run games, 3.45 ERA

* = Rowe win, loss, game appearance

R = relief appearance

R[s] = relief appearance and save

World Series

Date	Opp	IP	H	SO	BB	W	L	Score	CG
Oct 4	hStL	12	7	7	0		*	3-2	*
Oct 8	hStL	9	10	5	0		*	4-3	*
Oct 9	hStL	1/3	2	0	0	St.L		11-0	R
3 G (2 starts)		**21 1/3**	**19**	**12**	**0**	**1-1**			**2**

2.95 ERA

Opponent	W-L	IP	ER	ERA
New York	5-0	46	9	1.76
Cleveland	3-0	26.1	7	2.39
Boston	5-1	46.2	15	2.89
Philadelphia	3-2	49.1	30	5.47
St. Louis	2-2	27	15	5.00
Washington	2-1	27.1	12	3.95
Chicago	4-2	43.1	14	2.91

Low-Hit Games		Low-Run Games	
Three hits	2	Shutouts	3
Four Hits	1	One run	3
Six hits	5	Two runs	4

Pitcher, Major League All-Star Team

Tied AL Record with 16 consecutive wins. Led league pitchers with most chances in perfect fielding record.

Batting

G	AB	R	H	2b	3b	HR	RBI	BA
51	109	15	33	8	1	2	22	.303

Won games of May 7 and July 29 with home runs, game of August 10 with a sacrifice fly, and game of August 25 with a single in 9th inning.

It was Fred Tenney of the Boston Nationals, not John McGraw, who wanted to sign William Clarence Matthews, "Harvard's famous colored shortstop," to a major league contract in 1905

William Clarence Matthews

Karl Lindholm

I think it is an outrage that colored men are discriminated against in the big leagues. What a shame it is that black men are barred forever from participating in the national game.

A negro is just as good as a white man and has just as much right to play ball.... This negro question on the diamond might as well be settled now as any time. If Burlington sticks by her guns as Harvard did, men of my race will soon be playing ball in the Big Leagues.

—William Clarence Matthews, 1905

To baseball historians and their readers, William Clarence Matthews is the black player rumored in 1905 to be heading to a National League team in defiance of the "Gentleman's Agreement" in organized baseball.

Between the symbolic poles of Cap Anson's perfidy in 1887 and Jackie Robinson's breakthrough in 1945, Matthews is a significant figure. He was introduced to modern fans of the game's history by Robert Peterson in his seminal *Only the Ball was White* (1970). Peterson described Matthews as a great college player at Harvard in the first decade of the century and cites his rumored entry into the National League. Subsequent studies of the African-American contribution to the national game repeat this information.

The dissemination of the rumor springs from one crucial documentary source, Sol White's *History of Colored Baseball*, published in 1907. In his history, White wrote:

Karl Lindholm, Ph.D. *is the Dean of Advising and an Assistant Professor of American Literature and Civilization at Middlebury College. He is working on a book on the life of William Clarence Matthews.*

It is said on good authority that one of the leading players and a manager of the National League is advocating the entrance of colored players in the National League with a view to signing 'Matthews,' the colored man, late of Harvard.

Readers of White's words have long speculated on the identity of the manager brave enough to confront entrenched values by proposing to add a black player to his team. John McGraw naturally came to mind. White himself, in the paragraphs immediately after his discussion of Matthews, described McGraw's effort in 1901 to sneak Charlie Grant, second baseman of the Columbia Giants of Chicago, a black team, onto his roster as Tokohama, a full-blooded Cherokee Indian.

In *Only the Ball was White*, Peterson suggests "it could have been McGraw...then leading the Giants" who was pursuing Matthews." Negro Leagues historian Jerry Malloy, in his excellent introduction to the University of Nebraska reissue of White's history, indicates that "White most likely was concealing the identity of John J. McGraw, blustery, innovative manager of the New York Giants who is said to have employed two black stars, Rube Foster and Jose Mendez...at various times to coach his pitchers."

Tenney needs an infielder—However, an examination of White's own words leads elsewhere. He says ambiguously, "*one* of the game's players and a manager *is*" interested in Matthews.

There was only one player-manager in the National League in 1905 and that was Fred Tenney of the Boston

Nationals. Tenney was the slick-fielding first baseman for Boston (he made the 3-6-3 double play a standard part of the infield repertoire) who led them to pennants in 1895 and 1897, and was named player-manager in 1905 and again in 1907. Tenney had every reason in 1905 to be casting a longing eye at Matthews.

The Boston Nationals were in desperate need of a little punch in their infield. By mid-July, 1905, they were mired in seventh place, only a slender half-game from Brooklyn and the cellar. Their second baseman, Billy Raymer, was not much. He hit .211 in 1905 and .218 in his truncated three-year big league career. A player of Matthews' caliber would have solved Tenney's infield problems. In the summer of 1905, Matthews had finished at Harvard and was playing his first and only professional season in the "outlaw" Northern League for Burlington, Vermont.

On July 15, 1905, the Boston *Traveler* announced in a headline on the sports page, MATTHEWS MAY PLAY BALL WITH TENNEY'S TEAM. The article went on to say:

> It is very probable that [Matthews] will become a member of the Boston Nationals very soon.
>
> It has been hinted at for the past few days. Now it is rumored that it will transpire.
>
> A person 'on the inside,' one who generally knows whereof he speaks, has this to say: 'Captain Tenney has long been hunting for a lively second baseman to strengthen his infield. On hearing of Matthews' remarkable ability, and after following the career of the young negro collegian-professional while at Harvard and Burlington, (he) decided that William C. was just the laddybuck he needed.'

The source "on the inside" then offers a rationale for Matthews' acceptance where others would fail:

> As Matthews is a Harvard man, he should prove a great attraction…. Matthews is a well-educated, gentlemanly fellow, as well as a clever ball player.
>
> If Harvard men do not object to associating with and idolizing the negro, certainly none of the National League players will object to breaking bread with him.

The article concludes with the proviso that, "Of course, Captain Tenney will have to consult with the magnates, but there is little fear of objection on their part."

This same article also offered Matthews' response to the Tenney rumor. In a compelling statement to "a Vermont newspaper man," Matthews asserted:

> I think it is an outrage that colored men are discriminated against in the big leagues. What a shame it is that black men are barred forever from participating in the national game. I should think that Americans should rise up in revolt against such a condition.
>
> Many negroes are brilliant players and should not be shut out because their skin is black. As a Harvard man, I shall devote my life to bettering the condition of the black man, and especially to secure his admittance into organized base ball.
>
> If the magnates forget their prejudices and let me into the big leagues, I will show them that a colored boy can play better than lots of white men, and he will be orderly on the field.

"What shall we do with Matthews?"—A few days later, on July 19, 1905, a long story on the Matthews signing appeared in the *Traveler* under the headline MATTHEWS DEAL AROUSES IRE OF SOUTHERN FANS. *Traveler* reporter Dan Coakley asks at the outset, "What shall we do with Matthews?" and declares that "this question is now echoing around the baseball world."

Coakley claimed that "hot-headed southerners are so roiled" by the Matthews' case that they will withdraw and form their own outlaw Southern League if Matthews joins a "National Agreement nine":

> Men below Mason and Dixon's line look upon the playing of Matthews in the Vermont League as the entering wedge of the negro in big league ball.
>
> Southerners believe that Matthews has queer notions about the equality of the negro, and that he is using his prestige as an educated and petted Harvard man in a mission to pave the way so that negroes can play ball on the same teams as white men.

This article reprinted editorials from two national newspapers. In the Atlanta *Journal*, identified as "the most influential baseball newspaper in the South," Matthews is described as the "Human Chocolate Drop" with a "kinky dome." The editorial claims that the "verdict" of players is "he may be good enough for Harvard (…where a dark brown epidermis isn't any drawback), but he isn't good enough for us." The *Journal* editorial goes on to indicate that the National League would never take on this controversy and hand such an obvious advantage to the fledging American League.

The Chicago *Daily News* is more temperate, offering this realistic appraisal:

> There have been and are negro players with

as much ability as any white man can develop, but the prejudice against playing with them is too strong and the probabilities are that Tenney will find no way to get around the unwritten law which stands against them.

The "real" objection—Two days later, July 21, another story on Matthews appeared in the *Traveler*, this time an interview with "President Hart" of the Chicago Cubs. Hart indicated that he personally had "no objections to a negro playing baseball" but went on to reveal the "real objection" to integration:

> I do not think it is right to inflict (a negro) on others who have objections or forcing white players to sleep in the same car and associate as intimately as they would have to under such conditions.

Hart added that if Tenney succeeded in placing Matthews on his team, "President Pulliam would resign in a minute. His good southern blood would never stand for it." Harry Pulliam was president of the National League and certainly one of the magnates Tenney had to please in order to get Matthews on his club.

The *Traveler* writer couldn't help but add his own postscript to Hart's comments. "Matthews, the Harvard man," he said, "will be grossly insulted at what President Hart says about the negro inflicting himself on others in the sleeping car or at the table."

Matthews was not signed by Tenney. We are left to surmise what actually happened. Presumably the "magnates," Presidents Hart, Pulliam, and others, did not acquiesce. Coakley's story in the *Traveler* described Tenney's posture and predicted his response.

> Manager Tenney is maintaining a discreet silence during the controversy. Like all magnates when they are consummating important deals, he tumbles over himself to deny there is anything doing.
>
> Tenney is a fox and would be a fool to show his hand at this stage of the proceedings…. If Tenney is turned down the reporters will rush up to him and he will frantically deny that he has ever heard of Matthews.

Sure enough, in a story in the Boston *Herald* on July 21, a few days after the rumor surfaced, Tenney himself disavowed his interest. The *Herald* reported:

> Rumor had it that Matthews was willing to sign, but that the Boston management did not want to put the matter through until the consent of all the other clubs was given.

When Fred Tenney was seen in regard to the story, he laughed at it, and said that it was certainly information to him…. He denied emphatically that he had asked the consent of the other clubs to allow Matthews to play with the Boston Nationals.

The rumor died. Matthews was not signed. He played out the season in Vermont and got on with his life.

Was Matthews good enough?—Matthew was legitimate. In the first decade of the century, Harvard was arguably the best college team in the country and Matthews was its best player. Harvard's record in Matthews' four years was a combined 75 wins against only 18 losses. In 1902, Matthews first season at Harvard, 140 candidates tried out for the baseball team. The team's pitchers were coached that year by Cy Young of the Boston Americans and the batters by Brooklyn's Willie Keeler, the era's most "scientific" batsman.

In those days, before the minor leagues were organized, colleges were a fertile breeding ground for major league talent. The incomparable Christy Mathewson graduated from Bucknell University. In 1905, Big Ed Reulbach left the University of Vermont in Burlington just as Matthews was coming to town to play in the Northern League. That summer, Reulbach won 18 games for the Chicago Nationals, including 18- and 20-inning victories. Colby Jack Coombs played for Montpelier-Barre against Matthews in the Northern League in 1905 and then went on to a sterling fourteen-year major league career with Philadelphia and Brooklyn.

It wasn't particularly good form for Harvard men to go from their classical training in Cambridge to the questionable profession of baseball—but they did. The captain of Matthews' 1903 Harvard team, Walter Clarkson, was declared ineligible for the 1904 season because he had signed a contract with New York (AL). He played five years for the Highlanders and Cleveland from 1904 through 1908. Matthews' keystone partner, second baseman "Harvard Eddie" Grant, played for four major league teams from 1905 through 1915.

A major talent—At Harvard, Matthews was an outstanding all-round player, sound defensively, good with the bat, and fast on the bases. Clearly, he was a major talent, attracting attention beyond Cambridge and the Eastern intercollegiate world. In his three years as Harvard's shortstop (he injured his knee in his first year, missing over half the season), Matthews led his team in hitting each year. He batted .333 in 1903, had four homers, and stole 12 bases; the next year, he batted .343 with 3 homers and 8 steals; and in 1905, his last year, he batted .400 and stole 22 bases, playing in all twenty-five of Harvard's games. As Ocania Chalk says in his historical study, *Black College Sport*, "Had he been white, the majors would have been fighting to sign up this awesome talent."

His play was hardly without incident, however. In his first year, he was held out of games played in the South at Virginia and Navy. In his second year, Harvard called off its Southern trip altogether. Later that year, 1903, the Georgetown team refused to play if Harvard insisted on Matthews' presence in the lineup. Harvard said Matthews would play or there would be no game. Georgetown backed down, but the incident was reported in the Washington papers. The *Star* had this account:

Sam Apperious, Georgetown's captain and catcher, was not in the contest Saturday. He declined to go into the game because the Harvard men played Matthews, the colored shortstop, who comes from the same town in Alabama from which Apperious hails. Matthews displayed the abilities of a first-class ballplayer and conducted himself in a gentlemanly manner. Notwithstanding, there were hisses every time he stepped up to bat and derisive cheers when he failed to connect with the ball.

William Clarence Matthews,
"Harvard's best ballplayer."

The little shortstop took no notice of these demonstrations occasioned by the prejudice of a number of spectators.

Matthews in Vermont, 1905—These difficulties continued in the Northern League where Matthews was applauded for his play by fans and sportswriters, but also faced boycotts and dirty play on the field. Just a few days after finishing at Harvard, he was playing for Burlington in a Fourth of July doubleheader against Rutland, as fierce a rivalry as Harvard-Yale. Just a week after this first appearance, a story appeared in *Sporting Life* under the headline, ROW OVER BLACK PLAYER:

> The advent of William C. Matthews, the negro shortstop from Harvard, into the Vermont League, threatens to disrupt that organization. It is the first instance of record of a negro player in a professional league, and the other (sic) white players in the league do not take kindly to the innovation.

It turns out that the same Sam Apperious, the Southerner from Matthews' home town of Selma, Alabama, who captained Georgetown and boycotted Harvard games, was playing outfield and catcher for Montpelier. Apperious's refusal to step on the field with Matthews in Vermont caused an uproar in the Vermont newspapers. Most editorials condemned Apperious. This selection from the Wilmington (VT) *Times* was typical:

> ...up here in Vermont race prejudice has few supporters. Vermonters like to see good clean ball, and they are not fussy as to the color of the player who can deliver the right quality.

The Poultney *Journal* was more extreme in its criticism:

> There is a chap called Apperious in Vermont—came here to play ball. Hails from a state where the 'best citizens' burn people alive at the stake.... Scat! Vermont has no use for him. Better wash and go South. May get there in time to help burn the next 'nigger.' Move!

Some newspapers, mostly in the Montpelier area, defended Apperious, saying that he was only representing the values of the South. "Apperious would be false to the traditions, sentiments, and interests of southern whites if he should in any way recognize the negro as equal," a Montpelier *Argus* editorial said. "We can do it in the North. It cannot safely be done in the South."

The Boston newspapers and *Sporting Life*, also reported on the Matthews-Apperious matter. However, they saw it as evidence that blacks and whites could not play together. The headline in the Boston *Traveler* on August 9, 1905 read: HARVARD NEGRO DISRUPTING VERMONT LEAGUE.

"If Matthews goes, I go"—Matthews found support in Burlington and on his own club. His own manager, A.E. Whitney said: "Vermont is not a Jim Crow state.... A white man who would refuse to play ball with [Matthews], or even eat or sleep with him is a cad. If Matthews goes, I go."

Praise from the press, both for Matthews' deportment on the field and for his actual play, was frequent. Typical is this observation from the Burlington *Free Press* on July 9, 1905: "Matthews received the glad hand from the bleachers and grandstand when he first went to bat, showing that race prejudices did not blind the eyes of the spectators so they could not distinguish a good ballplayer and a gentleman."

At the end of the 1905 season, the Rutland *Herald* interviewed Rube Vickers, a veteran pitcher with major league experience who spent the season with Burlington as Matthews' teammate. Of the Apperious–Matthews' matter, Vickers said that Apperious "was the loser as far as favor with the crowds was concerned." As for Matthews specifically, Vickers called him a "first-class player" and "a brilliant young man, one who never causes trouble with any player."

On the field, Matthews' play was often celebrated because he was skilled at so many aspects of the game. The quality of his all-round play was often cited as in this account of a Burlington victory over Plattsburgh in the Rutland *Herald* on July 13: "The feature play of the day was made by Matthews who got first on a hit, stole second and third and then stole home."

Or this from the Burlington *Free Press* report of a doubleheader split before 1,500 fans in Montpelier: "Matthews hit the first ball pitched to him in the first inning over the fence and into the river and trotted around the bases for a home run."

At the plate, he got off to a fast start before tailing off severely near the end of the season. After thirteen games, he had 16 hits in 51 at bats for a .314 average. On August 1, he was batting .283 but by the final Labor Day game his average had dipped to .248.

His late-season slump may be accounted for by the crude play of his opponents, or he may simply have been worn down by the constant struggle of playing as the center of attention and controversy. On August 15 the Boston *Globe* reported:

> ...some few players on all of the other teams have been 'laying' for Matthews, with the result being that he has been spiked several times, and finally had to be put in the outfield from shortstop so that his chances for being hurt would be lessened.

Was Matthews strong enough?—As a baseball player, Matthews gained fame as "Harvard's famous colored shortstop" and as Tenney's would-be second baseman. His life, taken whole, goes far beyond baseball and bears testimony to his strength and resiliency. It is a fascinating American life, full of accomplishment and challenges confronted and overcome.

Matthews was born in the Deep South in Selma, Alabama in 1877. As a teenager, he attended Tuskegee Institute where he trained under Booker T. Washington. Washington saw promise in Matthews and arranged for him to be educated at the prestigious prep school, Phillips Andover Academy, in Massachusetts. Washington hoped that Matthews would return to teach at Tuskegee after being trained in the North.

In his four years at Andover, 1896-1901, Matthews was a star in three sports: football, track, and baseball, and became a school leader. He was the only black student in his class of ninety-seven young men. When he graduated, he was elected Class Historian and was presented a silver cup by his classmates to show their appreciation of him.

At Harvard as well he earned testimonials to his character and popularity. Charles Mason, a classmate, observed:

> He had to work hard for his education for he had to support himself through his college and law school course.... We held him in the greatest respect, and admired the way he undertook his duties, his athletic prowess, and his stand on social issues.

Matthews was held up as an "example and a moral" in a national magazine. In an article on the "College Athlete" in the *McClure's* of June, 1905, Matthews was singled out for his hard work, honesty, and determination.

The black "Matty"—At the end of the Northern League season in August of 1905, Matthews returned to Boston and enrolled in law school at Boston University. He was twenty-eight years old, with a Harvard education, and options outside baseball. He married in 1907 and worked as an athletic instructor at high schools in Boston to support himself through law school.

He passed the bar in 1908 and went on to a distinguished legal career. In 1913, he was appointed by President Taft as an Assistant United States Attorney in Massachusetts. In 1924 he was appointed to oversee the national effort to get out the Negro vote on behalf of Calvin Coolidge, a Vermonter. When Coolidge was elected President with the help of a million Negro votes, Matthews was rewarded with a federal position as Assistant to the Attorney General of the United States.

William Clarence Matthews died suddenly and prematurely of a perforated ulcer in 1928 at the age of 51. At the time of his death he was living in San Francisco, representing the government in "an important water adjudication matter."

His death was reported in all the major East Coast newspapers. The Boston *Globe* described him as "one of the most prominent negro members of the bar in America." The Boston *Post*, a major daily in the first decade of this century, cited Matthews as "no doubt the greatest colored athlete of all time...the best infielder Harvard ever had...[Harvard's] greatest big league prospect." In black newspapers throughout the East, his death drew page one headlines.

Like Christy Mathewson, William Clarence Matthews was "Matty" to his teammates and the public. His character, talent, determination, and achievement also linked him in many minds with Mathewson, the most admired white player of his era.

Baseball and Race—Baseball is a cultural institution that both reflects and affects American life. Filmmaker and baseball mythologist Ken Burns places Jackie Robinson in the very forefront, with Lincoln and Jefferson, in the pantheon of American heroes, so crucial is the connection of race and sports in American life. Matthews' rumored entry into the major leagues at the turn of the century stimulates the imagination.

What if Matthews had succeeded in finding his way onto a big league roster in 1905? Would he immediately have been forced out of the game like his predecessors in the 1880s—or would he have paved the way for John Henry Lloyd, Bruce Petway, Oscar Charleston, and other early African-American stars to express themselves, however problematically, in baseball? How would a Matthews breakthrough have changed American life in this century?

Of course, the discussion is moot. A Matthews breakthrough in 1905 was immensely implausible, given the dependence of baseball on the South for players and facilities and the racial divide in America—an America made legally segregated by the Plessy v. Ferguson Supreme Court decision of 1896. His difficulties in the Northern League dramatize the obstacles he faced.

Boston *Globe* columnist Harold Kaese, many years later in 1965, made the explicit comparison to a more famous legatee: "He was the Jackie Robinson of his age," claimed Kaese. Like Robinson, Matthews was smart, strong, educated, and experienced in the white world. If it had been within the capabilities of one man to challenge the baseball establishment over race in the first decade of this century, Matthews would have been an excellent candidate. He was an extraordinary baseball player and man. This black Matty was, indeed, the Jackie Robinson of his time.

The Helen Dauvray Cup

Larry G. Bowman

In 1887 Helen Dauvray, the New York actress, briefly played the role of a principal fan of the New York Giants, and through her attachment to major league baseball she also became one of the game's early benefactors. As an expression of her enthusiasm for baseball, Dauvray generously donated an expensive silver cup to serve as the trophy awarded to the victor in the annual playoffs for the "World's Championship of Baseball" between the two major leagues of the day. The Dauvray Cup was more than just an emblem of honor for a championship club. It was also symbolic of the acceptance of professional baseball as a vital part of American society. Even though organized professional baseball was less than two decades old in the mid-1880s, each year growing numbers of Americans became intrigued by the game and followed the outcome of league seasons and playoffs with avid interest. In the eyes of sports-minded Americans, the Dauvray Cup affirmed the growing notion that the game was an important part of the nation's culture and helped to elevate professional baseball to a new level of respectability.

By 1882 professional baseball featured two major leagues: the National League and the American Association. When the American Association was organized in 1881, the National League, which had been formed in 1876, attempted both to deride it and to ignore it. Those strategies failed, and in 1882 the two leagues entered into an agreement in which they grandly designated themselves "major leagues" and partisan fans

began immediately to speculate as to which of the leagues played better baseball.[1] The only certain measure was for the two leagues to compete against each other, but interleague play during the regular season was never given serious consideration. Postseason play was all but inevitable, but didn't get off the ground in an organized way until 1884.

The series between the champions of the Association and the League often proved controversial, the players often complained that they were not rewarded to participate in the games (sometimes the owners shared the profits with the players, and sometimes they did not), and the owners often quarreled among themselves and collectively grumbled about the antics of their players on and off the diamond. In its first four years of existence, no special award was given to the winning team, although its owner usually took the gate receipts after the expenses of the series were deducted. Nevertheless, the annual "World's Series" generated a good deal of attention, and Helen Dauvray was one of those watching.

The romance of the game—Helen Dauvray's real name was Helen Gibson. She had been born in San Francisco, California, on February 14, 1859.[2] She spent her earliest childhood years in Virginia City, Nevada, but when her family returned to California, she embarked upon a career on the stage. By 1870, after playing a series of child's roles in productions in San Francisco, the eleven-year old actress arrived in New York City with her family and pursued her career using the stage name "Little Nell, the California Diamond."[3] Helen later traveled to Australia with a

Larry Bowman *is a professor of History and Director of Cooperative Education at the University of North Texas in Denton, Texas.*

company of actors, and eventually went to France where she lived for several years, studied acting, became fluent in French, appeared on the stage in Paris, and took the professional name of Dauvray. She returned to New York in 1885, and promptly went on the stage of the Lyceum Theatre in a successful comedy, "One of Our Girls," which was probably her greatest personal acting triumph.[4]

Dauvray was not the most famous actress of her day, but she was a personality of some note. In addition to her work on the stage, she also attracted a good deal of attention to herself when she leased the Lyceum to produce several plays.[5] She quickly discovered that the routine business affairs associated with operating a theater interfered with her career on the stage, surrendered her lease late in 1886, and returned to being a full-time actress.

In additon to being a New York celebrity, Dauvray became an avid Giants fan. She was always seated in the balcony of the Polo Grounds grandstand next to the press box, and she was usually accompanied by one of her several sisters and a brother. Reporters noticed that Miss Dauvray kept score during the game, and if she missed a play, she asked one of the newspaper men how he had scored it. She was clearly devoted to the game. But she had another reason for attending the Polo Grounds so often. His name was John Montgomery Ward.

Ward was one of the great ballplayers of his era, but he was very different from most of his peers. He had attended Penn State, had earned degrees in political science and law from Columbia, and was noted for his good looks, his sophistication, his polished manners, and for allegedly being fluent in several languages. He was also a founder and leader of the Brotherhood of Professional Base Ball Players, which in a few years would confront the established order, create the Play-

Helen Dauvray in 1887. This cut appeared in The Police Gazette, and was captioned, "The clever actress who is now Mrs. J.M. Ward, wife of the well-known New York baseball player."

ers' League, and come within a hair's breadth of changing the structure of the professional game.

Dauvray was immediately attracted to this dashing fellow, and a romance blossomed. Sometime early in 1887 she and Ward secretly became engaged. According to one of Dauvray's brothers, the two believed that their career demands were such that they should wait until 1888 to be wed.[6]

The Dauvray Cup— Not long after the 1887 professional season got underway baseball fans across the country learned from the sports notes in their newspapers that Nick Young, president of the National League, had accepted a silver cup Helen Dauvray had generously offered to award to the winner of the annual series between the champions of the National League and the American Association. The sterling silver cup, estimated to be worth $500, caused quite a sensation in the baseball world. Its front featured a righthanded hitter at bat with flying pennants on staffs adorned by two baseballs and a catcher's mask located above the hitter's head. Crossed bats formed the handles, and the reverse side of the cup carried the inscription:

THE DAUVRAY CUP
PRESENTED BY
MISS HELEN DAUVRAY
TO THE PLAYERS WINNING THE
WORLD'S CHAMPIONSHIP[7]

The cup was to be awarded to the winning team each year, and if a team won the cup three times, that club was to be granted permanent possession. Dauvray also commissioned gold badges for the players whose team won the cup in its first year of existence. The gold badges featured the figure of a player in his batting stance engraved on a diamond shaped pendant suspended by gold links from crossed baseball bats.

Dauvray's generosity was frequently noted in newspapers along the East Coast, and she gained a good deal of favorable attention as a result of her actions. Only the *Police Gazette* criticized her. The editors of the magazine, which in 1887 had a rakish reputation, contended that it was all a publicity stunt and in their July 2 edition wrote:

> What is wrong with Helen Dauvray? Is she not of sufficient importance in the theatrical world, that she is seeking notoriety and cheap advertising in baseball circles by offering a costly 'loving cup' as a trophy for the world's championship, to be competed for by the winners of the League and Association pennants?

Throughout the summer and early autumn of 1887, the *Police Gazette* remained critical, and during October, as the playoffs were about to begin, the magazine observed that, "Helen Dauvray has worked the advertising dodge most admirably during the present season in the baseball arena."[8] The charge levelled by *The National Police Gazette* was unfair. During most of 1887, Dauvray's theatrical career was dormant as she sought to recuperate from an unidentified illness. Her attachment to the game was genuine, if enhanced by her still secret engagement to Ward.

Early in October, rumors of an impending wedding began to circulate. On the evening of October 11 a reporter for the New York *Times* called on Dauvray at her home and asked for confirmation or denial. She denied all, but the next morning she and Ward traveled to Philadelphia where they were married in the presence of several members of Dauvray's family. Why they were so coy remains unclear. Neither ever revealed why the reporter's visit prompted them into a hasty wedding. The New York newspapers reported the whole affair, and one observed that the union of Dauvray and Ward:

> …explains to a large extent the devotion to baseball recently shown by Miss Dauvray. All through the earlier part of the summer she was a regular attendant at the Polo Grounds and always aggressively and enthusiastically championed the home team.[9]

Larry Bowman

The Dauvray Cup

A few days after the wedding, the St. Louis Browns and the Detroit Wolverines, the teams competing for the World's Championship and the Dauvray Cup, played one of the series' games in Philadelphia, and the newly-married couple attended the event. Detroit had by this time won the eight of the fifteen games scheduled between the two teams, and had claimed the title of "World Champions." The members of the Detroit team had already received their gold medals, which they proudly displayed wherever they went off the playing field (At least two of these medals survive and today are in the collections of the Baseball Hall of Fame and Museum.) The Dauvray Cup was publicly displayed at the game. A Detroit reporter opened his account of the Philadelphia contest with the observation that:

> ...there was a rather expensive home plate on the Philadelphia diamond when the Detroits went on to practice this afternoon. The Dauvray Cup surmounted the rubber plate and the Wolverines were very careful not to hit it with the ball. They naturally did not desire to injure any of their personal property. The Browns regarded the property with wishful eyes.[10]

Once the series was concluded, the Detroit team took the Dauvray Cup home, and the proud owners of the Wolverines put it on display at Roehm and Sons Jewelers in downtown Detroit.[11]

Disappearance—For the next few years the Dauvray Cup was awarded to the victorious team in the series between the champions of the National League and the American Association. When the Association collapsed in 1891, the Cup was awarded to the National League pennant winner. In 1893 Boston won the cup for a third time and was awarded permanent possession. The Beaneaters were playing an exhibition game in Kansas City when the cup was awarded to them. The Kansas City *Star* reported the event and carried a likeness of the cup in its report of the ceremony. The cup dropped out of the public eye and has disappeared. The line art illustration of the cup displayed in the Kansas City paper on October 8, 1893, is the only likeness that I have found.

After the Dauvray Cup was retired in 1893, William Chase Temple, the wealthy owner of the Pittsburgh baseball team, donated an expensive silver cup to replace it[12]. The Temple Cup, which is on display at the National Baseball Museum in Cooperstown, became for a few years the coveted symbol of supremacy in professional baseball.

Dauvray's marriage to Ward did not endure. In 1888, while they were in St. Louis where the Giants were playing the St. Louis Browns in the World's Series, the couple had a nasty quarrel and Dauvray returned to New York City. After the Giants won the series, Ward joined Al Spalding's world tour and was away for months. Neither ever publicly revealed the nature of the quarrel, but many speculated that it centered about Dauvray's desire to resume her acting career. At the time of their wedding, Dauvray had announced that she was leaving her career as an actress, but by the autumn of 1888 she wanted to return to the stage, and Ward may have been opposed to the idea. After they separated, Dauvray went on tour with a road company early in 1889. She and Ward later attempted a reconciliation, but in 1893 she initiated divorce proceedings and the marriage ended. (An interesting sidelight to the domestic strife Ward and Dauvray endured was that in 1889 the great Giants pitcher, Tim Keefe, married one of Helen's sisters, and he and Ward were brothers-in-law for a brief time.)

In 1896 Dauvray married a naval officer named Albert Gustavus Winterhalter. Making her permanent home in Washington, D.C., she frequently traveled with companies that performed popular plays in major cities along the East Coast and in the Midwest. When she died in 1923, obituaries mentioned her stage career, but focused on her status as the widow of Admiral Winterhalter, who had commanded the Asiatic Squadron during the Great War.[13]

No mention was made of her brief, but passionate and eventful association with baseball.

Notes:

1. Charles C. Alexander, *Our Game: An American Baseball History* (New York: Henry Holt and Company, Inc., 1991), 37; Dean A. Sullivan, ed., *Early Innings: A Documentary History of Baseball, 1825-1920* (Lincoln: University of Nebraska Press, 1995), 128-30. Cited hereafter as, Sullivan, *Early Innings*.

2. James Grant Wilson and John Fiske, eds., *Appleton's Cyclopedia of American Biography* (New York: D. Appleton and Company, 1900), II, 80-81.

3. New York *Times*, January 4, 1885, 3.

4. Review of "One Of Our Girls," in the New York *Times*, November 11, 1885,

5. The unsigned review informed readers that Miss Dauvray as Kate Shipley in "One Of Our Girls" was, ". . . graceful, painstaking, and always self-possessed." *Billboard*, December 15, 1923, 238.

5. Oral Sumner Cloud and Edwin Mims, Jr., *The American Stage* (New Haven: Yale University Press, 1929), 272. *New York Clipper Annual for 1887* (New York: The Franklin Queens Publishing Company, 1887), 49.

6. New York *Times*, October 12, 1887; *Sporting Life*, October 19, 1887.

7. Kansas City *Star*, October 8, 1893.

8. *National Police Gazette*, October 8, 1887, 6.

9. New York *Times*, October 12, 1887, 1.

10. Detroit *Free Press*, October 18, 1887, 2.

11. ibid, November 1, 1887, 7.

12. New York *Daily Tribune*, October 15, 1894, 7; New York *Times*, October 15, 1894, 2; and New York *Times*, January 10, 1917, 13.

13. Washington *Post*, December 6, 1923, 5.

Harlem Globetrotters Baseball Team

Lyle K. Wilson, Esq.

No, you do not need to clean your glasses or get a new prescription. The title of this article is correct. In addition to the fabulous Harlem Globetrotters basketball team that we have all enjoyed, Abe Saperstein owned the Globetrotter baseball team that played from 1944 through 1950, and in 1954.

'44-'45—The Globetrotters baseball team appeared in August, 1944, playing a double-header against the House of David in Seattle. Included on the squad were Chip McCallister, R. T. Walker, Lefty Treherne, Collins Jones, Leaman Johnson, and Bill Bradford. The Davids won both games, played at Sick's Stadium, before a crowd of 4,000, by the score of 2-1. A long home run by McCallister and the excellent play of Treherne at first base were mentioned as some of the features of the game. In the fall of 1944 the Globetrotters played a series of games against the Pittsburgh Crawfords in Indianapolis and other Midwest cities. The team appeared again in September the following year, touring through the South with the Atlanta Black Crackers. Longtime Negro Leagues star "Double Duty" Radcliffe was the 'Trotters manager. Pitching, catching, and managing—sounds like "Triple Duty."

The roster included Rogers Pierre, who had played for the Ethiopian Clowns, Everett Marcel (the son of Oliver Marcelle), who also played for the Globetrotters basketball team, and Nap Gulley, who enjoyed a long career spanning from a start with the Kansas City

Monarchs in 1941 through several years in the minor leagues, ending in 1956. Gulley left the Cleveland Buckeyes to join the 'Trotters.

During '45 the 'Trotters played a series of games in the Midwest against the House of David, accompanied by Jesse Owens, who put on a running exhibition.

'46—The Globetrotters, as such, did not play in 1946. Most of the team played for the Seattle Steelheads in the newly formed West Coast Negro Baseball League. Former 'Trotters on the team included Gulley, Pierre, Marcel, Mike Berry, Collins Jones, Joe Spencer, and Stamp Holly. Saperstein was the president of the West Coast league, and Jesse Owens was the owner of the Portland franchise and vice president of the league. The Steelheads were managed by catcher Paul Hardy. Hardy's presence resulted in a ban against Negro American League teams playing Seattle, because he had signed with Seattle before being released by the Chicago American Giants. Gulley recalled that Saperstein had paid a percentage of the gate to the team in '45. They had been so successful that the arrangement for the Steelheads was changed to a salary.

Another team owned by Saperstein, the Cincinnati Crescents, had trained with the Steelheads in New Orleans at Xavier University. W. S. Welch, formerly of the Birmingham Black Barons, was the Crescents' manager, and "Double Duty" was still with Saperstein, handling the pitchers for the Crescents.

The Crescents played against most of the notable teams in the Negro American League and against the House of David. They had some success against these strong teams, and they were a good attraction. An

Lyle K. Wilson, *a member of SABR's Negro Leagues Committee, has a book out on the history of Seattle's African-American baseball teams, entitled* Sunday Afternoon at Garfield Park.

ZELL MILES

PROBABLE LINE-UP

FISHBAUGH, 2b
KITAMURA, SS
STRONG, 3b
SIMPSON, 1b
MILES, RF
S. WHEELER, CF
SMITH, LF
HARDY or BROOKS, C
J. WILLIAMS, P
MOORE, P
RATHEREE, P
CARSWELL, P
RAMSEY, P
BANKHEAD, P
J. WILLIAMS, Ind.
LEWIS, Ind.
L. WHEELER, OF

AMEAL BROOKS, Catcher

Action Pictures of some of the Harlem Globe Trotter Stars

JOE BANKHEAD

J. WILLIAMS

LEON WHEELER

Lyle K. Wilson, Esq.

evening game in Chicago against the Indianapolis Clowns in August drew 8,000 fans, twice as many as the White Sox had entertained earlier that same day.

Early in the season, Marcel, Al Sayler, and Collins Jones were included on the Crescents' roster, but before the summer was out, they were playing for the Steelheads. Some of the other Globetrotters from '45 also ended up on West Coast rosters. Bruce Wright played for the Portland Rosebuds and Wesley Barrow was the manager.

The West Coast league included six teams; Seattle Steelheads, Portland Rosebuds, Oakland Larks, San Diego Tigers, Los Angeles White Sox, and San Francisco Sea Lions. Initially, the league outlined an ambitious schedule of 110 games. Home games were to be played in Pacific Coast League ball parks while the home PCL team was traveling. Games were also scheduled in nearby locations, providing the opportunity for others to enjoy these teams and broadening the fan base. Records are sketchy, but it appears that Seattle was second in the league, with the Larks first, at the time the league disbanded about two months into its schedule. Many of the teams, or combinations of them, survived as barnstorming units. The Steelheads almost immediately became the barnstorming partners of the touring Havana La Palomas. The La Palomas featured comedian Ed Hamman, included several Cuban stars, and served as a farm team for the Indianapolis Clowns.

With their background as the Globetrotters baseball team, the Steelheads provided great entertainment. Many newspaper articles comment on the fact that the team was very quick and really hustled. The two teams played a series of games through the Midwest. In a July 27 article in the Chicago *Defender*, a parenthetical statement was included, defining a "Steelhead." Since the Steelheads were playing in places like Iron Mountain, Michigan, a definition probably seemed necessary, since the Midwesterners might have come up with a more ferric connotation.

In the fall of '46, Saperstein put together an all-star team, "Abe Saperstein's Negro All-Stars," touring Hawaii, among other places. Welch managed the team which included Goose Tatum, Globetrotter basketball and Indianapolis Clowns' star, and Piper Davis from the Birmingham Black Barons. Herb Simpson, Mike Berry, Sherwood Brewer, and Paul Hardy from the Steelheads played on this team. Brewer went on to become the last manager of the famed Kansas City Monarchs. Herb Simpson recalls the team winning fifteen of sixteen games in Hawaii and then returning to Oakland to play major league all-stars.

'47—In 1947 Saperstein applied for a franchise in the Negro American League for his Cincinnati Crescents. Two other teams also applied for franchises that year: the long-standing St. Louis Stars and a new team, the Detroit Senators. The Senators were owned by attorney and state senator Joseph Brown, W. S. Welch, Jesse Owens, and Cecil Rowlette, and claimed to have made arrangements for Sunday games at Briggs Stadium. Franchises were awarded to them and the Stars.

Undaunted, Saperstein decided to revive the Harlem Globetrotters baseball team for 1947. Although a Chicago *Defender* article states that the Globetrotters replaced the Cincinnati Crescents, Saperstein actually operated both teams in 1947.

It appears that the competition for the NAL franchise was friendly, since Saperstein opened his training in New Orleans with games against Welch's Detroit Senators. Many of the Seattle Steelheads were on the Globetrotters in '47, including Herb Simpson, Howard Gay, Stamp Holly, Zell Miles, Collins Jones, and Mike Berry. Blue Dunn and Eugene Hardin, other West Coast NBL players, also signed with the 'Trotters for '47.

Another player on the roster was Ulysses Redd. Before going into the service in World War II, he had played for the Birmingham Black Barons and planned to return to the Barons when he was discharged in 1946. However, his manager, Welch, was then working for Saperstein and managing the Crescents. Redd has fond memories of "Lucky" Welch, saying, "He was like a father to most of the fellows." Redd played for the Crescents for the balance of the Summer of '46, after his discharge. He recalls that it was a lot of fun to play for the Globetrotters.

Both Redd and Nap Gulley recall that the 'Trotters played straight baseball. Although they were sometimes accompanied by novelty acts, the Globetrotters were not the equivalent of their court counterparts. In Negro Leagues baseball, that niche was filled by the Indianapolis Clowns.

In '47 the Globetrotters were managed by Paul Hardy, who had been the manager for the Steelheads. They began the season with a barnstorming tour with their old partners, the Havana La Palomas. The 'Trotters toured all around the country, and their games included matchups against the Kansas City Monarchs and the House of David.

One of the new players in '47 was Jesse Williams, who had been the shortstop for the Kansas City Monarchs. Jim Riley's *Encyclopedia* describes him as a "flashy fielder with exceptional range and who could go to either his left or his right for grounders. He had the best throwing arm in the league and had quick hands, getting the ball away fast." Williams played both second base and shortstop for the 'Trotters. Redd held down third.

'48—The 1948 season started off with a bang, with Hardy's charges defeating Satchel Paige's All-Stars, in Dallas, Texas, 7-2, before a large crowd. Early in the summer, the Globetrotters toured with the Honolulu Hawaiians, and their victories in '48 included a win over Coors, the national semipro champions and Denver Tournament champions of 1947.

The 'Trotters' promotional material listed batting averages for the previous season. Zell Miles had led all of the hitters with .398, Herb Simpson had batted .397, and Jesse Williams had hit .355. Several others were over .300. Steelhead alums Miles, Simpson, Brewer, Hardy, and Cogdell, were still with the team, as were Blue Dunn, Sam Wheeler, Eugene Hardin, Louis Hutchinson, Jesse Williams, and Ulysses Redd. Some new faces were Preacher Henry, Othello Strong, and Joe Bankhead.

By the first of August, the 'Trotters had won 75 games and lost only 11. They played all over the country. On some of their dates they played in doubleheaders, where one of the games would feature a Negro National League team. This is reminiscent of the early days of the National Basketball Association, when the Globetrotters accompanied the NBA teams, to bring the fans out and increase interest in the league. Comedian Ed Hamman accompanied the team in 1948, providing the entertainment element.

'49—The opening game in May '49 was a bit more modest than the '48 opener, with the 'Trotters starting out against the East Chicago Giants. They followed up that game with a number of dates in the Midwest, including a 6-0 victory over the South Bend Studebakers. Paul Hardy was still the manager, and Steelhead alums, Herb Simpson, Paul Hardy, and Zell Miles remained with the team. New faces included Johnny Williams and Parnell Woods. Joe Bankhead, Sam Wheeler, and Othello Strong returned from the '48 squad. Second baseman James Fishback, from the Cincinnati Crescents, attracted a lot of attention. New shortstop Dick Kitamura had toured previously with the Honolulu Hawaiians.

The 'Trotters played a number of games against the Brooklyn Royal Giants around Memorial Day, and then headed south in early June, playing the New Orleans Creoles in Chattanooga, Tennessee, on June 5. Up to that game, they were undefeated. Later in June, they played a series of games against the House of David, and then defeated the General Electrics of Fort Wayne, Indiana, 9-6. The Electrics had been the national semi-pro Champions in '48. They continued on with several games against the Davids and local teams in several Midwest locales. The complete schedule was to include 140 games. By July they had won 75 percent of their games, including another victory over Coors.

'49-'50—There is little information about the '49 tour. Games were reported against the Black Yankees in the South, and as of August the 'Trotters had a record of 103-14. Ed Hamman again accompanied the team. Righthanded submarine pitcher Layman Ramsey put together an 18-game winning streak.

The next year the team reported to Monroe, Louisiana, on May 1 for spring training, with Hardy still at the helm. On May 7 the Globetrotters opened against the Brooklyn Cuban Giants, owned and managed by Brady Johnson. The 'Trotters' roster included Johnny Williams, Frank Carswell, Layman Ramsey, Joe Bankhead, Red Berry, Zell Miles, Herb Simpson, Parnell Woods, Sam Wheeler, and Jesse Williams.

In June they headed for the Pacific Coast and Canada, playing through the Midwest against local teams and the Cuban Giants. One of their stops was in Brandon, Manitoba, where they won a tournament. Johnny Williams threw a three-hitter versus the Brandon Grays in the tournament final, carrying a no-hitter through the eighth inning.

Encore—As with all great performers, the Globetrotters were called back for an encore in 1954. Welch managed the team in '54, and Paul Hardy re-turned as the catcher. The star attraction was none other than Satchel Paige, who had signed to pitch and serve as general manager of the team. A May 15, 1954, Chicago *Defender* article stated that Paige had turned down a $20,000 offer to pitch for the Los Angeles Angels of the Pacific Coast League. Responded Paige, "I'm worth much more than $20,000...I am still one of the best in the game. I'll prove it pitching for the 'Trotters...I can make anywhere from $25,000 to $30,000 with this team during the coming season. So, why should I pitch in organized baseball for less?" The 'Trotter games in '54 included appearances in Seattle and Tacoma, Washington. True to his word, Paige was on the mound in Seattle on August 8, 1954, pitching scoreless ball against the House of David, while giving up only one hit and walking two in a two-inning stint.

One of the stars for the 'Trotters in that game was Ezell King, who would later go on to be an all-star in the Negro American League. "Bobo" Nickerson, the famous comedian, was an added attraction on the '54 tour, and the House of David continued to entertain the fans with their famous "pepper" game in the fifth inning. The fans really got their money's worth when they went out to see these teams, with baseball and comic legends abounding. (Paige, of course would continue on well past '54, including an appearance with the Indianapolis Clowns in 1967, when it was my joy to see him pitch against our local Bellingham Bells. Paige, then over age 60, pitched the first inning against the Bells, getting two ground outs and then a strikeout to retire the side.)

As you look at the history of the Negro Leagues and independent black barnstorming teams, you see an explosion of activity after World War II. In the Pacific Northwest, for example, teams came through occasionally before the war. (See "Willie Foster and the Washington Browns," in TNP 96 for a partial discussion of this era.)

After the war, the floodgates briefly opened. New leagues, such as the West Coast Negro Baseball League and the United States Baseball League, were formed and, unfortunately, quickly passed out of sight, though some of those teams continued vigorously on as barnstormers. Things dropped off considerably after 1947. By the mid-'50s, the Negro Leagues were almost dead and few touring teams remained. By this time the Clowns often advertised themselves as the "Globetrotters" of baseball. Certainly, the level and style of play and entertainment were on a par with those of the fabulous basketball team. The real Globetrotters of baseball, though, had hung up their spikes some years before. They had traveled throughout the United States and Canada, providing good, entertaining baseball wherever they appeared, and they had held up the substantial reputation that had been established by Saperstein's basketball team.

The 1956 Los Angeles Angels

Jay Berman

They came. They won. They left.

They were the 1956 Los Angeles Angels of the Pacific Coast League. They won their fourteenth and final pennant that year, but never had time to enjoy it.

A few months after the season ended, the Brooklyn Dodgers bought the rights to the area. By 1958 the Dodgers were in Los Angeles and the Angels were gone.

Before they left, they gave the city a going-away present. They won the 1956 PCL pennant so convincingly that the last month of the season could have been mailed in.

They finished with 107 wins—sixteen more than second-place Seattle. They led the league with 202 home runs, scored 1,000 runs in 168 games, and had a league-high team batting average of .297.

Six of the eight starting players had more than 20 home runs, and four finished with more than 100 RBI. Baseball author-historian Richard Beverage calls the club one of the best offensive teams in the history of the minor leagues.

This year marks the forty-first anniversary of that club's success. It all came about before drug scandals, player strikes, agent-owner disputes, and seven-figure salaries had cooled fan interest in the game.

Seven-figure salaries? Some of these men had four-figure salaries. The average was about $10,000—not a lot of money even then—but virtually without exception, team members look back on that 1956 season as the highlight of their careers.

Jay Berman *is a retired journalism professor and an original member of the Pacific Coast League Historical Society. He and his wife, Irene Machuca, live in Manhattan Beach, California.*

All but four of the twenty-six men who played on the team are believed still to be living. All have left Los Angeles. They live in Naples, Florida.; Rocky Mount, North Carolina; Quincy, Illinois; Portland, Oregon; and Topeka, Kansas. Only three are in California. Ten of the old teammates reminisced about 1956 in a number of recent telephone conversations from their homes.

They talked freely about camaraderie, of a team without faction or friction. They remembered management warmly, calling general manager John Holland a father figure and manager Bob Scheffing someone who led and motivated them.

They spoke fondly of Steve Bilko, the massive (6-foot-1, 250-pound) first baseman whose 55 home runs, 164 RBI and .360 batting average all led the league—he was a unanimous choice as Most Valuable Player—but who was quiet and, by some accounts, almost shy. Bilko was probably the best-known athlete in Los Angeles during his three years with the Angels (1955-57). He went back to his home town of Nanticoke, Pennsylvania, and drove a milk truck until shortly before his death.

Nearly all singled out second baseman Gene Mauch, who went on to manage four major league teams—including the California Angels—as someone who had already displayed leadership skills and had a knowledge of the game's fundamentals that impressed them.

And at a time when baseball had been integrated for less than a decade and Lorenzo "Piper" Davis, a 39-year-old veteran, was the only black man on the team, many remembered him as one of the most important players on the club, in large part because of his off-the-field leadership.

1956 P.C.L. CHAMPS

LOS ANGELES ANGELS

They still recall details of games played in long-demolished parks as though they had taken place last season. A few of them offered, unsolicited, the observation that the 1956 Angels—a minor league team—would be a contender in the watered-down major leagues of today.

Nobody went on to major league greatness. Bilko spent all or part of ten seasons in the majors. Mauch was a big-league player for nine years. Center fielder Gale Wade had only 19 games in the major leagues. Catcher Elvin Tappe was a Cub for parts of six seasons (and later their manager), but never hit a big-league home run. Shortstop Casey Wise was in the majors for parts of four seasons, but never hit .200.

Unless you were there, you may not even know who George Freese, Jim Bolger, or Bob Speake were, but each had more than 20 home runs and 100 RBI in 1956.

It just all came together, as the old teammates will tell you today, and many say they could see as early as spring training that it was going to.

The youngest of them now is 62; the oldest, 79. Bilko died in 1978 at the age of 49, and pitcher Dick Drott died in 1985, also at 49. All the other members of the starting lineup survive. Most are retired.

After their baseball careers—in the 1950s baseball players still needed winter jobs and something to do

after their playing days—some stayed in the game. Among those who did not, Wise became an orthodontist. Davis, one of the PCL's first black players, became a minister. Speake is an insurance executive. Pitcher Ray "Moe" Bauer earned a doctorate and became a professor and athletic director at North Carolina Wesleyan College, retiring three years ago.

Steve Bilko—Today they are scattered in more than a dozen states, but in 1956, they lived in Hawthorne, Torrance, West Covina, Huntington Park, Glendale, Los Angeles, and elsewhere in a community they remember as being smaller and nicer than it is today.

Every day—the Angels played an almost all-daytime schedule in '56—they drove to Wrigley Field, the landmark ballpark built in 1925 by the same Wrigley family that owned the Chicago Cubs and that city's park of the same name. Wrigley was at 42nd Street and Avalon Boulevard, about a mile southeast of Los Angeles Memorial Coliseum. It was already a neighborhood that had seen better days, and off-street parking was almost nonexistent, but from the time it was built until the end of the line in 1957, the Angels were usually among the league leaders in attendance.

In 1956 those fans had plenty to watch.

"We never cared if we were a few runs behind,"

Wade, the former center fielder—later a rancher and farmer—said in a conversation from his home in Sebring, Florida. "We knew from the start that we were going to score a lot of runs, and we always felt we would win."

Wade, who had 20 home runs and hit .292 that year, was among the former Angels who spoke of Bilko's personality, as well as his 400-foot home runs. "Steve was one of the softest-hearted, kindest people I ever knew," he said. "His voice was soft; he never raised it. He encouraged the rest of us in his own quiet way.

"One thing I remember about Steve was that when he was at bat, he stood there with his shoulders kind of humped up, staring out at the pitcher. One day—I don't remember the pitcher—he delivered the ball and Steve swung and it went right back at the guy's head. He ducked down, somehow, and the ball kept on rising and hit hard off the center field wall.

"It was the hardest-hit ball I ever saw."

Third baseman George Freese, whose 22 homers and 113 RBI had earned him the No. 5 spot in the batting order, recalls a different Bilko story.

"Steve was an easy-going guy, a quiet guy, almost shy. The team's public relations man came up to him after a game—remember, we played mainly day games—and told him he wanted him to go to a TV show cast party that night for 'Sgt. Bilko.' The name of the popular situation comedy (later a film) had been chosen by star Phil Silvers because he was a baseball fan, had seen Bilko, and liked the sound of it.

"Steve told him, 'No, I'm not going. I don't want to do it.'" And George Goodale, the public relations man, said: 'Steve, I promised them. You've got to do it.' Steve looked around the dressing room and I was the only one left. He said: 'I'll do it if Freese goes with me.' I had to go into someone's locker to find a sport coat. It was a great party."

Bilko's widow, Mary, still lives in Nanticoke, where her husband was born and returned after his playing days ended. She said recently that while Bilko was aware of his celebrity status, it didn't inhibit their activities together. "We'd go to Disneyland or Knotts Berry Farm with the kids on an off-day," she says. "He was never really bothered."

As for wishing that he had played later, when stars became instant millionaires, Mrs. Bilko says of her husband: "He loved the sport. He played because he loved the game. So he didn't play when they were making big money. He played when it was fun. Times change, and you have to be happy with the times that you had.

"We would never have seen the places we saw without baseball. Steve played winter ball in Puerto Rico, Cuba, the Dominican Republic. We lived one winter in Havana. We couldn't have done that otherwise."

Of Bilko's success at Wrigley Field, Mary Bilko re-

members: "It was like second heaven to him there. He'd hit a home run and look at me and the kids as he rounded third base. Baseball has changed so much. Back then, you'd play even if you had an injury because you wouldn't want the manager to take you out of the game. Now, they miss the bus or just tell the manager they don't want to play."

Gene Mauch—Although Bilko was the team's top star, it was Mauch, who later managed the Montreal Expos, Philadelphia Phillies, Minnesota Twins, and California Angels for a total of 26 years, who earned their respect for his baseball knowledge. Catcher Joe Hannah said Mauch "was the leader. Gene was...knowledgeable about the game and was constantly keeping everyone in tune, reminding us of the strengths and weaknesses of the opposing players. He is one of the smartest baseball minds ever...."

Hy Cohen, who had pitched briefly for the Chicago Cubs and was 5-0 with the 1956 Angels: "Gene Mauch was the smartest guy I ever knew in baseball."

Shortstop Wise: "Gene had the thought process and demeanor of a manager. He was just always looking for a way to win."

One former teammate said Mauch—whose .348 batting average was third in the league that year—was so nervous during games that he occasionally threw up in the clubhouse between innings.

Left fielder Bob Speake, who contributed 25 home runs, 111 RBI and a .300 average to the lineup, has another recollection: "Gene batted second and I was third. We were playing Vancouver, and [Vancouver manager] Lefty O'Doul was on Gene like a cheap suit. Ryne Duren hit Gene with a pitch, and Gene figured O'Doul had told him to do it.

"The next time he came to bat, Gene told me, 'If Duren hits me again, I'm going after him. Keep the catcher away from me.' Well, the catcher, John Romano, was a lot bigger than I was, and I didn't like the idea.

"Sure enough, Duren hit Gene in the ribs again, and Gene ran out to the mound and jumped on him, and I turned toward Romano. He looked at me and said, 'We don't want any part of this.' We let Gene and Duren fight it out."

Lorenzo "Piper" Davis was remembered by his former teammates for other reasons. Davis, nicknamed for his home town of Piper, Alabama, had been a star on the Birmingham Black Barons before baseball was integrated. He was past his prime when the color line was broken. By 1956 he was only a part-time player, but still had six home runs, 24 RBIs, and hit .316 in 64 games. Bauer thinks Davis was as important as the starting players for his off-the-field leadership.

Bauer, 6-1 as a reliever in 1956, said of Davis: "The role players are much more emphasized now, but...Piper Davis could play anywhere and help you. He filled in at third, he pinch-hit, but most of our time was spent in the bullpen where he usually warmed me up. He said he liked that because 'all I have to do is hold this mitt there and you have to hit it.'"

Speake said of Davis: "He played a big part in the esprit-de-corps. He was a veteran, and he was well respected by all the younger guys."

Team chemistry—All remember the club as having no cliques or factions. Hannah, who shared catching duties with Tappe, said, "There was a chemistry of good will among the players that was special. I don't remember any arguments or jealousies toward other players."

Wise, the shortstop turned orthodontist, has similar memories: "Of course, it's easy to get along when you're winning, but we really did care about each other. There's an individual aspect to the game now that I don't like. The team isn't emphasized. I like Cal Ripken and Tony Gwynn—he's a marvelous hitter—but the loyalty and identification with a team seems to be gone."

Speake said of the 1956 team: "The chemistry was such that we all sat together on the bench, on the plane, or in the clubhouse. You didn't have the same guys always together at one end of the bench. We knew we were going to win, but we didn't even follow our own stats. We just followed Bilko's stats. The league record for home runs was 60, and we just wanted to see if he was going to break it."

Tappe, on the team attitude: "We all loved one another and we all loved the sport of baseball. It was a great team made up of great players and great men. It was my greatest year in baseball, and it all passed far too quickly."

Today, when players who make $3 million a year are openly contemptuous of management, it's hard to imagine the kind of bonds the former Angels speak of when they recall general manager John Holland.

"John Holland was a prince of a guy," said Wade. "Everybody loved him. We went first class all the way. People think the minor leagues always went by bus or train. We flew everywhere. Not just Seattle or Portland. We even flew to San Diego, in a DC6B. And we stayed in the best hotels."

Freese, now retired and living in Portland, remembers: "They couldn't do enough for us. They had a big team party at the Coconut Grove. Nat 'King' Cole sang. There were flowers for our wives. Everyone there had tears in their eyes. We didn't want the season to end. We didn't know when we'd see each other again."

Bauer says of Holland: "He was always fair, concerned, and interested in my career and what was best for me." Speake says Holland "was kind of like a dad. Everyone wanted to play for him and for Bob

[Scheffing]."

How would the Angels have fared in the major leagues? Several of the old teammates think they could have been competitive against today's teams, which they see as diluted by expansion.

Johnny Briggs, now a realtor in Camp Connell, in Northern California, was 5-5 as a starter and reliever in 1956. He says the Angels would not only be competitive today, "but just might have been good enough to win, given the fact that nobody has deep pitching."

Freese calls the team the best he ever played on and says, "I would put it up against many major league teams of that time or now."

Mauch went a step further, saying, "I might be prejudiced, but I think it was the best minor league team ever put together. I saw some teams in the big leagues that couldn't play as well."

The Angels moved into first place on April 24 and stayed there for a month, with Seattle and Sacramento close behind. Los Angeles' pitching was anything but overwhelming, but a team that averages six runs per game doesn't have to worry quite as much about its pitching.

Seattle caught the Angels on May 21, but the Angels then swept the Rainiers in a four-game series. In the last week of May, Bilko hit 10 home runs in 10 games.

By June 23 the Angels had dropped into second place, two games behind Seattle. Dave Hillman was the only consistent starting pitcher, but Bilko, Freese, Bolger, and Speake were hitting home runs on a regular basis to keep the club close.

On July 10 the team moved into first place to stay. Fittingly, this was accomplished with a 19-4 win over Portland which included a 12-run first inning.

By August 6 the lead was 7-1/2 games, and Seattle was fading. Bilko hit his 47th home run on August 12, as the lead moved to 12-1/2 games. There was no doubt who was going to win.

The only question was whether Bilko would hit 60 home runs to break the league record. He hit his 50th on August 26 and his 53rd came in the September 3 pennant-clinching win over Seattle.

"We wanted to clinch it in Seattle," Freese recalls, "and we did. We had to vote on whether we wanted championship rings or watches, and we voted for rings. Gene [Mauch] designed them. What a year that was."

Wrigley Field is gone. It was the home of the American League's Los Angeles Angels—no relation to the PCL club—in 1961. It was demolished in the mid-1960s to make way for a community center.

"I don't ever want to see where it was," says Wade, who has been in the Los Angeles area several times since he left the game. "There and Seattle. I have old friends in Seattle but I never go to where the ballpark used to be. I don't like to see where ballparks used to be."

Success and surrender

The Bernice Gera Story

Bob Fulton

The Finger Lake *Times*

Bernice Gera battled for five years to realize her dream of a career in professional baseball. But in an almost perverse twist of fate, that dream metamorphosed into a ghastly nightmare that left her shattered.

Gera shook the baseball establishment to its very core and was catapulted into the national spotlight twenty-five years ago as the first female umpire in a professional league. But after smashing through the gender barrier during a Class A game in Geneva, New York, she walked off the field for good, disillusioned, dispirited, disgusted.

"In my heart I regret that I ever did it," Gera said years later. "I went broke trying to fight all of baseball just to prove women could do the job. The only thing I've learned from baseball is how to be bitter."

No wonder. The woman who made history in a game dominated by men was reviled by many—even members of her own sex—for her unconditional surrender in the glare of the media spotlight. Gera had actually set back the cause of women, some suggested, not advanced it.

Wrote Nora Ephron in *Esquire* magazine, "In her first game she made a mistake. And broke down under pressure. And couldn't take it. And quit. Bernice Gera turned out to be human, which is not a luxury pioneers are allowed."

What's unfortunate is that Gera's only professional appearance—described as "brief, explosive and mysterious" in a *Finger Lakes Times* account—tends to

over-shadow her significant role as a trail-blazer. She opened doors not only for other women (for example, Pam Postema, who umpired six seasons at the Triple-A level), but for men who, prior to her landmark court victory, were also denied umpiring opportunities because of arbitrary standards.

Gera today holds a place of honor at the National Baseball Hall of Fame and Museum in Cooperstown, New York, where her photograph, pink whisk broom, and the uniform she wore on June 24, 1972, are displayed.

That night, not long after the remnants of Hurricane Agnes passed through the Geneva area, Gera stirred up a storm of her own. She worked the bases at Shuron Park as the host Rangers beat the Auburn Phillies, 4-1, in the first game of a season-opening New York-Pennsylvania League doubleheader.

Her call on a play at second base brought Auburn manager Nolan Campbell sprinting from the dugout, "his jugular veins popping," as Gera recalled in 1992, the year of her death.

In a matter of seconds, Campbell secured his own

Bob Fulton *is the author of* The Summer Olympics: A Treasury of Legend and Lore, *published by Diamond Communications. He resides in Indiana, Pennsylvania.*

place in professional baseball history: the first person tossed from a game by a woman. He appeared on the "Today" show the next morning, breezily discussing his ejection with ex-major leaguer Joe Garagiola. And the lady umpire? She just *disappeared*. Gera rushed to a waiting car after the game and sat sobbing in the back seat as it drove off.

"She let a lot of people down, all those people who fought for her in the courts and all the other women who supported her," said Geneva manager Bill Haywood, who was compelled to recruit an umpire from the stands to work the second game. "She made a farce of it."

A fine player—What should have been Gera's crowning achievement, the culmination of a remarkable five-year odyssey punctuated by unrelenting verbal abuse and even death threats, dissolved in a flood of tears and recriminations.

Ironically, the housewife from Jackson Heights, New York, had never fancied herself a crusader or an activist in the women's movement. Gera's motivation was simple: She just wanted to be part of the game she'd loved since her childhood in the western Pennsylvania mining town of Ernest. Of course, that's where Gera first experienced exclusion because of her gender. She wanted to play baseball with the boys; the boys had other ideas. Initially, at least.

"They wouldn't let me play baseball with them because I was a girl," Gera recalled. "But when the boys saw how I could catch and throw and hit the ball, they'd fight among themselves for me when it came time to choose sides."

She wasn't exaggerating. Gera developed into a player of uncommon all-around ability. She slammed baseballs 350 feet during charity demonstrations and once outslugged home run champion Roger Maris at Bat-a-Way on Long Island. Gera also drilled three hits off fireballing Hall of Fame pitcher Bob Feller in a batting exhibition.

The accuracy of her arm might well have rivaled Feller's. Gera became the scourge of amusement parks, repeatedly toppling objects with thrown baseballs and collecting armloads of stuffed animals, which she donated to children in hospitals and orphanages.

"Mrs. Gera has won dozens of prizes for her pitching skills at knocking over milk bottles, rag dolls or whatever else they might put in front of her at carnivals and amusement parks," noted a story in the Long Island *Star-Journal*. "In fact, Mrs. Gera's dexterity in the game has resulted in her being banned at various arcades."

Gera threatened those concessionaires with lawsuits, a prelude to later legal challenges when baseball sought to bar her. She had originally hoped to land a major league job in some capacity and mailed letters to each club, but none expressed interest. Undeterred,

Gera decided to try something different. Unprecedented, no less.

Another route—Over coffee one day with her husband, Gera declared her intention to become an umpire. Steve Gera would stand by his wife and offer unwavering support through the trials to follow, but that day, caught completely off guard, he nearly choked on his coffee.

It was a predictable response, as was that of the baseball establishment. To the hidebound men who acted as stewards of the game, welcoming a woman into the fold was more repugnant than lowering ticket prices. So they continually erected roadblocks in Gera's path, hoping to discourage her. But she forged on, even when the outlook was as bleak as an arctic landscape.

Umpire schools at first refused to accept Gera. She kept applying and finally gained admittance to Jim Finley's Umpire School, where harassment became as much a part of her daily routine as calling balls and strikes. Nighttime granted no respite from the emotional barrage. Beer bottles were tossed at Gera's door, the sounds of breaking glass accompanied by threats and taunts and obscenities. "It was a horrible, lonely experience," she said.

Gera somehow mustered the courage to continue and wound up graduating with high honors in 1967. But again she encountered resistance: no professional league would hire her. Gera was relegated to umpiring amateur and semipro games, where she gained a reputation for first-rate work.

Two years passed before New York-Penn League president Vincent McNamara offered Gera a contract. Thrilled, she immediately signed and returned it. But only days before her scheduled debut, the contract was voided by Phillip Piton, the president of the National Association, which oversees minor league baseball.

Barney Deary, the administrator of the umpire development program, quickly moved to forestall any budding controversy by affirming that Gera's gender had no bearing whatsoever on the decision. Women would be approved, he asserted, if they met the National Association's height (minimum: 5-10), weight (minimum: 175 pounds) and age (24-35) requirements. That effectively eliminated the 38-year-old Gera, who stood 5-2 and weighed 129 pounds.

Or so it seemed. Then a sportswriter pointed out that McNamara himself hadn't met the aforementioned requirements during his umpiring days. For that matter, neither had Hall of Famer Bill Klem, perhaps the most distinguished umpire in major league history. A crack had suddenly appeared in the National Association's armor.

Gera responded by filing a complaint with the New York State Human Rights Commission, contending her civil rights had been violated. In May, 1970 the Commission ruled that the National Association's requirements were "unjustified and discriminatory." When the association, after exhausting all appeals, still didn't offer Gera a job, she filed a $25 million lawsuit.

Seeming victory—Only then did the National Association capitulate. The New York-Penn League forwarded a contract for the 1972 season and Gera, flashing a rapturous smile, signed it before a phalanx of photographers on hand to record the momentous occasion. Who could have imagined then that after spending five years battling bravely for the right to umpire, she would hoist a white flag one game into her career?

Gera actually decided to quit *before* making her debut at Shuron Park. She discovered, to her chagrin, that while the legal system had upheld her right to umpire, others weren't so sympathetic to her cause. Telephone callers and letter writers spewed venom; some even threatened Gera with bodily harm.

"Male voices would tell me not to take the field, not to take the chance," she recalled. "I received threats that someone would shoot me if I went out on the field. Some of the letters I received were terrible."

Worse, Gera's fellow umpires offered virtually no support. She was treated as a pariah during a league meeting on the eve of the opener.

"I felt the cool resentment of the other umpires, like they didn't want me around," Gera said. "When I asked questions, they said there was nothing to discuss. I decided right then that I would resign after one game. Organized baseball never gave me a fair deal from the very beginning, so I don't feel I owed organized baseball anything."

One game—The first three innings of Gera's debut the following night were uneventful, the proverbial calm before the storm. But in the fateful fourth, she reversed a call.

Auburn's Terry Ford was leading off second when Geneva second baseman Jim Pascarella speared a line drive off the bat of John Dawkins. Pascarella quickly pegged the ball to shortstop Brian Doyle—the same Brian Doyle who would start at second base for the New York Yankees in the 1978 World Series. Doyle stepped on the bag before Ford could scramble back, completing the double play.

Except that Gera signaled safe. A moment later, after it dawned on her that no tag was necessary because a force was in effect, she changed her call. Campbell bolted from the bench as if shot from a cannon and, apoplectic with rage, went nose-to-nose with Gera.

"He kept yelling at me and spitting the tobacco he was chewing," she recalled. "I told him I made a mistake and he said it was the second one I had made. The first was putting on my uniform."

Campbell then suggested that Gera should have "stayed in the kitchen, peeling potatoes." Her right thumb immediately shot into the air.

What stung Gera even more than Campbell's sexist barb was the utter indifference of her umpiring partner. Doug Hartmayer never budged from behind the plate during the dispute. "That was *her* problem," he said contemptuously.

"Umpires must work as a team. But I went onto that field alone," Gera said. "I had no partner. And out there, the other umpire is your only friend."

After the final out was recorded, she marched into the office of Geneva general manager Joe McDonough. "I've just resigned from baseball," Gera told him.

Critics attributed her hasty surrender to the altercation, claiming she was intimidated by Campbell. But Gera scoffed at such charges.

"I wasn't scared off. I was disgusted. I was just fed up with it," she said. "Baseball fought me from the beginning and was going to fight me to the end."

Gera's groundbreaking achievement, marred though it was by that tempestuous appearance in Geneva, brought her arguably more media exposure than any minor league umpire in the history of the game. She appeared on television with Johnny Carson, Barbara Walters, Phil Donahue, Merv Griffin, and "Wide World of Sports" host Jim McKay. Game shows such as "What's My Line?" and "To Tell the Truth" welcomed Gera as a contestant. She hobnobbed with a host of celebrities and sports icons: former Miss America Bess Myerson, author Jacqueline Susann, Joe DiMaggio, Jack Dempsey, Roy Campanella, and fellow pioneer Gertrude Ederle, the first woman to swim the English Channel.

Gera could never have envisioned the far-reaching impact of her plunge into professional baseball. For though her career was fleeting, her fame and legacy endure. Even some of Gera's most impassioned critics eventually recognized her lasting contribution to the game and the courage she displayed in battling for five years against odds longer than Rapunzel's hair.

"I really admire her for what she went through," said Campbell, speaking years after their celebrated clash in Geneva.

Sadly, the experience—that game and the anguished struggle for acceptance that preceded it—took its toll on Gera.

"You've come a long way, baby. I tell that to myself," she said in 1972. "But it hasn't been easy. All through this case my heart was broken. I've wondered if this was worth it."

And was it? Only Gera could answer that question. And perhaps she did in a later interview.

"In a way they succeeded in getting rid of me," Gera said. "But in a way, I've succeeded, too. I've broken the barrier."

An Appreciation of Uncle Robbie

Jack Kavanagh

The rough and tumble time of "baseball's lost era," the nineteenth century, is being phased out by "modern historians." The icons of the receding past and their deeds fade as we approach another millennium. As fast as you can say, "Jackie Robinson," the fame of Wilbert Robinson disappears.

Wilbert Robinson was the hard-nosed team captain of the Baltimore Orioles of the 1890s. The team and its manager, Ned Hanlon, invented or polished much of the strategy still used by modern clubs. Later, Robinson was a convivial, jovial coach for rancorous John McGraw's New York Giants from 1911 to 1913. Next he became an easy-going manager, winning pennants with cast-offs and pitchers he rescued from the discard heap. Uncle Robbie was a dominant figure in baseball when games were played in sunlight and on grass.

Wilbert Robinson might be famous today for pennants won by the New York Yankees. One Yankee owner, Colonel T. L. Huston, wanted to hire him to manage the team. But the bankroll and ego of his partner, Jacob Ruppert, was bigger. He bought out Huston, and Miller Huggins got to win pennants with Babe Ruth and Lou Gehrig leading the way. Uncle Robbie was better suited, actually, to managing the ragtag teams of Brooklyn.

The player—The baseball career of Uncle Robbie, a rotund man with a sunny disposition, spanned more than fifty years, during which professional baseball

grew from a shaky proposition to a national institution. He came up in 1886, and was one of the best players of the 1890s. He once went seven for seven, a record which is still unmatched in a nine-inning game. Robbie began catching when cannon ball pitchers were only 50 feet away. When they were moved back to the present 60' 6", he caught the first no-hitter at that distance, pitched by William Hawke on August 16, 1893.

In the rapidly changing game of the nineteenth century, Robbie was one of the first catchers to dare to crouch directly behind the batter on every pitch. As a boy learning the receiver's trade, young Billy Rob, as the town of Hudson, Massachusetts, knew him, taught himself to deal with foul tips. Years later he reminisced, "Funny how I learned to catch behind the bat. I rigged up a clothesline in our back yard and fixed it just as high as my face when I leaned over. Then I would have a boy throw a ball to me." When the ball hit the line it would be deflected. Bare hands would adjust to the change in trajectory. Black eyes and swollen features were the price young Robbie paid to learn how to catch tips.

As the field leader of the Orioles, Wilbert Robinson was the team's "salver," pouring the balm of blarney on waters roiled by his tempestuous teammates. But he was tough, and he personified the spirit of "the old Orioles." When one of his fingernails was ripped off by a sliding base runner, he ground the bleeding digit into the dirt and roared, "Let's play ball." The tip of the bleeding finger was later amputated.

This and other injuries lent truth to the jest that shaking hands with an old catcher is like grabbing a bag of peanuts. But it was always known that the main

Jack Kavanagh *is writing a full-length biography of "Uncle Robbie" with co-author Norman Macht.*

Wilbert Robinson, young Orioles stalwart.

characteristic of a Wilbert Robinson handshake was not the broken digits it may have revealed, but the fact that it was his bond in any agreement. His hands might have been gnarled, but his handclasp was firm and more sincere than the manicured offering of a bank president.

On to Brooklyn—A wonder at salvaging or reinventing the careers of pitchers, Robinson gave up a comfortable Baltimore merchant's life in 1911 when his friend John McGraw persuaded him to come to the Giants spring training camp to coach the pitchers, especially the failed prospect, Rube Marquard. With Marquard finally living up to his potential, the Giants won pennants in 1911, with Robbie as a part-time coach, and with him on the coaching lines full time in 1912 and 1913. Each season he added another pitching star to McGraw's staff: Jeff Tesreau in 1912 and Al Demaree in 1913.

But the Giants couldn't win the World Series, and the genial but secure and self-confident Robinson could not accept McGraw's blame-shifting tirades. He left the Giants. The Dodgers, floundering and broke, hired him for 1914 and he crossed the bridge to Brooklyn. Two years later he brought the team a pennant, and repeated as National League champion four years after that.

Robinson was beloved by Brooklyn's fans, who renamed their team, "the Robins" in his honor. His genial good humor brought him the fond designation of "Uncle Robbie" after his friend and nationally read newspaperman Damon Runyon wrote about everyone's "Uncle Wilbert." It was said that he knew the game the way an old hound dog knows quail hunting, "by instinct and experience."

Uncle Robbie, regretfully, is remembered more for the foibles of the Daffy Dodgers in the late years of his career. Eccentric players gravitated to his roster and he patiently endured them even when three arrived at third base together. He couldn't cure the most colorful of them all, Babe Herman, from turning a fence clearing home run into a single by racing past runners jogging ahead of him. Herman did it twice in one season.

Brooklyn beat writers of the 1920s did not have to invent incidents to amuse their readers. They just observed and wrote about what actually happened. The Robins manager was like a fun-loving uncle romping with his favorite nephews. He made fun of his own ample girth. The rotund Robbie laughed at the idea that being late to arrive for spring training would delay Babe Herman's readiness. "He can just take a couple of laps around me and he'll be in shape," Uncle Robbie said.

Wilbert Robinson's image was shaped by a prank played on him in spring training in 1915. He accepted a challenge by reporters to catch a baseball dropped from an airplane. The old warrior lined up the plummeting pellet and grabbed it with his catcher's mitt. To everyone's merriment, and his own—eventually—it turned out to be a grapefruit which exploded on contact.

However, the bizarre incidents and the "Daffy Dodgers" of his later seasons fall far short of defining a career that began when organized baseball was only in its tenth season. Cap Anson and others who had played even before the National League was formed in 1876 were still major leaguers when Robbie debuted in 1886. When he retired after the 1931 season—against his will and the better judgment of the Brooklyn fans—he left a personal imprint on generations of players. His last big league pitching discovery, Van Lingle Mungo, who, until his arm went bad, was regarded as the peer of Carl Hubbell and Dizzy Dean, pitched into World War II baseball, ending in 1945, the year Jackie Robinson signed his Dodger contract.

After Uncle Robbie went to Atlanta for his twilight years, another big, hard throwing youngster impressed him. Hugh Casey, an Atlanta native, became a premier reliever and, with that other Robinson, brought Brooklyn a pennant in 1947. That was also the final playing season for Al Lopez, a Hall of Famer who broke in as a teenager under Uncle Robbie. Some of Robinson's managerial magic rubbed off on his players. Lopez won two pennants to interrupt runs of New York Yankee championships by Casey Stengel, who won ten. Stengel had played for Uncle Robbie's pennant winner in 1916,

The more familiar "Uncle Robbie" of the Brooklyn years.

Transcendental Graphics

and his antics helped set the eccentric style expected of Brooklyn players.

Legacy—Robinson's career extended through generations of baseball's development and improvement. He left the arena before artificial turf, domed stadiums, luxury boxes, batting gloves, million-dollar salaried utility men, the designated hitter, and interleague play were grafted onto the declining national pastime.

Uncle Robbie surprised baseball with two pennants in eighteen seasons in Brooklyn, in 1916 and 1920. He challenged better teams with near-miss finishes in 1924 and 1930. Other managers won more pennants and a few managed for more years. Their records reflect superior, dynastic teams more than inspired leadership. Robinson had no superior in extracting better performances from players than anyone—themselves included—had reason to expect. Few managers have been affectionately regarded for long, and none re-

mained a beloved leader longer than Uncle Robbie. Even Connie Mack angered the fans by selling off his star players and endured fifty years mainly because he owned the team.

Uncle Robbie always did his best with what he had to work with. He won more often than he lost, though not by much. In nineteen managerial seasons, eighteen with Brooklyn, he won one more game than he lost, 1,399 to 1,398. But you can't quantify a man like Wilbert Robinson. He is beyond statistical measurement. How do you weigh affability, honor, decency? How do you measure a warm smile, a hearty clap on the back? When Wilbert Robinson was everyone's Uncle Robbie, fan appreciation did not have to be orchestrated. Balls hitting scoreboard signs won the batter a suit of clothes. Now million-dollar scoreboards tell people when to clap their hands and make noise. In Uncle Robbie's time they knew…and they also knew that he would remain true to the love they gave to him.

Wild Jim McElroy

A. D. Suehsdorf

Let me tell you the story of Jim McElroy, pitcher, as far as I have been able to piece it together, for his short, melodramatic life is my outstanding example of the rewards and frustrations of baseball research.

His meager major league record of one win and thirteen losses in 1884 is attested to by both *Total Baseball* and "the Macmillan." Statistically the entries are identical. Factually, they differ on the date and place of his death. The *Encyclopedia* is right on the former: February 24, 1889; *TB* on the latter: Needles, California. Neither has his date of birth, but shortly before this article went to press, I found it: November 5, 1862. This was a reward, one I had been looking for, off and on, since 1988. Birth place? Now the frustrations begin again. He was born in Napa County, in the wine country north of San Francisco, but the town is not specified, and vital statistics of the county and the State Registrar's office do not go that far back.

My source for this statistic and a half is a rare and fascinating newspaper called the *California Spirit of the Times and Underwriters' Journal*, which was suggested to me by William Weiss, a SABR expert on nineteenth-century California baseball. He was unaware of Jim McElroy, but he knew that the *Spirit*'s baseball coverage was extraordinarily broad and complete for the 1880s. Indeed it is. Microfilm acquired on interlibrary loan from the California State Library in Sacramento reveals that the *Spirit* not only ran extensive play-by-play reports of games, but occasional player biographies. Among them, in the issue of July 7, 1883, is a 566-word bio of James D. McElroy.

It says that young Jim attended St. Mary's College, then located in San Francisco,[1] and was the star pitcher of its famous Phoenix Nine of 1880. He graduated that year with "high honors," but decided to make baseball his career. Incidentally, a roster of St. Mary's graduates and brief mentions of the Phoenix Nine in St. Mary's archives refer to Jim as James B.—not D. I'm inclined to think St. Mary's knew better than whoever tagged Jim with the sound-alike "D."

He played for and against a variety of well-known amateur and professional teams, and by 1883 he was with the Redingtons, one of four teams making up the California League, which played weekend games at San Francisco's Recreation Park. Perhaps Jim's greatest success came on June 17, when he beat the champion Haverlys (whose sponsor was the Haverly Theater), 4-3. "At the termination of this game," says the *Spirit* bio, "McElroy was fairly carried to the saloon by his excited friends...He is one of those good-natured players whom it is always a pleasure to see in a game." His speed seems to have been impressive. A frequently heard shout from the grandstand was "Drive them in hard, Mac!" Moreover, the *Spirit* adds, he "has at his command all the known curves, can change his pace and disguise it at will, is an intelligent base runner, and a fair batsman."

By the spring of 1884 *Sporting Life* mentions him as a promising hurler for the Baltimore Monumentals of a newly formed Eastern League. His salary: $50 per month.

Pitching from a distance of 50 feet and permitted a shoulder-high delivery, Jim does fairly well. He loses three to the Wilmington Quicksteps, by far the league's

---

A.D. Suehsdorf *finds baseball's humble toilers harder to excavate, but often as interesting as their betters.*

best team, and once to the Virginias, from Richmond, but tops Harrisburg twice. Of one loss to Wilmington, *Sporting Life* says, "McElroy pitched an excellent game and is worthy of better support." But he also reveals tendencies that will plague him throughout his career: walks, wild pitches, and errant deliveries scored as passed balls. In the Eastern League that year, incidentally, walks took seven balls. (Also in the American and Union Associations, although the National League was down to six.)

The Monumentals last about a month. Competing against Baltimore entries in the American and Union Associations, they are poorly supported and the franchise collapses under a load of debt after three wins and ten losses (one a forfeit). Jim's 2-4 record actually is the team's best. Within a week he signs with Harry Wright's Philadelphia club for $300. Struggling through their second year in the National League, the Phillies will finish in sixth place, 45 games out of first.

Jim pitches regularly and loses ten games in a row. In his first outing, he is whipped, 10-4, by Boston's Charlie Buffinton, who will win 48 this year. In his second, redoubtable Hoss Radbourne takes his measure, 9-2. In his third, it's Grasshopper Jim Whitney of Boston who scores an easy 10-1 victory. Our Jim then blanks Providence for seven innings before a couple of hits and four wild pitches are his undoing, 4-0. And in New York, the Phils get 13 hits off Mickey Welch, but still lose for Jim, 10-6.

For almost every game, the newspaper comments are the same: "McElroy...was very wild." "Only one base hit [was] made [against him] in the first seven innings. In the last two...however, the Grays pounded him for 10 hits." "McElroy was terribly wild and [catcher Frank] Ringo did remarkably well to hold him as well as he did."

Wright rests him for a week after the fifth loss and almost a month after the seventh. So his eighth is a horrible 17-3 beating by the Giants in which he gives up five walks and makes four WPs. He then loses a four-hit effort to Welch at New York. After eight well-pitched innings disaster strikes. Roger Connor hits a dinky infield fly that Jim and first-baseman Sid Farrar (opera diva Geraldine's father) both run for. "Farrar's name was called," says the Philadelphia *Record*, "but on seeing McElroy he stopped running, and McElroy muffed the ball." The next hitter "trundled [spun or rolled] one to McElroy which he first fumbled and then threw wildly to first." A hit by the next batter drives in two runs and turns a 2-1 lead into a 3-2 defeat. His tenth loss comes a week later at Providence, 6-1.

Finally, on July 22, Jim is the winning pitcher in a crazy 10-6 game with the Grays. Says *Sporting Life*: "[Charlie] Sweeney pitched seven innings, when Manager [Frank] Bancroft, thinking the game safe and wishing to give Sweeney a rest, put [Cyclone] Miller in the box, not without strong objection from Sweeney, who refused to play in right field, and Providence continued the game with but eight men." In the ninth, Miller was hit hard, his fielders went to pieces, and Philadelphia scored eight unearned runs, winning the game.

Jim's streak ends at one. Over the next two weeks there are two more defeats by Providence, 11-4 and 6-0, and as the Phillies depart for their first swing through the west—St. Louis, Chicago, Detroit, and Buffalo—McElroy is released.

Has anyone noticed that we don't yet know whether Jim is a righty or a lefty? I didn't know at this point, either. Then, grubbing through *Record* microfilm for the weeks Jim was with the team, I found this: "[Frank] Ringo and [Bill "Sparrow"] Morton, the Philadelphia club's lefthanded pitcher, have been practicing together all this week..." Well, if Sparrow's the one and only, what does that make Jim? Right!

Jim now enjoys a little stroke of luck. The Philadelphia Keystones of the Union Association disband and Wilmington is urged to replace them. Although the Quicksteps (51-12) have made a runaway of the Eastern League race, they have not drawn good crowds, and generous guarantees from the Unions encourage them to make the move. To strengthen their pitching they sign available Jim McElroy. In the week after his release by the Phillies he is given a $100 advance by the Quicksteps, joins the team in Washington, and goes to the mound against the Nationals. He is absolutely clobbered, giving up 16 hits, including four doubles and a triple, in a 12-1 beating. Toward game's end he is relieved. By mutual agreement the teams do not play the ninth inning.

Now the bad news. The Monday issue of Wilmington's *Morning News* reports that Jim was ineffective because "he had been drinking considerably...The next day he failed to appear, but was seen in a low saloon in Washington, very drunk. On Saturday he skipped the club with the $100 he had received as advance money."

Baseball always has had its alcoholics, some admired as men of heroic capacity, some tolerated as long as they got the job done, and some whose boozing wrecked their careers. Where does Jim belong in this group? And when did the trouble begin? Harry Wright was no pussycat. Did he have any sense of what was happening to his pitcher? Perhaps not. But in that laudatory bio in *Spirit of the Times* there is a clue. The "hearty, genial, wholesouled" Jim, carried to the saloon by cheering friends, evidently got himself there, from time to time, unaided. "Formerly," it says, Jim's "convivial proclivities would at times, perhaps, make him unreliable." The optimistic *Spirit* was persuaded that "that is all past," that success was Jim's tonic now. The reality was otherwise.

Shortly after the Washington disaster, The Wilmington *Every Evening* notes that McElroy has "reported for duty." *Sporting Life* predicts that he "probably will finish the season with the Wilmington club." A bad guess. The issue is barely on the stands when *Every Evening* learns that McElroy has stiffed Wilmington's Clayton House for his board bill and "departed no one knows where, and, except for Host Ortlip, no one cares." *Sporting Life* has the last word. "McElroy," it says, "seems to be an erratic sort of person."

The April start of the 1885 season finds Jim with Norfolk, Virginia, of the Eastern League.[2] He does reasonably well, winning three from Wilmington, now the league doormat, splitting pairs with Lancaster and Washington, losing a pair each to Richmond and Newark, and one to Trenton. Five and seven for a so-so team in and around sixth place is not bad. As usual, he averages four or five strikeouts, three or more bases on balls, a couple of wild pitches, some passed balls, and, now and again, a hit batter.

Inexplicably, in mid-June, he is released. He joins Springfield, Massachusetts, of the Southern New England League.[3] *Sporting Life*'s "Norfolk Notes" exclaim that in McElroy "the Springfields have secured one of the speediest and most effective pitchers in the Eastern League. Why Norfolk let him go is a conundrum here."

With Springfield, Jim has two wins and four losses, one an exhibition against the Buffalo National Leaguers, before the league collapses in August.

The season of 1886 is a blank. The Reach Guide has "J. D. McElroy" listed among fourteen players reserved by Memphis, Tennessee, of the Southern League. Yet in 1887, when he ventures west to join the Wellington Browns of the new Kansas States League,[4] the local *Monitor* reminds readers that Jim was with "last year's Topekas." I have no evidence that he played in either place.

He arrives in Wellington with Harry W. Smith, 31, who has been knocking about since his one major-league season in 1877. A hefty fellow, he becomes the Browns' field captain and Jim's personal catcher.

Jim appears to be in fine fettle. In a win against Wichita he twice fans a batter after running the count to 4-0, "a difficult feat...which goes to show that Mac's twirling abilities have not been overestimated." He wins three from Arkansas City, splits four with Emporia, and takes two of three from Wichita: a 7-2 season, plus service in the field when needed. He seems to have come a long way from the drunk in Washington.

In mid-August Wichita and Emporia desert to join the Western League. Wellington disbands, and in all the shuffling of players nothing is said of Jim McElroy or Harry Smith.

We pick up the trail in Albuquerque, New Mexico.

From the *Daily Citizen* of February 25, 1889, we learn that "McElroy came to this city two years ago as a base ball pitcher from Wellington, Kansas, being accompanied here by his catcher, Harry Smith..." They get "good jobs," Jim at "the Mint," a saloon on James Street, around the corner from the Central Bank. Albuquerque has put its reputation as a "rowdy and violent" frontier town behind it. Its streets still are unpaved and most of its buildings are of flatroof adobe construction. But traffic is light and the new Santa Fe railroad has put optimism, as well as coal smoke, in the air. Mention is made of a town ball team, though neither Jim nor Harry is in shape to play.

At some point Jim quits the Mint, gets "into trouble"—the story continues—"and on his fine being paid" he leaves for Needles, a perishingly hot spot on the eastern border of California, just below the point of Nevada. He tends bar there for six months or more, which pegs his arrival at August or September, 1888.

It is his appointment in Samarra. On February 25, 1889, a news brief on page one of the San Francisco *Evening Bulletin* reports that "J. D. McElroy of San Francisco died at Needles yesterday from an overdose of morphine." At San Bernardino, the county seat, Dr. Charles C. Wainwright, the coroner, and Charles N. Damron, an attorney, leave on the overland stage for Needles to conduct an inquest. There is speculation that murder or suicide may be the cause of death. On March 5, the San Bernardino *Daily Courier* reports their finding. McElroy "had gone to a Chinese dive while drunk and taken morphine, which killed him. The Coroner's jury returned a verdict of death from poison administered at the hands of some unknown person."

"John Eubanks," the story goes on to say, "who was pardoned from the county jail some time ago by Governor [Robert W.] Waterman, had a hand in the matter and was given short notice to leave Needles, which he did."

So, what happened? Hard to say. There seems to be no record of the "trouble" for which Jim paid a fine, or what got Eubanks into jail and interested the Governor enough to get him out. The California State Archives at Sacramento researched Governor Waterman's Letter Books and Pardon Files for me without finding a reference to either man. A researcher who checked San Bernardino city directories found Eubanks, a former grocery clerk, employed in 1895 as a Wells Fargo stage driver—a good citizen now in an innocuous line of work.

As for Jim, we know he liked his liquor. Yet the Chinese "dive" may not have been so sinister. Chinese laborers worked on the Southern Pacific railroad line across the Mojave Desert—it is said they survived the terrible heat drinking hot tea, while whites depending on ice water passed out—and some of them settled in

Needles. Undoubtedly, the dive was one of the few meeting places open to them and, obviously, a source of what we now call recreational drugs. According to the *Citizen*, the telegram that first informed Albuquerque of Jim's death said the overdose had been "administered to him by an opium fiend." Eubanks? No, he was not implicated, just told to get out of town. Who else? There is no more hard information, but perhaps no one. Reckless Jim, probably liquored up, possibly despondent, simply may have overdosed. ODs evidently were common then as they are now. Three days after Jim's death, the San Francisco *Morning Call* reported the death of "a Modesto man" who died from a similar overdose—liquid sulphate of morphine—which he was taking for insomnia brought on by "smoking cigarettes." So much for 1889 medical wisdom.

"In his prime," the *Citizen* concludes—sentiment overstating the facts—"he was a great base ball pitcher,

having twirled the sphere in some of the best clubs in the country, but of late years his arm became weak and his effectiveness as a pitcher departed.

"McElroy has many friends in this city who will regret to hear of his death. He was a native of Philadelphia."

Great? Best? Philadelphia?

Notes

1. Subsequently it moved to Moraga, in Contra Costa County, where it became a national college football power under Coach "Slip" Madigan in the 1930s.

2. And Jersey City, Newark, & Trenton, NJ; Lancaster, PA; Richmond, VA; Wilmington, DE, & Washington, DC.

3. A six-club league. Others are Bridgeport, Hartford, Meriden, New Britain, & Waterbury.

4. Plus Arkansas City, Emporia, Wichita, & briefly Winfield.

James D. McElroy, when not in his cups, was a genial, polite, and companionable sort of fellow and had many friends. He was also a clever minstrel and a prominent member of the Golden Gate Minstrel Club, with whom his songs and dances were a prominent feature. His end was that of many of his profession, the old, old story of "his own worse [sic] enemy." But why moralize? Surely the early demise of this young man is a sermon most profound in itself.
—*California Spirit of the Times and Underwriters' Journal*, March 16, 1889

Baseball Writers
Oppose Radio Use
Association Formally Protests
Broadcasting Details of
League Games

PHILADELPHIA, May 25.—The Baseball Writers' Association of America is opposed to the radio broadcasting of baseball results from major league parks throughout the country, it became known today when the association wired Baseball Commissioner Landis, and Presidents Heydler and Johnson of the National and American Leagues, protesting against alleged granting of a permission to a radio corporation to provide facilities for this purpose.

The telegram, signed by Frederick G. Lieb, of New York, President of the association, and Joseph M. McCready, of Philadelphia, Secretary, is as follows:

"Understand permission has been granted to a wireless corporation to broadcast results of games at Polo Grounds and other parks throughout the country, giving detailed results play by play. If this is permitted, it will kill circulation of afternoon papers and in the end will result in curtailment of baseball publicity.

"The Baseball Writers' Association is strongly opposed to allowing any wireless connection with the baseball parks which would give details while a game is in progress." (New York Times, *May 26, 1923.)*

—Joe Murphy

Herb Washington

Scott Pitoniak

Herb Washington walks across the spacious office above one of the five McDonald's he owns in Rochester, N.Y., and picks up the baseball bat that bears his name. He begins swinging the 34-inch, 32-ounce Adirondack Big Stick.

"Never did use the lumber in a game," Washington says, smiling broadly. "But I did get one offer."

That occurred late during the 1974 season. The Oakland A's had already clinched their third straight American League West title, when manager Alvin Dark walked down the dugout and asked the only "designated runner" in baseball history if he would like to pinch-hit. At first, Washington was like a kid who had been offered two scoops of his favorite ice cream.

"I'm thinking, 'Wow! A chance to bat in the big leagues. There are guys who would kill for this opportunity,' " Washington recalls.

But the more he pondered the circumstances and the historical ramifications, the less Washington was inclined to take his turn at bat.

"We were playing the California Angels that night and they had this guy by the name of Nolan Ryan on the mound," he says, his face lighting up as if the game were yesterday rather than two decades ago. "Now, Nolan wasn't exactly on the top of his game. He was having some control problems. One pitch would be down the pike. The next would be behind your back.

"I'm thinking that Ryan, a prideful, supercompetitive man, might not take too kindly to

Scott Pitoniak, *an award-winning sports columnist and feature writer for the Democrat and Chronicle in Rochester, N.Y., is co-author of* Silver Seasons: The Story of the Rochester Red Wings, *published by Syracuse University Press.*

having this rookie who hadn't hit in a game since high school come up to bat against him. He might take it as us rubbing it in, like when you try to steal when you're up 8-0. The thought that Ryan might want to retaliate by putting one of those 100 mile-per-hour fastballs into my ribs wasn't real appealing.

"But the main reason I didn't bat that night was that I wanted to keep my spot in baseball history. I was on the big-league club solely as a designated runner. I was part of Charley Finley's grand experiment. I figured if I ended my career without a single at bat, I would preserve the mystique, retain my unusual place in baseball annals."

And so Washington put down his lumber. Nearly a quarter of a century later, the bat and his legend remain in mint condition.

As long as they play baseball there will be stories about Herbert Lee Washington, the man Charley O. Finley once hired to steal bases and games.

You'll find him in the baseball reference books, tucked between two other Washingtons—Claudell and LaRue. Herb's career line for 1-1/2 seasons with Oakland reads: 104 games, 33 runs scored, 30 stolen bases and zero at bats.

"It is a pretty strange-looking stat line," admits Washington, who has made a successful transition from the sports world to the business world. "People look at it and say, 'This has got to be a misprint. How can you steal bases and score runs when you don't have any at bats.'"

Washington played a lot of sandlot baseball while he was growing up in Flint, Michigan, and was good at the sport. But he never dreamed one day he would be paid to play it. He figured his meal ticket would be as a sprinter, and for a while it was.

"The track and baseball seasons overlapped, and I had to make a decision between the two," he says. "It really wasn't a difficult one. If you run a 50-yard dash that's just a tenth of a second off the world record when you are a high school sophomore, you kind of know what direction you want to go."

Washington wound up receiving an athletic scholarship to Michigan State, where he starred in track and football. As a sprinter he was talented enough to beat Olympic medalists such as John Carlos and establish a world record in the 50-yard dash. As a wide receiver he was good enough to be drafted by the Baltimore Colts of the National Football League and the Toronto Argonauts of the Canadian Football League.

After graduating from Michigan State, Washington worked part-time as a reporter with a television station in East Lansing. He also continued to compete in national and international track meets, and continued to weigh offers to play pro football. One night after returning from an interview he had conducted with a pretty fair high school basketball player by the name of Earvin "Magic" Johnson, Washington received a phone call at the station.

The receptionist told Washington that Charley Finley was on the line waiting to talk to him. Washington thought one of his coworkers was pulling a prank.

Twenty-three years later he recalls the conversation going something like this:

FINLEY: "Herb, this is Charley Finley, owner of the world champion Oakland A's."

WASHINGTON: "How are you Mr. Finley? This is Herb Washington, the world's fastest human."

FINLEY: "That's precisely why I'm calling you, Herb. How would you like to play some baseball?"

WASHINGTON: "Mr. Finley, I'm not sure I'm following you. Sir, I haven't picked up a bat since high school."

FINLEY: "Herb, it's not your bat I'm interested in, it's your legs. I want you to become a full-time pinch runner for us. Over the course of the season, I figure you could win a handful of games for us with your baserunning."

The idea intrigued Washington, and he flew to Finley's office in Chicago in February, 1974, and finagled a $50,000 no-cut contract from the A's owner. A week later the world-class sprinter reported to spring training and began learning about the art of basestealing from Maury Wills, the ex-Dodger great Finley had signed as a part-time consultant.

The news of the designated runner experiment wasn't greeted with open arms. Baseball purists thought this was just another eccentric stunt being pulled by an owner who brought us mules as mascots and mechanical rabbits that popped out of the ground behind home plate to provide umpires with new baseballs.

Several veterans on the A's resented the fact a roster spot was being "wasted" on someone who hadn't paid his baseball dues.

"The outcry wasn't nearly as bad as what Michael Jordan received when he took up baseball after retiring from basketball, but it was the same mind-set," Washington recalls. "The baseball establishment has never been quick to change or accept different ideas, and this experiment definitely was something different. It took me a while to convert my teammates. Some of them never warmed to the idea."

Finley knew there would be opposition to the experiment, but he didn't care. "I never ran my teams as if they were popularity contests," said Finley in a 1993 interview, three years before his death. "I didn't care if some of my players didn't like it or if baseball didn't like it. I was looking for any edge I could find. I saw Herb as a way of winning a few extra games. And that's what wound up happening. He had an impact."

Like many experiments, this one succeeded only after much trial and error. Washington quickly discovered that speed is only part of the baserunning equation. Deciphering a pitcher's pickoff move and gauging a catcher's arm were every bit as important.

After being thrown out often early on, Washington got the hang of things, and finished with 29 steals in 45 attempts. The stats didn't reflect those occasions when his speed enabled him to score on short sacrifice flies or take the extra base in situations when most other runners would have been gunned down.

Unfortunately for Washington, the most memorable moment of his baserunning career occurred in Game 2 of the 1974 World Series when Dodger reliever Mike Marshall picked him off first base in the ninth inning with the score tied. It wound up being the only game Los Angeles won during the Series.

"I was sitting in the box seats when that pickoff happened, and I was more embarrassed than he was," Finley recalled. "If there had been an ejection button on my box seat I would have pushed it. And I'm sure he would have wanted to join me. But I wasn't mad at him. In fact, I saw him later that night and I told him not to worry about it. Hell, he had won a bunch of games for us, had helped us get there."

In fact, Washington had scored the winning or tying run in ten of Oakland's 91 victories that season. Little wonder Finley called the investment in Washington "money well spent."

The experiment ended midway through the 1975 season. When Finley lost pitching ace Catfish Hunter to the New York Yankees, he could no longer get by with just nine pitchers on his staff. Washington was released to make room for an extra arm.

"I wasn't bitter toward Charley," Washington says. "I

Herb Washington today, in front of one of his restaurants.

understood the business. I knew what he had to do. He was good about it. He even offered me a chance to go to the minors to work on my hitting and perhaps come back as an everyday player down the road. But I was ready to move on with my life. It had been fun, and I left the game with something most guys aren't fortunate enough to have—a World Series ring."

Washington used the money he earned from baseball to purchase a McDonald's in Rochester. Today the 46-year-old owns five restaurants in the area, with an eye on other business pursuits. Four years ago, his entrepreneurial skills received national recognition when he was appointed to replace former Secretary of State Cyrus Vance on the prestigious Federal Reserve Board. He also has received numerous honors for his extensive community service work.

But baseball history buffs will forever associate Washington with fast feet rather than fast food. Washington never swung a bat or chased down a fly ball or threw a pitch in the big leagues, but he still managed to secure a permanent, off-the-wall spot in the game's lore.

Tim Hurst

Joe Dittmar

Joe Dittmar

Arbitration on the ballfield around the turn of the century was a hazardous profession. There was no union, employment could be terminated at any time, and with little support from owners and league officials, umpires faced raucous crowds and unbridled players who behaved with impunity. Afforded little respect or appreciation, the men in blue were routinely and publicly blamed for any subpar performance of a club or individual. Usually working alone, they were fed a staple diet of verbal abuse from throngs that sat within easy earshot, and often were targets of physical abuse as well. Rotten eggs, pop bottles, and seat cushions were common rebuttals to unfavorable decisions, and fist fights between umpires, players, and patrons were chronic. It didn't help that solo arbiters often worked entire home stands, lending credence to the adage that "familiarity breeds contempt."

The harrowing work left a shameful legacy of one-year umpiring careers in the baseball encyclopedias. Between 1890 and 1909, when the NL employed no more than twenty full-time umpires at any one time, forty-three individuals could bear the invective for one season or less. Many of these victims were former players who quickly learned that calling balls and strikes was akin to flirting with the coroner.

Small but feisty—Tim Hurst was one of the more colorful and probably the toughest umpire in the major

leagues. Despite standing only 5'5" and weighing 175 pounds, he had more fights with ballplayers than any other umpire. The bow-legged, sorrel-topped powder keg never backed down from anyone and didn't know the meaning of the word "afraid." Hurst's attitude was bred in the impoverished coal regions of eastern Pennsylvania. The second of six children, Tim was born on June 30, 1865, in Ashland, where residents remembered him as a devilish and boisterous lad. He later worked picking slate and learned how to handle his fists during the daily lunchtime boxing matches by which the men established their pecking order. Hurst never played professional baseball, but leaped from the

---

Joe Dittmar *has been an active participant in several SABR committees and Philadelphia regional meetings as well as the author of the newly released* Baseball Records Registry *(McFarland).*

coal pits to a career wearing blue. Progressing from the Pennsylvania State League to the Southern League and then to the Western Association, Tim was eventually called by National League president Nick Young in 1891.

Players often baited Hurst just to hear his Gaelic retorts and brogue. Once a player, who was having a good game, began giving the Irishman an earful. Tim coolly told him, "Now you're getting a bit chesty. I see you made a couple of good stops, knocked out a couple of hits, and you think you're solid with the crowd. Well, I'll just tell you something. I'll give you the key to my room at the hotel where everything is nice and quiet, and when we get there alone, I'll break that jaw of yours so you can't kick for the rest of the season. I'll see that you get out quietly so you can explain your injury by saying you fell down somewhere." The complainer chose not to take the key.

On July 6, 1896, Hurst absorbed repeated verbal attacks during a game from Pittsburgh's Jake Stenzel and Pink Hawley. After the game Tim followed both men out of the park, asked them to repeat their remarks, then knocked each to the ground with a blow to the jaw. Hurst's rough and tumble style of diamond enforcement led him from one tumultuous episode to another. But he relished the excitement and considered events such as crowd riots as merely enhancing his image.

Marathon man—Tim often umpired in a cap with the letter "B" on it. When asked why, he replied, "It signifies I'm the best." He also officiated boxing matches, bike races, and marathons, although league president Ban Johnson frowned upon these. Once, while umpiring behind the plate in Philadelphia, Hurst needed to catch a train to referee a marathon in New York. In the ninth inning of that game, Kid Elberfeld scored what obviously appeared to be the tying run. But Hurst wanted the game to end, so he called the runner out at the plate. An argument followed in which Elberfeld pushed Hurst. Tim calmly picked up the catcher's discarded mask and drove it full force into Elberfeld's head, knocking him unconscious. He then calmly tossed the mask aside and walked off the field. The incident warranted a $100 fine and a one week suspension. Hurst, however, made $500 for refereeing the New York marathon and got to spend a week's vacation in his favorite city.

In addition to his fighting prowess, Tim possessed a sarcastic wit. Joe Kelley of the notorious Baltimore Orioles once tried to offend Hurst by saying, "If I was Hanlon [the Orioles manager] you'd never umpire another game in Baltimore." To which Tim replied, "What? Not be allowed to umpire in this city for a lot of swell gentlemen like your crowd? Now Kel, don't say that, old boy, for you know all the umpires are stuck on you people."

Hurst delighted in relating another of his favorite stories about the rowdy Orioles. With Tim working alone behind the plate in Baltimore, the visitors had a runner on first who started to steal. As the runner left the bag, he spiked first baseman Dan McGann who retaliated by tripping him. Undaunted, the runner recovered, dashed for second, and tried to spike shortstop Hughie Jennings. Meanwhile, the batter hit the catcher, Wilbert Robinson, on the hand with his bat in an effort to prevent the throw. Robinson tramped on Hurst's toes with his spikes and shoved his glove into Tim's face so he couldn't see the play. When Hurst was asked what decision he made, he said: "Well, I punched Robbie in the ribs, called it a foul, and sent the runner back to first."

Stories abound about how Hurst spurned the usual protection, refusing to wear shin guards, mask, and often a chest protector. Once he was clipped by a foul ball off his ear which bled profusely. Despite pleas from the players he refused to stop the game for medical attention. After the game, a doctor was called into the locker room to sew up his ear.

Hurst also refused to wear spikes. He preferred patent leather dress shoes. Once in the heat of an argument, New York manager Clark Griffith purposely stepped all over Hurst's shoes, puncturing them with his spikes. About an inning later, as Hurst bent over to dust off the plate, he discovered what had happened. Tim raised his hand and called, "Time out!" He sauntered over to the water bucket in the New York dugout and began drinking from a cup with his left hand. Griffith sat beside the water bucket. Suddenly Hurst delivered a right fist to Griffith's chin and knocked him out. He then strolled back to the plate and yelled, "Come on boys, let's go."

Reports also claimed that Hurst didn't always call them as he saw them. One day while working behind the plate, Jim Delahanty was at bat. Tim called a ball that the catcher insisted was a strike. Ever the diplomat, Hurst agreed to leave the decision to Delahanty. "Now, me boy, what was it—a ball or a strike?" Delahanty, recognizing an opportunity to embarrass Hurst, replied that it was a perfect strike, that it had cut the heart of the plate, and that if Hurst weren't so blind he would have seen it. "It did, eh, James me boy? Well, that is very fine to know." From then on everything the pitcher threw to Delahanty was called a strike—a perfect strike right through the heart of the plate.

Another instance of stretching the truth occurred in Cleveland where Hurst had been having a running feud with Indians manager Patsy Tebeau. One day, playing Chicago in front of an overflow crowd, fans filled the seats and circled the field. They stood twelve deep, kept in place by a loosely strung rope. Chicago's Jimmy Ryan, who made a habit of cricketing low pitches down the third base line that either were fair or foul by inches, had precipitated many arguments during the day between Tebeau and Hurst. After one particularly heated discussion, Tebeau screamed at Hurst: "You blankety-blank Irishman. If you make another decision like that, I'll cut the ropes and let the crowd in on you." The next time Ryan came to the plate, he hit another ball down the line, but seeing it would be foul, didn't run. Hurst stepped beside him and said: "Run, Jim, run. It's fair, I tell ye. Run." Then turning to Tebeau, Tim shouted, "Cut the ropes, ye spalpeen, cut the ropes." It was a challenge that went unanswered. (Spalpeen is an Irish derogatory term meaning a mischievous, unprincipled person.)

TIM IN TRAINING AS UMPIRE

AT PITTSBURG

AT ST. LOUIS

HURST

Joe Dittmar

short tenure at the helm, he also turned against his former peers and established a reputation as one of the worst umpire-baiters in the league.

Years later, Hurst also was dismissed from the American League after an argument with Eddie Collins on August 3, 1909, in which he allegedly spit in Collins' face. A near riot ensued and both police and players had to fight to save the umpire from an outraged crowd. When later asked for an explanation of this breach of etiquette, Hurst replied, "I don't like college boys."

Once his umpiring days ended, Tim became a wealthy man managing the events of Madison Square Garden and later working in the real estate business in Far Rockaway, New York. In 1915, while returning to Pennsylvania to attend the funeral of a rela-

It did no good to argue with Hurst. One day he called a strike on George Moriarty after calling the first pitch a ball. "Why, that strike was worse than the one you called a ball," complained Moriarty. "What! It was really worse than the other pitch? Then I made a mistake, me boy. The first one should have been a strike also. Strike TWO!" Moriarty turned around to argue the point further, and Tim called him out on the pitch that came while George wasn't looking.

Dismissals—Hurst's confrontational style eventually led to his banishment from both the National and American Leagues. He was fired from the senior circuit over an incident in Cincinnati on August 4, 1897, when, after being bombarded with beer mugs, he tossed one back into the stands and injured an unwary spectator. Amid a near riot, only a heroic effort by the police saved Tim from the vengeful crowd.

His friend and owner of the St. Louis club, Chris Von der Ahe, rescued Tim by naming him the manager of the Browns for 1898. Alas, Tim's fancies turned to dust as his squad finished twelfth in the twelve-team league at 39-111. It's been reported that in an effort to ignite his club, Hurst fought with just about every member at some time during the season. Ironically, during his

tive, he was stricken with acute indigestion and died on June 4 at the age of 54.

Concerning the lot of an umpire, he once remarked, "It gets monotonous having several million people threatening your life every year. You get awfully hardened to abuse. When they tell you you're rotten, you get to feel proud of their superior judgment." Later he reflected, "I also learned what the fans in various cities knew of me and my family history. They often knew things that I never suspected myself."

Tim Hurst, despite his much publicized confrontations with many players, was truly their friend. On more than one occasion he went to the aid of players who were being mobbed by spectators, incurring their wrath. He also left the umpiring profession with an elevated level of respect. At a time when baseball was being played at its crudest levels and weak league leadership fostered disrespect and abuse, Hurst stood tall and held his ground against tremendous odds. Connie Mack claimed that Hurst did more to stamp out rowdyism than any other official he ever knew. Though some of his techniques could be questioned, Tim's rough-and-tumble style paved a road for the next wave of arbiters who would be afforded an improved level of dignity and support from league officials and fans.

A rediscovered image

The Earliest-known Baseball Photograph

Tom Shieber

For decades baseball historians and researchers have heralded the familiar half-plate daguerreotype of six members of the Knickerbocker Base Ball Club as the earliest known baseball photograph. Reproductions of the photograph are found in a number of readily available sources, including Geoffrey Ward and Ken Burns' *Baseball: An Illustrated History* and the Spring, 1984 issue of *The National Pastime*. But are these fellows really Knickerbockers? Should this image truly be considered a *baseball* photograph? Let us consider what is known about the famous picture.

Of the six fellows seen, only Alexander Cartwright (top center) has been positively identified. Numerous photographs of Cartwright support this identification. Cartwright had been a member of the Knickerbockers from the date the club was formally organized, September 23, 1845. Indeed, he had been playing ball with fellow Knickerbockers long before that day. But on March 1, 1849, the promise of California gold lured him away from his New York home. As it is extremely doubtful that the photo was taken anywhere other than New York City, this latter date is an upper limit for when the photo was taken.

Harold Peterson, author of *The Man Who Invented Baseball*, has conjectured that the clean shaven fellow at the top left of the image may be Cartwright's younger brother, Alfred. Indeed, the two young men are similar in appearance and each has an arm around the other's shoulder. But according to club records, Alfred was never a member of the Knickerbockers

It has also been proposed that the individual at lower left is Duncan Curry, first Knickerbocker president. This is a tenuous identification based solely upon comparison with a photo of a much older Duncan Curry found in Albert Spalding's *America's National Game*.

Recently, two photographs of Knickerbocker Daniel Adams have been discovered. The cigar-smoking chap at lower center bears some resemblance to Dr. Adams, though the conjecture is by no means definitive.

Finally, what of the fact that each man appears to be wearing a straw hat? Was it not the case that just such a hat was, along with a pair of blue woolen pantaloons and a white flannel shirt, a well-documented element of the Knickerbocker uniform? Yes, but it was not until a club meeting held April 24, 1849, that the Knickerbockers officially adopted their uniform, and by that time Alexander Cartwright was halfway across the continent. On the other hand, the uniform (while not necessarily official) may have been in use prior to 1849. And what are the odds that all six fellows would be wearing such hats? Is that not indicative of some sort of mutual affiliation? Perhaps.

Picture identification, especially of nineteenth century photographs, is an inexact science. What appears to be a similarity to one researcher may be less than convincing to another. Furthermore, a baseball historian's hopes, whether conscious or unconscious, may hinder unbiased research. It would be wonderful if we could identify each of Cartwright's companions as Knickerbocker club members, but objectivity must al-

Tom Shieber *is the chairman of SABR's Pictorial History Committee and is an authority on antebellum baseball research. In his spare time he operates a solar telescope at the Mt. Wilson Observatory. A version of this article has appeared in* The Vintage & Classic Baseball Collector. *The author wishes to acknowledge the aid of Joy Holland, Mark Rucker, Barry Sloate, Corey Shanus, and A.D. Suehsdorf.*

ways remain the watchword of the photo researcher. In an attempt to insure this objectivity, I have made every effort to get the opinions not only of other baseball photo historians, but also of individuals with no knowledge of early baseball history.

The best we can say about the daguerreotype is that it may be a portrait of six members of the Knickerbocker Base Ball Club. It may also be a portrait of Alexander Cartwright and five unidentified companions, some or none of whom played baseball. We cannot state that this is definitively the earliest known baseball photograph.

We are left, then, with the question: What is definitively the earliest known baseball photograph? The answer is an exciting and interesting find—an impressive photo only recently rediscovered.

The "Brooklyn" photo—Buried in the files of the Brooklyn Collection at the Brooklyn Public Library is a photo purported to be of the Atlantic Base Ball Club of Brooklyn, 1855. Unfortunately, the photo, twice published in the Brooklyn *Daily Eagle* in the 1930s, is a copy, the original nowhere to be found.

The picture is unquestionably of a baseball team. Nine players are dressed in uniform, while three other club members sit in dark suits and top hats. At far left, the club's pitcher holds a baseball in hand, while two balls can be seen on the table at right. Identifications of each individual are noted at the bottom of the image, as is the date, "1850," which has been crossed out and replaced with "1855." On the reverse of the image is written "Atlantic Baseball Club of Brooklyn." It should be noted that both the date of "1855" and the information on the reverse of the image are written in pencil on the photo. In other words, that information is not contemporary. However, the date of "1850" and the caption identifications were evidently on the original image. These identifications read as follows:

Van Cott, Pitcher
Wm. Burns, Catcher
Wm. H. Van Cott, President
J. McCosker, 3d Base
O. Teed, Short
Phil Sheridan, Left-field
R.H. Cudlip, 2d Base
G. Van Cott, Umpire
I. Vail, 1st Base
H.M. Platt, Game-Keeper
Winslow, Center-Field
Chas. Comerford, Left-Field

Surprisingly, these are not names of members of the Atlantic B.B.C. In fact, these names are of members of the Gotham Base Ball Club of New York City. How this photo came to be mistaken for one of the Atlantic club is unknown, but it is ironic that the Brooklyn *Daily Eagle* unwittingly published a picture of a club from the other side of the East River and embraced them as their very own Brooklyn boys.

The Gotham Club officially organized in the spring or summer of 1852, the exact date being unclear. The club was an amalgamation of veterans from the Washington Club of New York City along with a few new players (or, at the very least, new names). Among the "old-timers" joining the Gothams were William Van Cott, Thomas Van Cott, Elisha Davis, and Messrs. Winslow, Vail and Murphy. A gentleman named Burns also played with the Washington Club, though it is unclear whether or not this was the same fellow as the Gothams' William Burns.

As records are incomplete and information sketchy at best, dating the photo is a difficult task. The original date of 1850 is an impossibility. The Gothams did not form until 1853. The handwritten date of 1855 was apparently added in the 1930s, probably at the same time that the photo was misidentified as the Atlantics, so that date is unreliable. Only two boxscores are known in which the Gotham lineup exactly matches the players pictured. Both of those games took place in late October of 1856. Thus, the photo was probably taken at the end of the 1856 season, or in the off-season that followed.

The players—Described below are the club members pictured.

William H. Van Cott was the first president of the Gotham B.B.C. and remained in that position throughout the 1850s. He was so well regarded that he was elected first president of the National Association of Base Ball Players when it formally organized in 1858. Judge Van Cott (he was a lawyer and justice by profession) was also frequently asked to referee match games, a position reserved for only the most well-respected members of the ball-playing community. A photo of a much older William Van Cott appears in Spalding's *America's National Game*.

By 1855, *Thomas Van Cott* had established himself as the Gothams' premier player. He was the club's regular pitcher, one of their leading batters, and, as far as can be determined, missed only one match game in the Gothams' first five years of existence. Incidentally, that game resulted in a loss to the Eagle Base Ball Club of New York City, a team the Gothams had otherwise manhandled. A drawing of Thomas Van Cott (based on this very photo) can be seen at the top, third from left, of a woodcut published in *Frank Leslie's Illustrated Newspaper*, November 4, 1865.

Mr. Winslow is a bit of a mystery. This Winslow is probably the same fellow found in the lineup of the "New York" nine that defeated the Knickerbockers in the so-called "first" baseball game played at the Elysian

Brooklyn Public Library—Brooklyn Collection

WM.BURNS
CATCHER

J.McCOSKER
3RD BASE

O.TEED
SHORT

PHIL·SHERIDAN
LEFT·FIELD

R.H.CUDLIP
2D BASE

G.VAN·COTT
UMPIRE

I.VAIL
1ST BASE

H.M.PLATT
GAME·KEEPER

WINSLOW
CENT·FIELD

WM.VAN·COTT
PRES.T

1860/855

Fields, June 19, 1846. Interestingly, Winslow also appears to have played for the "New York Ball Club" in an earlier baseball match against the "Brooklyn Players" on October 21, 1845, at the same locale. (The discovery of this earlier game was first announced in the New York *Times*, October 4, 1990.)

Two Winslows, a Senior and Junior, are found in the lineup of the first match game played by the Gotham club. Over the next few years the name Winslow appears with a number of clubs. In 1854, an Albert Winslow played with the Knickerbockers. Two years later, a Winslow is found with the Gothams. Finally, in the summer of 1857, Winslow apparently jumped from the Gothams to the Eagles, where he played first base and pitcher. Are all of these individuals Albert Winslow? Is Albert the Senior or Junior Winslow—or neither? Early baseball research is inevitably accompanied by such mysteries.

Mr. Vail, like the Van Cotts and the Winslows, took part in the Gotham's first contest, a 21-12 loss to the Knickerbockers, July 5, 1853. He remained a regular with the club until September of 1857, at which time his name disappears from all records. Like Winslow, Vail's first name is unknown. A first initial given in the photo caption is "I," but no first name or initial can be found in contemporary accounts. It is probable that this is the same Vail who played alongside Winslow in the baseball match of October 21, 1845. In 1858, a John W. Vail was associated with the Lady Washington B.B.C. of Brooklyn and the following year with the Reindeer B.B.C. of the same city. Are any or all of these Vails one and the same?

While the above players all took part in the very first Gotham baseball match, *William Burns'* name does not appear with the Gothams until 1855. Perhaps, therefore, this Burns is not the same Burns who played with the old Washington Club. Whatever the case, Burns was an active player for the Gothams in 1855 and '56. By 1857 he disappears from Gotham records.

Other than the above noted players, the only other individual in the photograph to have taken part in the Gothams' first match game was *Reuben Cudlipp*. Cudlipp, like Thomas Van Cott, was a stalwart, rarely missing a game. But, like Vail and Winslow, Cudlipp disappears from club records in the summer of 1857.

While *Gabriel Van Cott* never played on the Gotham first nine, he often served as the club's umpire, a role quite different from today's arbiter. Prior to 1858, base-

ball matches were officiated by a group of three individuals. Two men known as "umpires" represented each of the contesting clubs, while a mutually agreed upon "referee" came from a neutral club. Changes in the rules for the 1858 season eliminated the three-man crew, and called for a lone, impartial umpire to officiate the match.

H.M. Platt, probably Henry Platt, a jeweler by trade, was the Gothams' "Game-Keeper." Platt actually played in the Gotham first nine during the season of 1854, but afterward he wielded the pen, not the bat, as he was relegated to the duties of club score-keeper.

Charles Commerford is first found playing with the Gothams in 1854. He was widely recognized as an excellent shortstop, and later organized the Waterbury Club of Waterbury, Connecticut. A woodcut and short biography of Commerford was featured in the August 25, 1866, issue of *Frank Leslie's Illustrated Newspaper*.

Like Commerford and Platt, *Phil Sheridan* first began playing with the Gothams in 1854. By 1858, however, Sheridan was seen more often as an umpire than a player. Like Commerford and Platt, Phil Sheridan first began playing with the Gothams in 1854. By 1858, however, Sheridan was seen more often as an umpire than player. This Sheridan should not be confused with the more famous Philip Henry Sheridan of Civil War renown. The future leader of Union cavalry was posted in Texas for much of 1854 and stationed in the Pacific Northwest by the fall of 1855. Alas! We are left with yet another Civil War general who has nothing to do with the early history of the national pastime.

Little is known of *Mr. Teed*, including his first name. The photo caption gives the letter "O" as his first initial. Other sources refer to an "A.D Teed." Teed was a regular with the Gotham first nine in 1855 and '56.

John McCosker did not appear in a Gotham match until late in the summer of 1856. He immediately secured a position on the first nine as the club's third baseman. In a match game played between the Gotham and Empire clubs in September of 1857, McCosker hit a home run with the bases full. While he was most probably not the first to accomplish the feat, the description in the New York *Clipper* is the earliest known recounting of what would later be termed a grand slam: "The Gothamites ... scored 4 beautifully in their last innings, chiefly owing to a tremendous ground strike by Mr. McCosker, bringing each man home as well as himself."

Ron Shelton

Rob Edelman

In the baseball fantasy *Field of Dreams*, the spirits of various diamond greats come to play ball on a field rising out of Midwestern corn stalks. "Ty Cobb wanted to play," chuckles Shoeless Joe Jackson. "But no one could stand the son-of-a-bitch when we were alive, so we told him to stick it."

In 1994 this "son-of-a-bitch" was the subject of a film all his own. It was *Cobb*, written and directed by Ron Shelton.

On the field, Tyrus Raymond Cobb, the Georgia Peach, had an exemplary major league career, lasting from 1905 through 1928. No other batter has matched his lifetime average of .367. Only Pete Rose has bested his total of 4,191 hits.

The story goes that, in 1958, Lefty O'Doul was questioned about how Cobb would fare against contemporary pitching. O'Doul responded that Cobb might hit .340. Why so low, he was asked? "You have to remember," he replied, "the man is 72 years old."

Off the field, however, Ty Cobb was something else altogether. He was an unabashed racist who lamented the South's loss of the Civil War. He constantly carried a loaded gun. He was a vicious, foul-mouthed brawler and tyrant. It is no surprise that he was so disliked by his fellow players.

"Cobb was the original trash talker," Shelton explained, in an interview just after his film's release. "He

was a Southern redneck who taunted everybody all the time, even his own teammates." This is the Ty Cobb that Shelton depicts on screen.

But *Cobb* does not focus on the man in his playing days. It is set in the twilight of Cobb's life, and examines what Shelton described as the "curious relationship" between Cobb (played by Tommy Lee Jones) and sportswriter Al Stump (Robert Wuhl). In 1960 Stump was hired to ghostwrite the faded legend's whitewashed autobiography, *My Life in Baseball: The True Record*.

The two spent nearly a year together. A truer picture of the man emerged in Stump's 1994 book *Cobb: A Biography*, in which Cobb is portrayed as an argumentative, sickly, booze-soaked old man who was, as Stump writes, "contemptuous of any law other than his own."

"He's in very poor health now," Shelton said of Stump, who has since died. "But I got to know him very well before I began writing the film. For this reason it's filled with many anecdotes about Cobb that had never before been printed."

Shelton is one for making literary references, in both his films and his conversation. He contrasted the Cobb-Stump relationship to what might have been "if Samuel Johnson hired Boswell at gunpoint." In *Bull Durham*, his instant-classic baseball film which came to theaters in 1988, one of his characters is noted for quoting Walt Whitman and William Blake.

But while the subject of *Cobb* is a Hall of Fame ballplayer, Shelton does not at all consider it a baseball film. He sees no relation between *Cobb* and *Bull Durham*, which is as pure a baseball film as has ever

Rob Edelman *is the author of* Great Baseball Films *(Citadel Press), which chronicles the manner in which baseball has been depicted on screen from 1898 to the present. His most recent books, both cowritten with his wife, Audrey Kupferberg, are* Angela Lansbury: A Life on Stage and Screen *(Birch Lane Press) and* The John Travolta Scrapbook *(Citadel Press).*

been made.

"I am fascinated by people like Ty Cobb, who can be so sociopathic and dysfunctional outside their craft and so brilliant in it," he said. "Cobb was a fascinating set of contradictions. He was an uncommonly brilliant athlete who was equally uncommonly obsessed. You can only marvel at his numbers—and also at his abominable social behavior."

He added that his film also "is about an old man who's been called immortal, and how he faces his mortality."

In *Cobb*, Shelton asks questions which are well worth pondering: Why do we in America make heroes out of people like Ty Cobb? Why do we forgive the abysmal behavior of a man whose main contribution to society is the ability to hit .367?

Not all less-than-saintly sports heroes—not even an Albert Belle!—are as downright appalling as Cobb. Others simply are uncouth. "Deion Sanders, for instance, can get away with his outrageous behavior because he's so damn good," Shelton noted. "He can pull off all his jive. But if he wasn't Deion Sanders, he'd just be another boor."

Others, meanwhile, are more paradoxical. Shelton reported that his conception of Cobb was being contrasted to O.J. Simpson. It is a comparison he does not buy.

"O.J. Simpson is a man with a public image and a

A cheery Ty Cobb, as played by Tommy Lee Jones.

private reality," Shelton explained. "Ty Cobb was completely different. His antics were not hidden. All of them made the front page. But nobody cared. Because he hit .367, he was able to meet with presidents. If he had hit .267, he would have been in jail."

The critical reaction to *Cobb* has been what Shelton described as "most curious" and "schizophrenic." He explained, "I could show you 400 reviews. Two hundred of the critics loved the film; 200 hated it. There's been no middle ground." This fact plus the inability of Warner Bros., the film's distributor, to properly market *Cobb*, resulted in a limited release for the film.

On the other hand, *Bull Durham*, Shelton's first feature as director-writer, was a smash hit. That film contrasts an aging catcher for the minor league Durham Bulls (Kevin Costner) and a raw rookie hurler (Tim Robbins) with a "million-dollar arm, but a five-cent head." The third major character—the one who cites Whitman and Blake—is a sexy baseball groupie (Susan Sarandon) who each spring selects one Bull as a season-long lover.

Bull Durham is a knowing ode to minor league baseball and a realistic depiction of the everyday lives of ballplayers, stressing the fact that, in the end, pro sports is a business. "It's about the players as people, the very real pressures they face," Shelton noted. "For example, are they gonna get promoted? Are they gonna lose their jobs?"

While researching the book *Great Baseball Films*, I queried real-life major leaguers on their feelings toward baseball movies. Phil Rizzuto commented that ex-ballplayers, among others associated with the sport, should be involved in the production of baseball movies, to make them more realistic.

And that is exactly where Shelton fits in. During the late 1960s and early 70s, he toiled in the bushes for five seasons as a second baseman in the Baltimore Orioles' farm system, and lived the life of corny ballpark promotions and all-night bus rides portrayed in *Bull Durham*.

That film was well-received by critics, audiences—and professional ballplayers. "I thought it was a great movie," Don Mattingly told me, in a Yankee Stadium pregame conversation. "I played in the South Atlantic League, (and the film) was pretty close to capturing life in the minor leagues. It was pretty cool."

"When it came out," reported Shelton, "Will Clark (then of the San Francisco Giants) was passing out garter belts in the locker room. Apparently, the Giants really embraced the movie."

Shelton's reason for making *Bull Durham*, he explained, is that he "felt no one had made a sports movie right."

The majority of baseball films focus on the glory of the game, on-field drama, underdog heroes hitting game-winning home runs in the last of the ninth or striking out a fearsome opponent's heaviest hitter with the bases loaded. "I generally don't like them," he explained. "They're not relative to anything other than a publicist's idea of their subjects."

For example, Shelton cites two celluloid biographies of Babe Ruth: *The Babe Ruth Story*, a 1948 film starring William Bendix; and 1992's *The Babe*, with John Goodman.

"Neither of them worked," he said. "The first in particular is nothing more than a campy exercise. How can you believe William Bendix, who looked to be about 45 when he made this film, in his scenes (playing Babe) as a sixteen-year-old orphan?"

Shelton's experiences as a pro have enabled him to grasp the reality behind the myths of baseball. "Fans don't understand that athletes don't hate other athletes," he said. "The Dodger players don't hate the Giant players. The fact of the matter is that they all hate management. They all have much in common with labor.

"My view of sports is from the field, the locker room, the team bus. I tend to tell stories from the field, not the thirtieth row of the bleachers."

Such also is the case in his nonbaseball sports films: *White Men Can't Jump* (1992), the story of two urban basketball hustlers (Woody Harrelson and Wesley Snipes); and *Tin Cup* (1996), about a self-destructive golfer (also played by Kevin Costner).

However, even where baseball is not the focus of the story, Shelton manages to sneak references to the sport into his scenario. For example, in *Tin Cup*, it is revealed near the finale that the hero, Roy "Tin Cup" McAvoy, won his nickname as a schoolboy baseball player. And, in one sequence, McAvoy yells out, "Louisville Slugger" as he belts a golf ball with a baseball bat. Shelton began his film career as a screenwriter. He was inspired to become a director because, as he explained, "I wanted to direct my own words. I didn't like the way they'd been interpreted on screen."

One exception was *Under Fire*, whose script Shelton coauthored with Clayton Frohman: a 1983 drama set in Nicaragua just before the fall of dictator Anastasio Somoza to the revolutionary Sandanista forces. "I was pleased with the way that one was made," Shelton said.

One of the secondary characters in *Under Fire* is Pedro, a bomb-throwing Sandanista who feels an affinity with then-Baltimore Orioles pitcher Dennis Martinez. Pedro autographs a baseball and instructs an American reporter to give it to Martinez when she returns to the United States. With a grand gesture, he dons an Orioles cap and hurls a grenade with pinpoint accuracy, just as his idol would burn in fastballs.

"Kid's got a hell of an arm," observes a photojournalist. Pedro then declares, "Dennis Martinez, he is the best. He is from Nicaragua. He pitches major leagues…You see Dennis Martinez, you tell him that my curve ball is better, that I have good scroogie…" Seconds later, Pedro is felled by a bullet.

"I didn't want to make an ideological movie about the Nicaraguan revolution," explained Shelton. "I didn't want to make a movie for the already converted. But how could I make the Sandanista point of view understandable to audiences?

"I decided to do it through baseball, by having a young revolutionary infatuated with baseball." Pedro is a character who, as Shelton said, "is not gonna talk about Karl Marx. He's gonna talk about Earl Weaver."

In *Under Fire*, Shelton honors the type of little-known but devoted ballplayer with whom he feels an affinity by naming one of the characters, a political flack, after career minor league pitcher-manager Hub Kittle.

Kittle entered baseball as a player in 1936, and began managing in 1948. Even though his last full season as a pitcher was in 1952, he periodically hurled through 1969. Kittle eventually made the majors for the first time in 1972, as a Houston Astros pitching coach.

Hub Kittle may be a relatively obscure baseball professional. Ty Cobb may be one of the most famous names in baseball history.

But which one would you rather have coaching your kid's Little League baseball team?

Fritz Maisel for Joe Jackson?

Lyle Spatz

Rumored trades that do not get made are usually quickly forgotten and seldom mentioned again. That being said, I would like to resurrect a trade rumor that was being hotly discussed in the New York and Chicago newspapers more than three-quarters of a century ago. I noticed it while researching the February, 1916, sale of Frank "Home Run" Baker to the Yankees. And although I knew this proposed deal between the Yanks and the White Sox was one that would not get made, the seeming one-sidedness of it induced me, read on. But it was not until I learned the reason *why* it didn't get made that I decided this little sidebar of baseball history was worth sharing.

According to reports coming out of both cities, White Sox owner Charles Comiskey, and his manager, Clarence "Pants" Rowland, were en route to the American League meetings in New York intending to make a trade for Yankee third baseman Fritz Maisel. The White Sox had been seeking a third baseman ever since Harry Lord had jumped the team in 1914. Two forgettable players, Jim Breton and Scotty Alcock, had filled the position that year, while most of the playing time in 1915 went to the weak-hitting Lena Blackburne. Comiskey had actively pursued Baker, the former A's star who was returning to baseball after sitting out the previous season. His going to New York was a disappointment to the White Sox. Nevertheless, it led them to assume that with Baker now available to play third base the Yanks would be willing to trade Fritz Maisel. Before boarding a Chicago-to-New York train, Rowland

told reporters, "We are ready to make one or two offers for one or two men we have in mind, and I think the offers are so big that they will be given attention. If we get either one of two men I am negotiating for, the fans will not be sorry that we didn't land Frank Baker."

The player Chicago appeared willing to trade to New York in exchange for Maisel was outfielder Joe Jackson, one of baseball's most feared hitters. Presumably, the Yankees' hesitance to part with Maisel was the only reason they did not make the trade. Astonishing as it is that the White Sox would propose such a trade, even more baffling is the Yankees' reluctance to accept.

Two questions immediately jump out at someone reading this with the benefit of eighty years' hindsight. Why were the White Sox willing to trade Jackson, who in five full seasons had compiled a .366 batting average, for the punch-hitting Maisel? And why did the Yankees not escort the train to New York to make sure nothing happened to make Comiskey and Rowland change their minds?

Perhaps we can gain some insight from the New York press, no less an influential force then than they are today. Many of the local dailies questioned whether wily old Comiskey was trying to put one over on inexperienced Yankee owners, Jacob Ruppert and Til Huston. Might it not be, they wondered in print, that the 26-year-old Jackson had seen his best days, while Maisel, although just six months younger, had his in front of him? The Sox had sent three players and cash to Cleveland to get Jackson the previous August, but he batted just .272 in 45 games for them. His season's average was .308, a drop of 30 points from 1914, 110 points from 1911, and the fourth consecutive year in

---

Lyle Spatz, *whose book,* New York Yankee Openers, *has just been published, is the chairman of SABR's Baseball Records Committee.*

which his batting average had declined. Maisel, meanwhile, had led the American League in steals with 74 in 1914 and followed that by batting a career-best .281 in 1915 with 51 stolen bases.

Also, he scrappy Maisel was very popular with the New York fans. In an unsigned article, the gentleman from the New York *Tribune* counseled that this would have been a terrific deal for the Yankees two years ago,

Fritz Maisel

but it would not be so today. "For all the power of Jackson's bat," he cautioned, "there are reasons for believing he is not so valuable a ballplayer as Maisel." He then went on to say that while Jackson has a first-class throwing arm, his fielding ability is limited and his base-running is "almost negligible." This is in contrast to Maisel, who, the anonymous *Tribune* writer maintained, did all these things well. Furthermore, he claimed that the other teams in the league would be in an uproar if the Yankees gave the White Sox such an outstanding player as Maisel.

There are countless thought-provoking scenarios suggested by a player of Joe Jackson's ability joining the Yankees in 1916. Wherever you follow one it leads to a chronology of major league baseball radically different from the one we know. For instance, had the deal been made, would the White Sox (minus Jackson) have won pennants in 1917 and 1919? Even if they did win in 1919 (Jackson hit .351 that year with a team-leading 96 RBIs), would we have had the Black Sox scandal?

The Yankees did not win their first pennant until 1921, a year after getting Babe Ruth from Boston. With Jackson on the team, might they not have won before then? And think about the Yankee teams of the early 1920s that would have included both Ruth and Jackson? Then again, had Jackson led the Yankees to pennants in the late teens, would Ruppert and Huston still have gone after Ruth in 1920? Just imagine how different baseball's next fifteen years would have been if Ruth had remained in Boston or gone to another team. It's difficult to envision the Babe Ruth legend developing in quite the same way if the Babe had never played in New York. And we have to wonder whether Ruppert would have built Yankee Stadium without Ruth. If he had, would we call it "The House That Jackson Built?" Among the more intriguing questions to ponder is the one concerning the relative positions of the two men in baseball's hagiology and how they would have changed. It certainly seems possible that Joe Jackson would have been among that first group of men voted into the Hall of Fame in 1936.

Fascinating as it is to speculate on the repercussions of a Jackson-Maisel trade, reality intrudes. Chicago not only failed to get Maisel, they also were unable to acquire the other third baseman that Rowland claimed would make the fans not sorry that they "didn't land Frank Baker." Instead, the manager found the third baseman he was seeking playing shortstop on his own team. He moved Buck Weaver, his shortstop for the past four seasons, to third base where he remained until his career ended following the 1920 season.

Jackson's career, of course, also ended after the 1920 season, but not before he put together four more outstanding years for Chicago. (He missed most of the wartime season of 1918.) Maisel, whom the Yankees obviously believed was a more productive player than Jackson, lost his third base job to Baker and played in 53 games in 1916 as a utilityman. He hit .228 and followed that with a .198 season in 1917 as the Yankee second baseman. In January, 1918 the Yanks traded Maisel, the man who might have brought the great Joe Jackson to New York, along with four other players to the St. Louis Browns for second baseman Del Pratt. Maisel played one season for the Browns and then was gone from the big leagues .

There is an addendum to this story, one that further illustrates that owning a ballclub does not necessarily make someone a good judge of baseball talent. On April 7, 1916, the New York *American* revealed that at those American League meetings in February in which Ruppert and Huston had vetoed the Jackson-for-Maisel trade, they also had discussed a deal for Tris Speaker with Red Sox president Joseph Lannin. Speaker, 28, was in the prime of his career, but he was having salary problems with Boston. The Yankees offered to buy him, but Lannin also wanted a player in return. Guess who? The Sox felt that veteran third baseman Larry Gardner was fading and they wanted Maisel to replace him. However, the Yanks, while willing to pay a substantial amount of money for Speaker, refused to give up Maisel. "We would like to have Speaker," Huston said, "but we won't let Maisel go. Why should we trade a young fellow who has ten good years ahead of him for a veteran who may last only three or four years more at the most?" As in the Jackson case, the age component of the Yankees' rationale for not making the trade is particularly difficult to comprehend. Speaker was only twenty months older than Maisel.

By the way, Speaker's comments about the possible trade are especially instructive to those who think the absence of player loyalty to the cities in which they perform is a new phenomenon. "I'd like to play in New York," he said, "although I prefer to stay in Boston. It's simply a case of where I can get the salary I want." That place turned out to be Cleveland. A few days after the *American* story surfaced, Boston sent Speaker to the Indians for pitcher Sam Jones, second baseman Fred Thomas, and $55,000. Speaker, of course, lasted a lot longer than "three or four years." He won the batting championship in his first year with the Indians and accumulated 2,187 more hits before he retired in 1928.

Some of the same questions about how Jackson's joining the Yankees would have affected the game's future may also be asked about Speaker, particularly as they pertain to Ruth. Evidently, neither one became a Yankee in 1916 because Ruppert and Huston were unwilling to part with Fritz Maisel. One more thing. A thorough search revealed no instance of the Yankees turning down an offer of Maisel for Ty Cobb.

Home Run Derby

David Gough

More than four decades before the home run hitting contest became a popular event at each summer's All Star Game, the best sluggers in the game often competed in similar match-ups between games of doubleheaders. In efforts to lure larger crowds into the ballpark, club owners conspired once or twice each season to pit a visiting team's top two or three longball threats against the big names of home favorites. The fans loved seeing the head-to-head competition involving the biggest names in the game, and the players generally were eager to pick up a few extra bucks for participating in the contests. These events were so well received that they gave rise in 1960 to a short-lived but long-remembered television program entitled "Home Run Derby."

The birth of "Home Run Derby"—The idea for the program was largely that of veteran sportscaster Mark Scott, who had gotten his start by doing radio recreations of major league games. Leaving the confines of the studio, he spent many years calling Piedmont League and Pacific Coast League games, and for one season was the broadcast voice of the Cincinnati Reds. Scott arrived in Hollywood in 1952 as the play-by-play man of the Hollywood Stars, and quickly gained repute among show-business magnates as an aggressive and amiable broadcaster. With the arrival of the Dodgers on the California scene in 1958, minor league clubs like the Stars and the Los Angeles Angels were forced out. No longer in the broadcast booth behind the plate,

Scott remained active by hosting radio programs such as "Meet the Dodgers" and "Mark Scott's Press Box," as well as appearing in a number of motion pictures including the boxing film, "Somebody Up There Likes Me."

In 1959 Scott collaborated with ZIV Productions in proposing a weekly television program matching two of baseball's premier sluggers in a home run hitting contest. The winner of each week's "Home Run Derby" would return the following week to meet another challenger. The proposal was accepted, and production was scheduled to begin near the end of the year. Scott himself, of course, would be the program's host. In time his opening greeting, "Why, hi there everyone. I'm Mark Scott saying, 'Welcome to Home Run Derby'," would call viewers across the country to sit down in front of their sets and marvel at the longball power of baseball's top home run hitters. For most fans it was a unique opportunity to see players that they likely had only read about in those days of limited national television exposure. It was also a chance to watch a little baseball during the off-season.

Park and players—Wrigley Field, located in south-central Los Angeles, was chosen as the site for "Home Run Derby." It was an aging stadium which, following the National League's invasion of California, had lain dormant for two seasons. Named for chewing gum tycoon William Wrigley, Jr., who in addition to owning the Chicago Cubs had purchased the PCL's Angels in 1921, the park had been built in 1925 and served as the team's home from then until 1957. The Hollywood Stars also were tenants from 1926 through 1935 and

David Gough *has taught and coached baseball at Washington Bible College in Lanham, Maryland, since 1986.*

again in 1938. Its dimensions of 340 feet and 339 feet down the left and right field lines, respectively, and 412 feet to center were deceptive, because its power alleys, just 345 feet, caused hitters of just average power to salivate. It was a longball hitter's dream, making it the ideal place to showcase baseball's leading sluggers. Not even a 15-foot-high concrete wall in left field, covered with ivy (*a la* Chicago's Wrigley Field) in its latter years, or a nine-foot screen in right field could contain

what in most other ballparks would have been routine fly balls. Batted balls on occasion lodged in the ivy, and were ruled doubles during games. The bottom of a light tower in left center field was in play. Any ball that hit the standard above a painted white line (parallel with the top of the wall) was ruled to be a home run. Repeatedly, throughout its history, hitters would shell houses located behind the left field wall on 41st Place with home run missiles. When the American League expanded into California in 1961, the newborn Los Angeles Angels played their first season in Wrigley Field. Not surprisingly, a major league record 248 home runs were hit out of the stadium that year, an average of more than three a game.

If the new program were to be successful, it had to attract the major leagues' premier sluggers. Nineteen marquee players, including nine future Hall of Famers, agreed to participate in the inaugural season. Fifteen of the sixteen major league clubs were represented, with the American League champion Chicago White Sox the lone omission. Despite winning the pennant by five

games, the "Go-Go Sox" were a team built on speed, pitching and defense. They hit fewer home runs than any other team in baseball in 1959 (97), which may explain their absence in the contests, although arguments could be made for the inclusion of Sherm Lollar (22 homers) and aging Ted Kluszewski (three round-trippers in the World Series against the Dodgers). As if the absence of the defending American League champs wasn't strange enough, the last-place Washington Senators ironically had the most representatives (three: Harmon Killebrew, Bob Allison, and Jim Lemon). "We couldn't catch the ball very well and we didn't have very good pitching, but we could throw a little thunder at you," Lemon remarked years later, defending the presence of the Senators' power-hitting triumvirate.

Other notable absentees from the program were Ted Williams and Stan Musial, who were both nearing the end of remarkable careers. Just as conspicuous was the inclusion of other participants who have never been mentioned among the game's elite power-hitters. Kansas City's Bob Cerv, for example, would hit only 105 home runs in twelve big league campaigns, and more than one-third of them (38) came during the 1958 season. Nevertheless, the cast was an illustrious collection of major league talent.

Whirlwind filming schedule—Necessity dictated that the episodes be filmed sometime after the conclusion of the 1959 World Series and prior to the opening of spring training camps, meaning essentially a three-month window of opportunity (November-January). The Southern California winter would not pose a problem. Filming actually began in December. Players were flown to Los Angeles the day before their contest and housed in a local hotel for the night. Most of the next day was spent at the ballpark. Including a round of batting practice, it took about four hours to film what would be seen by viewers as a thirty-minute episode. The losing player was flown back home, usually the same day, while the winner remained to play another contest. Two episodes were filmed each working day, one in the morning and the other in the afternoon. Amazingly, twenty-six programs were filmed over a three-week period.

Lemon, who drew the unenviable task of facing Hank Aaron and Willie Mays, recalled his experience on two trips to Los Angeles in January. "I hadn't swung a bat since October and I wasn't in swinging shape. When I left my home in Roanoke there was a foot of snow on the ground. The fellas who lived in warmer climates probably had an advantage because at least they could be out playing golf or something. There could have been many more homers hit, but here we were swinging so hard trying to hit home runs, that I remember being sore the next day. I enjoyed it, even though I lost both of my games."

The first contest, which served as the "pilot" for the program, featured the most popular sluggers of the day, Mickey Mantle and Willie Mays. The opening was awkward, as were other technical aspects of this episode. But by the second filming, the telecasts settled into a comfortable format and "Home Run Derby" was on its way. Each week, after greeting the viewers, Scott would introduce the players and explain the rules of the contest: Nine innings. Three outs per inning. Any ball that was not hit for a home run was an out. A called strike by the plate umpire was an out. The player with the most home runs after nine innings was the winner, and received $2,000. The loser received $1,000. A player who hit three home runs in a row received a bonus of $500, plus another $500 if he hit four in a row. Any consecutive home runs beyond that total was worth a bonus of $1,000. It was big prize money for players who, for the most part, were still earning in the low five figures.

The setting was as natural as an empty ballpark could be. Claiming to use "multiple cameras," meaning two or three at the most, production was low-budget. Cameramen were positioned in front of the stands behind home plate and near the first base dugout. Close-up shots were filmed after the contest, dubbed in later by the film editor. Interviews were taped during the contests, Scott talking with one player from a booth located behind home plate at field level, while the other player batted. "We could not believe we were on television and we didn't know what to say," Ernie Banks commented in recalling his awkwardness at being interviewed on camera. "Mark Scott was very relaxing. He kept asking us various things, but we were told to keep it going and make comments. But we didn't know how to make comments because it was very new to us."

American League veteran umpire Art Passarella, who had spent eleven seasons in the '40s and '50s calling balls and strikes, agreed to be the home plate umpire for the contests. Passarella was a well-respected arbiter, having worked three World Series before retiring. His "crew" consisted of umpires stationed along both foul lines to be certain balls cleared the fences in fair territory. The pitchers were described as "batting practice pitchers." Throwing alternate innings, their job was simply to put the ball in the strike zone, and the one who yielded the most home runs would also receive a "bonus." Like the pitchers, the catcher and outfielders were local college or minor league players who were never identified and whose efforts went virtually unnoticed.

Classic match-ups—Mantle and Mays were the last two players at that time to have hit 50 home runs in a season, and the first contest lived up to its billing. Mays lost a coin toss and was designated the "visiting team." He stepped into the batter's box and promptly belted the first pitch over the left field wall, officially inaugurating the program. Before the top of the first inning was over, Mays had hit three more home runs to stake himself to a 4-0 advantage. After five innings, the "Say Hey Kid" had increased his lead to 8-2, making things look bleak for "the Mick." But Mays did not hit another home run, while Mantle chipped away at the deficit, hitting three in the seventh (including a "controversial" shot that hit the light standard in left-center field requiring a ruling from head umpire Passarella) and two in the eighth to tie it. And then Mantle ended the contest on the first pitch in the bottom of the ninth with a wall-clearing blow to left. Declared the first champion on "Home Run Derby," a smiling Mantle was presented with his $2,000 check by Scott, who promised viewers that Mickey would be back the next week to face Ernie Banks.

Mantle's stay on top extended over two more contests, as he defeated Ernie Banks, 5-3, and Jackie Jensen, 9-2. In the fourth inning of his game with Jensen, Mickey became the first player to hit three home runs in a row, earning him the $500 bonus. One of his blasts was a towering shot which cleared 41st Place and hit the roof of a house well beyond the left field wall. In the next contest he appeared to be well on his way to a fourth consecutive win, holding a 7-3 lead over Harmon Killebrew going into the seventh inning. His margin had melted to 7-6 going into the ninth, when Killebrew muscled up for three homers to grab a 9-7 advantage. Like the champion that he was, however, Mantle led off the bottom of the ninth with a home run to close to within one before three outs forced him off the throne. Even in defeat "the Mick" flashed the boyish grin for which he was so well known, no doubt consoled by the $7,500 in prize money that he had collected for his four appearances on the program.

Rocky Colavito posed Killebrew's first threat in the next contest, which was billed as a "playoff" between the two men who had tied for the American League lead in home runs the previous year with 42 apiece. Both players started off tight, but Killebrew held a 2-0 lead through five innings. In the top of the sixth Colavito broke loose with a four-homer barrage (the most in one inning to date), including three in a row. Killebrew tied it in the seventh, and very nearly took the lead when his long drive to dead center field hit the ivy-covered wall just below the 412-foot mark. Both players homered in the ninth to send it into extra innings, the first overtime contest on "Home Run Derby." Colavito made a bid in the tenth, but his drive died at the wall in left. That left it up to Killebrew, whose one-out drive hit the top of wall in left center and bounced over to end the showdown.

Killebrew next went down to defeat against Ken Boyer, who wrapped a ninth-inning homer around the left field foul pole to usurp the crown. Sitting in the booth literally with his fingers crossed as Killebrew batted for the last time, Boyer became the first National League winner on the program. For his success, he drew the unenviable task of meeting Hank Aaron, who not only went on to become the all-time home run leader in major league history but who would begin a run of six consecutive victories on "Home Run Derby." In addition to Boyer, "Hammerin' Henry" disposed of Jim Lemon, Eddie Mathews, Al Kaline, Duke Snider, and Bob Allison, prompting Scott to exclaim, "Hank, you're making a career of 'Home Run Derby'." In the process Aaron piled up $13,500 in earnings to become the program's all-time money winner. Up to that time, no World Series share had equaled that purse.

Aaron's contest with Mathews was notable for two reasons. First, it would prove to be the only time on "Home Run Derby" when players from the same team were pitted against one another. With Braves bragging rights as well as the winner's share at stake, Aaron hit a two-out shot in the ninth just to the left of the light standard to beat his Milwaukee teammate, 4-3.

Home Run Derby Game-by-Game Results

Winner		Loser	
Mickey Mantle	9	Willie Mays	8
Mickey Mantle	5	Ernie Banks	3
Mickey Mantle	9	Jackie Jensen	2
Harmon Killebrew	9	Mickey Mantle	8
Harmon Killebrew	6	Rocky Colavito	5
Ken Boyer	3	Harmon Killebrew	2
Hank Aaron	9	Ken Boyer	6
Hank Aaron	6	Jim Lemon	4
Hank Aaron	4	Eddie Mathews	3
Hank Aaron	5	Al Kaline	1
Hank Aaron	3	Duke Snider	1
Hank Aaron	3	Bob Allison	2
Wally Post	7	Hank Aaron	4
Dick Stuart	11	Wally Post	9
Dick Stuart	7	Gus Triandos	1
Frank Robinson	6	Dick Stuart	3
Bob Cerv	8	Frank Robinson	7
Bob Allison	4	Bob Cerv	3
Willie Mays	11	Bob Allison	3
Willie Mays	7	Harmon Killebrew	6
Willie Mays	6	Jim Lemon	3
Gil Hodges	6	Willie Mays	3
Ernie Banks	11	Gil Hodges	7
Jackie Jensen	14	Ernie Banks	11
Jackie Jensen	3	Rocky Colavito	2
Mickey Mantle	13	Jackie Jensen	10

Mathews became the first lefthanded slugger to appear on the program, prompting plate umpire Passarella to explain prior to the contest what constituted a home run to right field. Because of the

preponderance of right handed sluggers on the program, only seven of the 302 homers hit during the 26 "Home Run Derby" episodes were hit to right field. Aaron's reign finally ended when he fell to Wally Post, 7-4. Perhaps feeling the effects of his seventh contest on four consecutive days of filming, Hank just missed four home runs which would have extended his run. Two of the balls hit the top of the ivy-covered wall in left, one dented the screen in front of the right center field bleachers, and another landed just to the right of the 412-foot sign in dead center field. Despite the defeat, the man who eventually bettered Babe Ruth's

career home run mark had captured more wins and more earnings than any other "Home Run Derby" participant ever would.

Post's first defense of the title was also his last as he

dropped a dramatic ten-inning affair, 11-9, to gum-chewing Dick Stuart. Ten home runs flew out of the park in the sixth inning alone, both sluggers hitting five apiece. The eleven home runs clubbed by Stuart and the twenty belted by both players set new "Home Run Derby" highs. Stuart went on to vanquish Gus Triandos, 7-1, earning his second straight $500 bonus for belting three home runs in a row. Triandos' lone homer did not come until one out in the seventh inning.

The next opponent for Stuart was Frank Robinson who, for some reason, Scott insisted on calling "Frankie." The youthful Cincinnati slugger wrested the title away from Stuart, 6-3, but immediately surrendered it to Bob Cerv. Cerv in turn yielded the crown to Bob Allison, who was the first player to make a return appearance. Willie Mays ended Allison's short reign as champion by taking a lopsided 11-3 win and tying the mark for most home runs on the show. It was the first of Mays' three straight victories over Washington Senators as Killebrew and Jim Lemon also fell to the "Say Hey Kid."

Mays finally ran out of muscle against Gil Hodges, who had the distinctions of being the final player to make his debut on "Home Run Derby" as well as being oldest player (age 35) to appear on the program. Between innings, Scott complimented the Dodger slugger by assuring him that the Hall of Fame certainly had a spot reserved for him. More than three and a half decades later, many still wonder how Cooperstown has managed to pass him by. Hodges failed in his attempt to defend his title against Ernie Banks, who returned to the program on an overcast and drizzly day to wrest the crown in a record-tying 11-7 performance.

The rain intensified in the next contest with Jackie Jensen challenging Banks in what was at times a heavy downpour. But not even the elements could dampen what turned out to be the highest scoring and perhaps the show's most thrilling match-up. Jensen returned to the program with a vengeance, belting fourteen home runs, a new record. A total of twenty-five homers, also a new standard, flew out of Wrigley Field. For the second game in a row Banks hit eleven balls over the wall, but on this day they weren't enough.

In a match which bore a resemblance to the previous one only in that it was played in the rain, Jensen defeated Rocky Colavito, 3-2. The twenty consecutive "outs" made by Colavito in starting the contest before hitting his first home run was a "Home Run Derby" record for futility. A drive that cleared the fence just foul with two out in the ninth ended his frustrating performance and left him staring at the spot where the ball went out. The game provided the final opportunity for most fans to see Colavito in a Cleveland uniform. By the time this episode was aired, he had been traded to Detroit for the American League's defending batting champion, Harvey Kuenn.

Jensen's second visit to "Home Run Derby" was much more successful than his first. Rather than moving on to spring training, however, the former University of California All-American running back voluntarily retired from the game to take care of personal and family problems before returning for one final year in 1961. A career-long fear of flying would have no doubt kept him out of "Home Run Derby" had he not already had roots planted in California.

In the final match-up of the series, Mickey Mantle returned to reclaim the title in an exciting 13-10 win over Jensen. Both sluggers clubbed mammoth home runs, including one of Mantle's which appeared to hit a bird on the roof of a house behind the left center field wall. It was the type of contest Scott had in mind when he came up with the idea for the program, and his ex-

citement was manifest. Jensen hit five homers in a row (six total) in the fourth inning, picking up a $2,000 bonus and setting a standard no one had come close to. Jensen displayed a huge smile following the inning, causing Mantle to quip, "I don't blame him for smiling. I'd be rolling on the ground laughing up there if I did it!" Then it was his turn. "The Mick," who genuinely seemed to be having fun, answered with four home run blasts of his own (including three in a row) in the top of the sixth, prompting Scott to exclaim "I hope we have plenty of baseballs today!" Filled with highlights and sound bites, this program was a fitting conclusion to the program's initial season.

Home Run Derby Record and Earnings

Player	W-L	HR (Avg)	Earnings
Hank Aaron	6-1	34 (4.9)	$13,500
Mickey Mantle	4-1	44 (8.8)	10,000
Jackie Jensen	2-2	29 (7.3)	8,500
Willie Mays	3-2	35 (7.0)	8,000
Dick Stuart	2-1	21 (7.0)	6,000
Harmon Killebrew	2-2	23 (5.8)	6,000
Ernie Banks	1-2	25 (8.3)	4,500
Bob Allison	1-2	9 (3.0)	4,000
Frank Robinson	1-1	13 (6.5)	3,500
Wally Post	1-1	16 (8.0)	3,000
Gil Hodges	1-1	13 (6.5)	3,000
Bob Cerv	1-1	11 (5.5)	3,000
Ken Boyer	1-1	9 (4.5)	3,000
Rocky Colavito	0-2	7 (3.5)	2,500
Jim Lemon	0-2	7 (3.5)	2,000
Eddie Mathews	0-1	3 (3.0)	1,000
Al Kaline	0-1	1 (1.0)	1,000
Duke Snider	0-1	1 (1.0)	1,000
Gus Triandos	0-1	1 (1.0)	1,000
Totals	**26-26**	**302**	**$84,500**

The end(uring) of "Home Run Derby"—Tragically, Mark Scott suffered a sudden and fatal heart attack within six months of filming the final episode of "Home Run Derby." He had been the driving force behind the program, and his death at the age of 45 left its future in doubt. Because the telecast first aired in the summer of 1960, it is doubtful he ever saw the complete run of episodes in their final form. Scott concluded the last program by inviting the viewers to "Join us at home plate for another exciting series when the top sluggers of the American and the National League will compete on Home Run Derby." But there would be no second season as the project was shelved with the death of its prime mover. For more than two and a half decades, the original twenty-six episodes on reel-to-reel film collected dust in an MGM studio. In 1988 ESPN managed to acquire the rights to re-televise them. Fans who had only heard of Mantle, Mays, Aaron, Banks, Killebrew and other legends of the game were able to witness these legends as youthful and in the prime of their careers. Following a two-year run on ESPN, Classic Sports Network purchased the broadcast rights in 1995 and began airing the program once again. To date no videotape sets of the program have been produced, even though fans in recent years have clamored for them. MGM continues to own the rights to the program and has no immediate plans to mass produce videos for public consumption.

Thanks to its recent revival via cable and satellite, "Home Run Derby" is more popular today than it was when it originally aired thirty-six years ago. In a technical sense, the black-and-white program pales in comparison with today's multiple camera angles and slow motion replays, and Mark Scott could be cited for an occasional *faux pas* and fan-like effervescence. But the program still conveys a love for the game rarely seen today. From Scott's glee to the players' own boyish grins at seeing one of their batted balls clear the wall, "Home Run Derby" was representative of a purer and simpler national pastime, one which many of us long to see again.

Mark Scott once gave an interviewer his statement of broadcast philosophy: "What I hope to do as a sportscaster is to make the game so interesting to the listeners that no matter who he is rooting for and no matter what the score happens to be, he keeps his radio on and his ear pitched to every word that I say. When I can achieve those results, I will know that I am doing my job well." Though he did not live long enough to receive the appreciation due him for fulfilling that purpose, "Home Run Derby" remains his lasting legacy. When we watch the program today, so many years later, we can still sense Scott's enthusiasm for the game and his desire to infect his listeners and viewers with a similar appreciation.

A Tragic Link

J. Kent Steele

The Philadelphia Phillies arrived at the Baltimore & Ohio train station on Thursday, February 24, 1910, for the trip south to their spring training camp at Southern Pines, North Carolina. At trackside waiting to board the train was my great uncle, Harry Welchonce, and the balance of the veterans and newcomers invited to make the trip by owner Horace Fogel. Among the veterans were new manager Charles "Red" Dooin, future batting champion Sherry Magee, dentist Mickey Doolan, and the Harvard-educated lawyer and third baseman, Eddie Grant.

Grant was a fine infielder and a fast baserunner. He was not known for his hitting, but was a valuable lead-off man who twice led the National League in at bats. Grant went 7 for 7 in an extra-inning game against the great New York Giant pitchers Rube Marquard and Christy Mathewson. He enjoyed a ten-year career in the major leagues and retired from baseball in 1915 to practice law in New York.

Also appearing at the train station that day was an unusually tall (variously described as ranging from 6'3" to 6'8") German-born rookie pitcher from McDonald, Pennsylvania, named Robert Troy. Twenty-one years old, Troy was by all accounts a shy and homesick young man, away from his family for the first time.

Due to his uncommon height, Troy immediately caught the attention of one newspaper reporter who had joined the team for the trip south. This reporter observed that, unlike the other Phillies, Troy did not wear an overcoat in the bitterly cold weather, but kept himself warm by flapping his arms. A preboarding photo reveals that virtually all of Troy's teammates were dressed for the weather in overcoats and derby hats. Troy alone wore a straw hat.

This same journalist noticed Grant's arrival and reported that the lawyer was possessed of a "pocketful of briefs so as to be ably prepared to defend third base next season." As Grant and the other players boarded the train, our most observant scribe claimed that, "At the last minute it was found that Troy was too tall to get inside the Pullman, so he went to Southern Pines sprawled on all-fours in the baggage coach ahead."

Teammates—Eddie Grant and Robert Troy undoubtedly met for the first time at that Philadelphia station. They traveled south as new teammates and lived together at the Piney Woods Inn in Southern Pines until about March 20, 1910.

Of course, Grant and Troy trained together and played against each other in games pitting the "Yanigans" against the "regulars." In a team picture taken on March 5 at Southern Pines, Troy towers over all of his teammates. He is almost shoulder to shoulder with Grant in the back row of the photo and they are separated only by the head of Mickey Doolan in the background.

Being young, shy, and retiring, and taking everything very seriously, "Bun" Troy naturally became the target of the team's practical jokers. It was noted, however, that his teammates were pleased with the good-natured way in which the youngster took the constant kidding.

In early workouts Troy impressed Dooin with his

J. Kent Steele *is a lawyer living in Idyllwild, California. He has a wife, Jana, and two sons, Sean and Brendan.*

velocity and control. Unfortunately, he did not survive the first rookie cut that spring, and by March 21 he had been sent down to the Worcester, Massachusetts, minor league club. Troy is not heard from again as a Phillie. In fact, his entire major league career consisted of 6-2/3 innings pitched in a losing game for the Detroit Tigers in 1912.

Teammates for such a short time, Troy and Grant were destined to be linked once again. Three major league ballplayers died in Europe during World War I. Alex Burr, who appeared in one game for the New York Americans in 1914, but who had no major league at bats, died on October 12, 1918, when his plane crashed at Cazaux, France.

It is well known that Eddie Grant was killed in battle.

Captain Grant was leading a mission to rescue the "Lost Battalion" behind enemy lines in the Argonne Forest offensive when he was killed by German machine-gun fire. He died on October 5, 1918, only five weeks before the Armistice was signed. Grant was buried in the Meuse-Argonne Cemetery in France, and a memorial was constructed in his memory and dedicated at the Polo Grounds in New York in 1921.

What is less well known is that, on October 7, 1918, only two days after Eddie Grant met his death, Sgt. Robert Gustave Troy was also killed in action in the Argonne. Grant and Troy, whose baseball careers brought them together, however briefly, on the 1910 Phillies, were joined again in death on the fields of France.

The 1910 Philadelphia Phillies at their Southern Pines, North Carolina, Spring Training site. Robert Troy is the tallest man in the back row (with the MAC on his cap). Eddie Grant is two men to Troy's left, with the plain white cap. Mickey Doolin stands between the two men. Manager Red Dooin is to Troy's right.

The '37 All-Star Game

Oscar Eddleton

Wednesday, July 7, 1937, dawned in Washington D.C. with a forecast of sunny, hot, and humid, a normal weather pattern for the nation's capital in July. But an event far beyond the range of normality would occur that afternoon at Griffith Stadium where the fifth major league All Star Game would be played before a gala throng of 31,391. It would be the first All Star Game in Washington and the first to be attended by a President of the United States, in this instance Franklin D. Roosevelt.

Seated in the pavilion section along the right field line was an awe-struck youth of eighteen, a child of the Great Depression, attending his first All Star Game in a state of wonderment and anticipation. Yes, I was there. I saw all that my eyes could behold, from batting practice to Frank Demaree's final groundout. Now as a septuagenarian I realize my good fortune in being able to recall the events of that memorable afternoon.

My pavilion seat provided an excellent view of President Roosevelt and his entourage as they entered through a gateway in right field, driving slowly toward the infield. The President, attired in his familiar seersucker suit and panama hat, waved to the cheering crowd and also to the players now standing along the baselines awaiting his arrival.

Mr. Roosevelt was escorted to his box, decked in bunting behind the American League dugout, amidst senators, congressmen, and cabinet members in addition to baseball commissioner Kenesaw M. Landis, Senators president Clark Griffith, rival managers Joe

McCarthy and Bill Terry, and other diamond luminaries. A delegation of Boy Scouts attending the National Jamboree in Washington assisted in the flag-raising ceremony and national anthem after which President Roosevelt threw out the first ball and the game was under way.

The presence of the President along with official Washington added prestige to an event still striving to solidify its position as a permanent feature. The signature event of the '37 All Star Game by which it is usually identified and recalled occurred in the home half of the third inning. The starting pitchers, Lefty Gomez of the New York Yankees for the American League and Dizzy Dean of the St. Louis Cardinals for the National League, were locked in a scoreless duel. Dean had retired Red Rolfe and Charlie Gehringer on groundouts. Joe DiMaggio then singled to center field. Lou Gehrig was next at bat. After driving Dean's second offering foul over the right field roof, Gehrig belted a 3-2 pitch high over the right field wall for a two-run homer.

The pavilion roof was low so that I was unable to follow the path of the ball. Rather, I watched right fielder Paul Waner drift back, eyes on the ball. When his head dropped and the crowd cheered, I knew that Gehrig's blast was out of the park.

Earl Averill was next up and grounded to the right side of the infield. Second baseman Billy Herman fielded the ball and threw to Johnny Mize for the third out. Unfortunately, however, Averill's smash had caromed off Dean's left foot, seriously injuring his big toe.

At the time I was learning to score. I recently located the game program in my files and checked the scoring

Oscar Eddleton *is a retired minister who lives in Richmond, Virginia. He is the author of "Under the Lights," an article on night baseball that appeared in the 1980* Baseball Research Journal.

of that play. I had marked it 4-3, failing to credit Dean with an assist. But my scoring did indicate that Averill's shot was so sharply hit that its contact with Dean's foot was not sufficient to alter its course appreciably. Second baseman Herman handled it without difficulty.

From the stands, I did not detect that the ball had struck Dean's foot. I have searched my memory often over the years, but I can only recall that the Cardinal ace walked off the mound to the dugout just as he had the previous two innings, without any visible indication of injury.

It is well documented that in the heat of a pennant race Dean returned to the mound too soon following the All Star Game. In attempting to compensate for the toe that was broken, he adopted an altered delivery which damaged his pitching arm permanently and shortened his career. Those of us at that game saw Dizzy Dean, the resplendent power pitcher for the last time.

The American League added to its lead with three runs in the fourth inning off Giant ace Carl Hubbell, scored another off Cincinnati's Lee Grissom in the fifth and two more off Van Mungo of Brooklyn in the sixth to win the game handily, 8-3.

The National League's scoring consisted of single runs in the middle three innings off Detroit's Tommy Bridges. Mel Harder of Cleveland worked the final three innings and gave up five hits, but no runs.

One defensive play deserves mention. It came in the sixth inning when the National League attempted a rally. With one run scored, Burgess Whitehead was on second base running for Gabby Hartnett, and Dick Bartell was at first. With two out Rip Collins, batting for Grissom, singled to right. For some reason I took my eyes off the ball and watched Whitehead round third and head for home. Suddenly Bill Dickey whipped off his mask and got set. The ball came in to him about waist high with no bounce. Whitehead was out at the plate with a little to spare. Joe DiMaggio playing right field, possibly in deference to Earl Averill's seniority, had made a remarkably accurate throw. Joe was only in his sophomore year in the majors, but even then he played with that regal air and poise that belied his youth.

It was not until 1962 that Most Valuable Player selections were made at All Star Games. Had there been a selection in 1937, it would almost certainly have been Lou Gehrig. The great Yankee first baseman with his homer in the third inning and double in the sixth drove in half of the American League's runs, and fielded his position flawlessly. Gehrig appeared to enjoy the game immensely, frequently smiling and talking it up on the infield.

For the National League, Joe Medwick, left fielder of the St. Louis Cardinals, turned in the strongest offensive performance with four hits including two doubles and a run batted in. This was Medwick's banner season. He went on to win the Triple Crown— the last National League player to accomplish that feat.

In those depression times before television and the jet age, many of us at Griffith Stadium that day had little opportunity to see National League players. The All Star Game provided that special treat.

In conclusion, comment should be made regarding the contrast in All Star Game strategy over the years. Today the game serves as a showcase for the best players in the major leagues. It has become an exhibition in which winning is important, but playing as many stars as possible—often fifty or more—is of equal importance. Managers accept that approach to the game. Not so in 1937. The game plan then was play to win regardless of who played or who didn't.

At that time each team consisted of twenty-three players, selected by the eight managers in each league, to be used at the discretion of the managers of the two previous World Series teams. Seven of the nine players from each league who started that day are now in the Hall of Fame, indicating that McCarthy and Terry made wise choices.

The American League used the eight starting position players throughout the entire game. Four of those were from McCarthy's Yankees, a dynasty team that would win four consecutive pennants and World Series during 1936-1939. Although Terry called on six pitchers in an effort to check the American League's batters along with three pinch hitters, he made only one position change, lifting catcher Hartnett for a pinch runner, Whitehead, in the sixth inning and bringing in his own backstop, Gus Mancuso, to finish the game.

As a result, only thirty-one players were used by both managers. Fifteen All Stars saw no action including four future Hall of Famers Lefty Grove, Hank Greenberg, Rick Ferrell, and Ernie Lombardi. Jimmie Foxx appeared as a pinch hitter. Much to the dismay of Washington fans the three Senators selected, Buddy Myer and the Ferrell brothers, Wes and Rick, all sat out the game.

It would be my privilege to attend two subsequent All Star Games in Washington, the 1956 contest, also at Griffith Stadium, which featured some of the greatest home run hitters of all time, and again in 1962 at the new District of Columbia Stadium when another president, John F. Kennedy, attended. But the 1937 game sixty years ago remains my favorite. I was young and impressionable back then, and the glow of youth has kept the treasured memory of a distant day bright and clear. Much that I saw appeared larger than life. For there were giants on the earth in those days.

Eddie "Smoke" Stack

Ray Schmidt

Most of the baseball record books that are weighing down historians' bookshelves these days present a picture of baseball as an overwhelming torrent of numbers, percentages, and other mathematical gymnastics. While a player's career is usually judged solely by the length and sheer volume of his statistics, what is often forgotten is that most of the men who have helped shape baseball's storied past actually compiled rather undistinguished major league records. Many of these players also contributed greatly to the colorful history and lore of baseball through their participation in the game's venues outside the "big show".

One such player was pitcher Eddie Stack, notable for his jump directly into the major leagues in 1910, after just two seasons of college and semiprofessional baseball in the Chicago area. This was a period in baseball's history when not all the talented players, especially college players, were eager to endure the hardships and low pay of the minor leagues. The resulting top-flight local baseball during the first two decades of this century represents the golden era of semipro ball in the United States, and so Stack's accomplishment was not considered all that unusual at the time.

He was born William Edward Stack on October 24, 1887, in Chicago, to his parents Edward and Mary. His father was from Ireland, and the family had settled in what was a very tough neighborhood on the near West Side of the city. Part way through high school, in 1904, Eddie's parents felt it best for him to begin attending

St. Viateurs College (also a high school) in Bourbonnais, Illinois, about fifty miles south of Chicago.

By the spring of 1908, in his junior year of college, Stack had matured into a top-flight pitcher, who also played center field and second base as the Saints finished 18-1 and claimed the cochampionship of the western universities. Before the college season ended, he had also begun pitching on Sundays for the top-level semipro team, the Joliet Standards. But in late June the Standards brought in a former major league pitcher named Harry "Klondike" Kane, and Stack moved over to the Chicago Marquettes.

The spring of 1909 found Stack serving as the team captain in his final year at St. Viateurs, as the Saints again claimed the western college baseball title. He had again been pitching for the Joliet Standards while the college season was still in progress, and he demonstrated his development by winning six of seven appearances, including a pair of two-hitters over top Chicago semipro outfits. In late June of 1909, Stack left Joliet and signed with former major leaguer Jimmy Callahan and his famous Logan Squares team on Chicago's north side. On July 3 he out-dueled Rube Foster to shut out the Leland Giants, 5-0, on three hits, on the way to an overall record of 17-8 for the season. But on July 7, 1909, controversy had broken out over Stack's services when it came to light that both the Chicago Cubs and the White Sox were claiming ownership of his major league contract.

Contract problems—Stack, believing himself free of his Joliet contract, had signed with president Charles

---

Ray Schmidt *, a SABR member since 1982, is primarily interested in pre-1920 baseball. He is the author of a history of the 1890s Illinois-Iowa League, and also serves as director of the College Football Historical Society.*

Comiskey of the White Sox for an undisclosed amount. But two days later it came to light that owner Billy Moran of the Joliet team had sold Stack's contract to president Murphy of the Cubs for $100, on the basis of Eddie having made a verbal agreement with Manager Frank Chance of the Cubs for $400 per month.

When the dispute went to the National Commission, Murphy provided an affidavit claiming that Stack had called on him and accepted terms for the 1910 season, while Comiskey contended that Stack had called on him prior to meeting Murphy and had accepted terms with the Sox. At first Stack insisted that he had accepted terms with the Sox prior to the Cubs, but under questioning by chairman Herrmann the pitcher finally admitted that he had in fact first accepted the terms offered by the Cubs.

His contract was then awarded to the National League club, and for his actions in the case he was fined $50 and ruled ineligible until he refunded $109 which he had accepted from the White Sox. *Sporting Life* noted that, "This is but one of the many cases showing the lax notions of ballplayers regarding contractual and financial obligations and illustrates...the imperative need of just such a body as the National Commission to control players, to do justice to players and magnates alike."

Stack accompanied the Cubs to spring training in 1910 as a mature pitcher with a good curve, a spitball, and a heavy fastball. But the Cubs were ready that year with another great team, and even though Frank Chance was impressed by the young pitcher, Stack was sold to the Philadelphia Phillies on May 26, 1910, without having appeared in a game for Chicago.

The Philadelphia story—Eddie made his major league debut against the Cubs on June 7, 1910, at Philadelphia. He made Chicago fans feel that the team made a mistake in selling him. For the first six innings he held the Cubs hitless until his future roommate, Frank Schulte, led off the seventh with a single. Eddie finished with a

Eddie "Smoke" Stack

masterful three-hit 1-0 win, which prompted sportswriter Ring Lardner to launch a good-natured attack on the kid from Chicago's West Side, with a game account headlined STACK IS TRAITOR. Stack made three more starts between June 14 and 22 and pitched complete game victories in all three, but he was inconsistent through the rest of the seaon, and ended with a 6-7 record in 20 appearances.

In 1911 Eddie was back with the Phillies and hoping for a good season, but manager Red Dooin stayed mostly with a rotation of Grover Alexander, Earl Moore, and George Chalmers until mid-August, when Stack was moved into the regular rotation. On August 19 in St Louis he beat the Cardinals, 5-2, followed within days by a 3-2 win over Pittsburgh, and then a five-hit, 3-1 win at Cincinnati.

With three complete game wins in eight days behind him, Stack squared off against the equally hot Rube Marquard of the New York Giants on September 1 in the second game of a doubleheader, with 12,000 fans looking on. For seven innings the teams remained scoreless. In the eighth Eddie gave up his only walk, to Art Fletcher, followed by a single to Chief Meyers. Misplays by the Phillie infield let in two runs and the Giants prevailed, 2-0, as Marquard finished with a one-hitter. Eddie remained in the rotation until the end of the season, finishing with a 5-5 record in thirteen appearances as the Phillies ended up in fourth place.

On to Brooklyn—In November twelve players from the Reds and Phillies, including Stack, made a twelve-game tour of Cuba, where over 14,000 fans turned out in Havana for the opener against the Alemendez club. It must have come as a shock to Eddie when he was traded in mid-December to Brooklyn in exchange for pitcher William "Doc" Scanlan, who was coming off a 3-10 season. The Phillies would come to regret this trade. Doc Scanlan never appeared in another major league game.

After getting married on January 3, 1912, to Miss

Kathryn Gilson Dwyer of Chestnut Hill, Pennsylvania, Eddie went to spring training that year with a definite chance to be a starter for a Brooklyn club that was coming off a seventh-place finish in 1911. On April 20 he stepped into the regular rotation and stayed there for most of the summer, although he pitched inconsistently. On September 4, though, Eddie pitched the finest game of his major league career as he worked all thirteen innings and held the Boston Braves to just three hits at old Washington Park, outdueling "Hickory" Dickson for a 2-1 win. In Eddie's final 1912 start on September 27, he defeated the Phillies, 3-1, on a five-hitter in front of fewer than 150 fans at Washington Park.

The 1913 season would prove to be the best of Eddie's major league career. He got off to a good start on April 25 by scattering six hits for a 7-1 win over Boston. In May, Eddie beat the Braves two more times, including a 2-0 shutout on May 31, while starting to appear more in relief roles.

Back home—On June 27 Stack won his final victory for Brooklyn as he stopped the Phillies, 6-1, with a three-hitter. On August 5, 1913, he was traded back to the Chicago Cubs in an even swap for Ed Reulbach, the long-time Cub legend.

Manager Johnny Evers of the Cubs gave Stack an immediate start on August 7 against the Phillies and he responded with a complete game 5-2 win, giving up only four hits. On August 12 Evers tried to capitalize on Eddie's ability to beat the Braves, but the magic was gone as Boston shelled him for seven runs. On September 9 Stack threw his final big league shutout with a 4-0 win over St Louis. His last major league win came on September 28, 5-3 over Cincinnati. He ended the 1913 season with a composite record of 8-6 in 34 games.

In 1914 Stack was back with the Cubs, but he pitched ineffectively, as an increasing stomach problem restricted him to only seven appearances and an 0-1 record. He was released after spring training 1915.

Faced with a choice between going to the minor leagues or accepting the realities of life, Eddie wisely decided to begin preparing for a second career. He satisfied his baseball desires by returning to the fast-paced Chicago semipro competition on the weekends, worked at different jobs during the week to support his family, and began studying for a teacher's degree at Chicago Normal College.

Back to semipro company—In 1915 Stack began pitching for the Chicago Tigers of the City League. His opening win on May 9 merited a banner headline across the top of the entire sports page of the Chicago *Tribune*. Eddie "Smoke" Stack was still a big name in Chicago baseball, and overflow crowds jostled for space every Sunday that he was on the mound. In July

Eddie jumped to the famous Niesen's Gunthers, where he eventually finished with an overall record of 16-6, while leading them to the Litzinger Cup title.

On August 22 the Gunthers traveled the forty-five miles to Joliet to take on the strong Rivals before a large crowd. During an argument between the Gunthers and the umpire, Rivals' owner and manager James Sime began taunting Stack, and in no time flat the two were in a full-fledged brawl, which quickly included several fans who jumped from the grandstand to join in the attack on the former big league hurler. With players from both teams in the scrap, it took a fleet of Joliet police to restore order and clear the field. Such were the hazards of old-time semipro baseball.

The quality of top semipro baseball in Chicago was still at an outstanding level in 1915. Former major leaguers still played on the top teams, and current big leaguers often appeared using assumed names, to the delight of the press, which usually went along with the open secret and did not reveal the true identities of the players.

From 1905 on, the top semipro clubs of Chicago had regularly played post-season games against major league teams. In 1906 the Logan Squares had swept the National League champion Cubs and the American League champion White Sox on the same weekend. Minor league teams also came through Chicago for exhibition games, with the local semipros more often than not coming out on top. In July, 1915, the Mutuals team brought in most of a Three-I League club to play under their name against the eventual pennant-winning White Giants. To no one's surprise the White Giants crushed the Mutuals' hired guns, 13-5. Later in the season the White Giants defeated the Chicago Whales, Federal League champions of 1915, 2-1.

In 1916 Eddie spent the spring pitching for the Gunthers before jumping to the Garden City club in May, and then eventually to a team in the northern suburb of Glenview. On January 26, 1917 he received his teaching certificate and embarked upon a thirty-nine-year career as a teacher and administrator in the Chicago school system, including a twenty-year stint at the Montefiore School, which was for the more troublesome students of the city. In 1917, Eddie returned to his old club, the Logan Squares, and compiled a 17-8 record in 28 games. His 2-1 win over the Gunthers on June 3 was accomplished before over 3,000 fans at the Squares' park.

Eddie began the 1918 season with the Squares. One of his best outings came on May 26 when he lost a 2-1 decision to the Gunthers and Jeff Pfeffer of the Brooklyn Dodgers, now a navy trainee at the nearby Great Lakes base. By mid-June the Chicago League had dropped its schedule because of the war effort, and the Logan Squares began playing service teams exclusively. On June 23 approximately 5,000 fans mobbed the Squares park to watch the Great Lakes team, with several major leaguers in the lineup, blast Stack. In mid-August Eddie went to the Cicero semipro club and pitched there for the rest of the season, eventually leading them to the McGurn Cup title.

The season of 1920 was Stack's last as an active player, and it was probably fitting that he spent the entire year as a member of the Logan Squares. He experienced a comeback of sorts, with an 8-5 record in fifteen games. Eddie ended his pitching days with two brilliant performances, as he scattered seven hits over twelve innings on October 3 in beating the Gunthers, 1-0, and then defeated the Normals, another longtime foe, on October 10 by a 4-3 score. The Normals pitcher was Jack Quinn, just off an 18-10 season for the New York Yankees, who had been brought in specifically to beat Stack and the Squares.

His playing days were now over. Eddie Stack had pitched five years of major league ball and eight years of top-flight semipro ball during the Golden Era of the game in Chicago. His lifetime major league record was 26-24 in 102 games, and his documented semipro record was 89-42 in 142 appearances.

Early in the 1920s the stomach problems he had suffered for years became so bad that Eddie went to the Mayo Clinic, where it was determined that he had been suffering from a duodenal ulcer, for which he then underwent surgery. In the late 1920s Eddie became active in baseball again, this time as an umpire in the Chicago semi-pro leagues. After enduring a few years of the physical attacks and other hardships regularly visited upon the umpires working semipro games, Stack and Ed Weinstein organized the Chicago Umpires Protective Association in the early 1930s to improve pay and working conditions. The group eventually became so large and powerful in Chicago baseball that its members worked all semipro and amateur games in the city. Stack served six years as the union president.

Eddie received numerous assignments to umpire college games over the years, and so was a logical choice to serve as a freelance scout for the Detroit Tigers and Chicago White Sox, before finally retiring from umpiring in the late 1940s. He and his wife Kathryn raised a family of four boys, and Eddie finally retired from the classroom in 1956. He died in Chicago on August 28, 1958, aged 70. After a career of forty years in teaching, and nearly four decades of service to the game of baseball, it could safely be said that Eddie Stack had led a full and colorful life devoted to young people and his beloved sport.

Why One Scribe Didn't Vote This Year

"To be named to the Hall is supposedly the highest honor you can bestow on a ball players,' observes Joe Williams, sports columnist of the New York World Telegram. 'Do they appreciate it? Well, last year we voted four of them into the shrine—Frank Frisch, Lefty Grove, Carl Hubbell and Mickey Cochrane—and not a single one showed up. They just couldn't be bothered. So this year Mr. Ken Smith and his fellow historians can include me out ... The only player to show at Cooperstown last year was Ed Walsh, who had been voted in by a special old-timers' committee. Walsh, a 40-game winner for the White Sox in 1908, composed and read a poem for the occasion. In Walsh's day, you see, the ballplayer had a great respect for the game he lived on and with." (The Sporting News, February 18, 1948.)

—Andy Moursund

Hitting Bob Feller

Larry D. Mansch

Van Meter, Iowa, is not unlike hundreds of other small towns in the Midwest. It's a quiet place, shady and pleasant. It is surrounded by mile after mile of deep-green fields of corn and soybeans, interrupted only by straight country roads and white, two-story farmhouses. The pace of life is slow. It is still a big event when the evening freight train rolls through town, loaded with grain and headed for Omaha. Kids on bikes stop to watch, and housewives and store clerks drop what they're doing to watch, too. Van Meter is about the same size, 800 or so folks, as it was seventy-five years ago. It has weathered droughts and floods, the Depression of the 30s and the farm crisis of the 80s, and it's still pretty much as it's always been.

There is one big difference, though, between this small town and others. Van Meter is the hometown of baseball legend Bob Feller, and it sports a brand-new museum and exhibit dedicated to Feller and his Hall of Fame career.

On a trip here in July, 1996, I am to get a private, after-hours tour. My good friend from law school, Dan Manning, lives and works in Des Moines, about fifteen miles away. His father Pat played against Feller in high school in the '30s. Pat and long-time Van Meter resident and the museum's curator, Fletcher Jennings, have agreed to meet me, show me the museum, and talk about their famous friend.

The museum itself is a colonial-style brick building located in the middle of town. Bas-relief sculptures of Feller in his baseball prime adorn one outside wall, and a pitching mound and home plate are embedded in the

sidewalk leading up to the entrance. Inside, I find a treasure trove of memorabilia from Feller's career, mostly donated by him: trophies, photos, autographed balls, framed newspaper articles describing no-hit games. Behind a glass case lie more precious artifacts, including a Babe Ruth-autographed baseball. (Nine-year-old Bob got it during Babe's 1928 barnstorming tour that came through Des Moines. He earned money to buy the ball by killing gophers and collecting the bounty of ten cents per claw.) I thumb through a scorebook, circa 1933, from Feller's amateur days. Later, Fletch takes me downstairs for a look at mementos not yet ready for public display: dozens of balls, awards, uniforms, and photos. Bob Feller was easily one of the greatest pitchers—and perhaps the fastest thrower—of all time, but for all his baseball accomplishments memorialized in this impressive collection, I learn that he is proudest of something quite different: his World War II service.

On December 7, 1941, Feller was driving across Iowa on his way to Chicago to sign his contract for the coming year. The radio program he was listening to—after several successful years with the Indians, he could afford a radio in his '41 Buick Century—was interrupted with a bulletin about the attack on Pearl Harbor. Feller enlisted in the Navy the next day, despite his 3-C classification (Bill Feller, Bob's father, was terminally ill with cancer, and Bob was his family's sole support). Anxious to get into the thick of things, he volunteered for gunnery school and served aboard the U.S.S. Alabama in the Atlantic, where his ship was awarded eight battle stars. A photograph of Bob's induction—he was sworn in by ex-heavyweight champion Gene Tunney,

Larry D. Mansch lives in Missoula, Montana. His biography of Rube Marquard will be published in 1998 by McFarland.

who ran the Navy's physical fitness program—is prominently displayed in the museum.

After my tour we sit down to talk baseball. Fletch was born in 1925, making him six years younger than Feller. He graduated from Van Meter High in 1943 and went into the service. After the war he attended Iowa State University and began his careers in teaching, business, and farming. How well did he know Bob Feller as a boy growing up in Van Meter? "Everybody knew everybody in this town," he laughs. "But my first recollection of Bob was hearing that he couldn't attend freshman initiation because his parents had him on a tight schedule. Bedtime was at a certain time, and his dad would work out in the fields as late as he could and still have time to play catch with Bob. They'd play in the barn under the lights his dad installed."

Many baseball fans know that Bill Feller built the first (real) Field of Dreams on his Iowa farm as a place for local kids to play ball. Fletch tells me that the place was carved out of a cow pasture a quarter-mile or so from the barn, which still stands. It had a dirt infield and a tiny set of bleachers, "all homemade out of chicken wire and sticks." Home plate was crafted out of a piece of tree; seven-year-old Bob wrote a story about it for school:

> When I was a tree, and my brothers and sisters, there were many of us there but there is not many of us now. Many of us have been cut down and made into lumber and it came my turn and they cut me down and made me into a big board. And Mister Stucke's manual training boys got me and made me into a home plate for the baseball diamond. And that's the end.

The field was called Oakview, because a stand of oak trees divided the hilltop diamond and the Raccoon River about a mile away. (The pasture itself is no longer owned by the Feller family, but Fletch gives me directions so that I can see the place for myself.) You might say that Bill Feller was dedicated to his son's career. Not only did he built the field for him, but he switched his crop from corn to wheat because of the earlier harvest, thus allowing Bob more time to play ball.

Games at Oakview were held on Sundays, Fletch tells me, which drew only mild protestations from some of the "stricter Methodists" in town. Bill Feller managed the Oakview team himself. He recruited the players, hired the umpires, and set up the schedule against nearby amateur teams. Fletch remembers that adults were charged a dime or maybe a quarter for admission, but kids were always free. He saw dozens of games there in the early '30s (he was too young to play himself then), and he recalls that Bob was a good-hitting shortstop when he wasn't pitching. The Oakview team had its own uniforms, and for a while those uniforms were loaned to Van Meter High when the school could not afford its own. Sometimes, when there were doubleheaders, Mrs. Feller served sandwiches and lemonade to the players between games.

Feller dominated local baseball, even at the age of 13 or 14 and playing against older boys. He starred for Oakview, of course, and also for the American Legion team out of nearby Adel. In 1935 his Des Moines Farmers Union team won the state amateur title and competed in the national tournament in Ohio. One day that summer while out in the fields, Bob on a tractor and his dad on a combine, a man with a sportcoat slung over his arm came walking out to visit. He was Cy Slapnicka, a scout for the Cleveland Indians. Slapnicka signed Bob to his first contract, getting the signatures on the fender of the combine. The handwritten contract, now on display at the museum, was for exactly one dollar—Bob's bonus was a signed Indians baseball—and was technically with the Fargo-Moorhead Twins of the Class D Northern League. It was agreed to keep the signing quiet, so as not to jeopardize Bob's high school playing career. He had not yet begun his junior year.

I have to ask the obvious question: just how fast was Bob Feller? Pat Manning has lived and farmed in nearby Granger for all of his 80 years. He played baseball for Assumption High School in the spring of 1935 and has very vivid recollections of batting against Bob Feller.

"We were anxious to play against Van Meter, because we'd all heard so much about him, and we wanted to see for ourselves what all the fuss was about," says Pat. "And we found out quick enough. It was almost impossible to believe a guy could throw so hard. He didn't really need a team behind him, just a catcher. Most of us were lucky to get a piece of the ball off him, maybe a pop fly or something. That ball came in—whoooooosh was all you heard—and then the pop of the catcher's mitt. Our coach just told us to swing at anything if it seemed close, and who knows, maybe we'd hit something." Pat laughs when he recalls one of his teammates. "This poor kid got hit on the shoulder or something his first time up. The next time, it looked like he wanted to stand over by the third base coach instead of in the batter's box! I couldn't really blame him, though. Feller was so fast...aw, hell, you couldn't see the damn thing."

Bob did play basketball his junior year (Van Meter had no football program, and Fletch doubts that Bob would have been interested in, or allowed to play, that sport and risk injury.) The basketball team was led by its star player Carroll "Kelly" Gutshall; Bob, at six feet the tallest on the team, was the steady if unspectacular starting center. The team captured the Dallas County championship, plus the sectional and regional titles, and qualified for the Iowa state tournament, to be held at the Drake University Fieldhouse in Des Moines. But word leaked out of Feller's signing with Cleveland the previous summer, and the High School Association had to decide if he was ineligible and if Van Meter must forfeit its championship trophies. (The complaining school came from Logan, whose team had been defeated by Van Meter in Districts.) But because the contract was for a nominal amount, and was in a different sport anyway, Feller was allowed to play. And that year, 1936, marks the one and only time Van Meter has made it to the Iowa state basketball tournament.

One reason that Logan officials were so sure that Feller had signed a lucrative contract, Fletch tells me, is because Bob's girlfriend had been seen around town in an expensive fur coat. The girl, La Vaun Jennings, just happened to be Fletch's older sister. "Our aunt Jessie had just passed away," Fletch says, "and our uncle gave my sister the coat!" Sixty years later, telling that story still makes him laugh.

Bob never did play minor league ball but reported to Cleveland during the summer of 1936. His record that abbreviated rookie season was 5-3, including a 17-strikeout performance—the figure matched his age—against Philadelphia.

He came back to Van Meter in October to begin his senior year. (It would be a short school year. He left again in February for spring training, coming back in May only for graduation.) I wonder how his old schoolmates reacted to his celebrity status. "Bob was always a very popular kid, and even more so when he came back to town," says Fletch. "He was elected class president, you know. I think there were about seventeen in the class that year. We all looked up to him, of course. Remember, everyone, from grade school to high schoolers, were all in the same building. But he was still the same guy, a great guy. He did the chores for his dad, rode the school bus with his little sister Marguerite—they were very close, by the way—and he still went down to the gym in the winter to play catch with Kelly and the others. He brought his lunch in a bucket just like he always did. I remember how we all used to save a seat for him, you know, so that he might sit next to us. Of course, since he was dating my sister, I had the advantage there!"

I ask if anyone doubted whether Bob would be successful in the majors. "Listen," says Fletch. "Bob wasn't cocky, but he was very confident. He didn't just think he'd make it, he knew he'd make it. And the rest of us knew it, too. From the time he was a young kid, everyone in town was behind him." Pat agrees. "Anyone who saw him pitch knew he had what it takes," he says.

It's getting late, and the tour and interview are just about over. I thank Fletch and Dan, and remark that it must be quite a thrill to know one of the greatest players of all time and to have seen him play. "But you know," says Fletch, "I saw somebody else who was just as fast."

You mean you saw Walter Johnson, I ask, or Lefty Grove? "No," he says, "and I don't mean Nolan Ryan either. A guy from right here in Van Meter named Max England was just as fast as Bob Feller. They played together at Oakview. Max played minor league ball up in South Dakota for a while, but it didn't last too long." Fletch and Pat smile and nod at each other. "Old Max used to party a little bit."

I am stopped in my tracks. You guys have to be putting me on, I say. What are the chances that not one, but two, of the hardest throwers of all time came out of the same small town in Iowa, and at the same time? Fletch is ready for me, though. "If you don't believe me," he says, "let's call Bob up right now and you can ask him yourself. I imagine he'll tell you the same thing." He walks over to the front desk and begins dialing the telephone. And the next thing I know, I'm talking with Bob Feller. No, Bob says, we are not interrupting him. He is happy to take a call from Fletch any time. He is watching the Indians and Blue Jays from his home in one of Cleveland's suburbs. He is glad I have enjoyed the museum, and he tells me about an upcoming trip he and his wife Anne are planning to my home state of Montana. And he wouldn't mind answering a few questions. "Absolutely," he tells me. "Max England was just as fast as I was. He didn't have near the same movement on his fastball, though. He used a different grip, and didn't have the same wrist action. But he certainly could throw as hard as me." I ask why Max's baseball career didn't work out, and there is a slight pause before he says, "Let's just say Max didn't follow the strictest of training regimens."

Later, we are back at the Manning farm in Granger. We have enjoyed a beautiful sunset—"one of the prettiest you'll ever see," Pat says, and I believe him. My kids are out on the front lawn laughing and playing, trying to catch fireflies. This is their first trip to the Midwest and they've never seen such things. Pat's wife Mary Kay brings out the liquid refreshments to celebrate this special night, and we drink a toast to Bob Feller, who put Van Meter, Iowa, on the map. And then I offer one to Fletcher Jennings and Pat Manning, who help keep it there.

Harold Seymour (1910-1992)

George Grella

On clear nights in the tranquil hamlet of Cooperstown, capital city of our dreams, the sky seems close and palpable, a black velvet canopy decorated with thousands of stars, the perfect foil for a special diamond, just the right backdrop for the contemplation of eternity. In the cool darkness of such an evening in early June of 1995, an assortment of fans—at least enough to staff a couple of teams—gathered in Doubleday Field to attend not a baseball game but a kind of funeral, a burial and memorial service for a man who had devoted most of his life to the study of the game. Mostly academics from a variety of disciplines, they assembled in the grandstand above the darkened field along the first base line to remember the life and work of the baseball historian Harold Seymour and to witness and participate in the scattering of his ashes on the field itself. Although the occasion and the ceremony may seem strange or even comical—as they did initially to a few of the company—they turned out to be sweetly appropriate, somewhat lighthearted, and yet oddly touching, not at all a bad way to bid farewell to a distinguished scholar of the great American game.

The small crowd might properly deserve the oxymoron of professional amateurs, serious scholars of the game who also love it with the intensity that no other sport and few human endeavors can evoke. Coming mostly from universities and colleges all over the country, they had assembled in Cooperstown for the Seventh Annual Symposium on Baseball and American Culture, at which they spent a considerable amount of

time delivering, listening to, and discussing papers on any number of relevant subjects, including the history, literature, cinema, art, aesthetics, and philosophy of baseball (Seymour himself had addressed the gathering in a keynote speech in 1990). They attended dramatic readings of baseball poetry and prose, and earlier in the evening they even played their annual game of Town Ball, a direct and immediate ancestor of the modern game. Not only as scholars but simply as enthusiasts they did what all fans do: they talked baseball, perhaps the best talk of all, providing an all-too-uncommon version of what intellectual discussion should be, a discourse lively and literate, passionate and profound, grounded on both love and knowledge.

Alvin Hall, dean of continuing education at the State University of New York at Oneonta, the genial, loquacious host and energetic organizer of the Symposium, presided over the occasion. Tom Heitz, former director of the Baseball Library and Archives at the National Baseball Hall of Fame, read a eulogy that Seymour's widow Dorothy, also in attendance, had helped prepare; he touched on the several major aspects of Harold Seymour's long and rewarding career in baseball, as player and coach, teacher and student, and above all, as the ground-breaking historian of the game. Others read excerpts from some of Seymour's best-known and most representative works, including his monumental three-volume history, *Baseball: The Early Years* (1960), *Baseball: The Golden Age* (1971), and *Baseball: The People's Game* (1990).

Although the occasion, of course, was intended as a solemn final tribute to an important pioneer who

---

George Grella *is a professor of English and film studies at the University of Rochester who has published extensively on baseball.*

blazed the way for innumerable followers, it never sank into the maudlin or the lugubrious. Many of the passages of Seymour's work examined their subjects in humorous terms, especially those from his reminiscence of his service as a batboy for the Brooklyn Dodgers in the era of the colorful Wilbert Robinson, where the young man advanced his knowledge of two languages, "English and profanity." In *Baseball: The Golden Years* he wrote about the tendency of players of the past to contract venereal diseases, which the newspapers reported as "malaria." (America must have been a swampy, mosquito-ridden place in the early part of the century to allow those stories to fly—in recent years the "pulled groin muscle" has served a similar purpose.)

The readings also helped remind the crowd of the importance of Harold Seymour's achievements to the serious study of the game and therefore to those attending the Symposium. In the face of considerable opposition and even scorn from his department at Cornell, he wrote the first doctoral dissertation on baseball, the longest ever submitted at the university, which formed the basis for his magnum opus. Unlike the previous histories, his works proceeded from a thorough grounding in basic research, a meticulous regard for fact, and a refreshingly disinterested point of view; he did not, like many previous chroniclers, stridently propagandize for the sport or employ it as an excuse to promote some narrow notion of nationalism. He discussed some of the actual history of the game, helping to lay to rest the apocryphal story— probably never more than half-believed—of Abner Doubleday's invention of the game there in Cooperstown in 1839.

Dorothy Jane Mills

Tom Heitz, who gave the eulogy, hands Dr. Harold Seymour's ashes to author, editor, SABR member, and former Seymour colleague Chris Jennison.

Most students of the sport and of Seymour's valuable work probably expected that the third volume of his study would follow sequentially from the first two, dealing with the game up to a point somewhere near the present time, perhaps bringing it into its second Golden Age in the 1950s. Instead, he wrote the aptly entitled *Baseball: The People's Game*, devoted to a rich and important chapter of baseball's crowded history, neglected by many scholars, the game as it was conducted outside the confines of Organized Baseball (his capitals).

In that volume he covers its endless incarnations in informal local contests in village greens, sandlots, and cow pastures, the various levels of amateur ball, its emergence as a college sport (including at women's colleges), baseball in the military, the beginnings of black baseball, and so on. That necessary book reminds us all that the best, the most authentic baseball takes place not in the sterile confines of some concrete tureen that owners call a stadium but in other venues far from the major leagues. Out there, all over America, it is truly the people's game as the people actually play it.

Despite the relative informality of the presentations and the resolutely secular nature of the ceremonies, the occasion, like so much of baseball, also hinted at the spiritual and the transcendent. Directly down the leftfield foul line, just beyond the outfield fence, a single light glowed in a church steeple, like some combination of Magritte and Norman Rockwell, underlining the vital connection between traditional religion and what Annie Savoy in *Bull Durham* calls "the church of baseball." We all know that ball parks are temples, holy places that combine the exuberant activities of sport and faith. The dark and empty field, further, was haunted by innumerable ghosts: the spirits of all those thousands who had played this beautiful game in this lovely place. It was even haunted specifically by those individuals, many of them Hall of Famers—players, owners, managers, and umpires—whose own remains had mingled with the mythic dust of that magical ball park. Now and then a trick of the dim light or a flicker of some fan's imagination coalesced around the image of some spectral figure patrolling the outfield or running the bases. Sitting in its dark bowl of stars, the stadium was peopled, moreover, by the millions more who loved the game and, correctly or not, regarded Doubleday Field as a site of special sanctity. No wonder Kinsella's protagonist in *Shoeless Joe* says that "a ballpark at night is more like a church than a church."

The simple fact of that location itself suggested some complex ironies. Although Harold Seymour had quite rightly rejected the mythology of Abner Doubleday's "creation" of the game, he also chose to have his ashes scattered at the purely imaginary location of that entirely fictitious occurrence. Some special wonder attaches to that choice of so completely mythical a spot, as if even to a historian the myth itself were more important than the historical fact … and, of course, it is. Doubleday Field is obviously the real field of dreams, or perhaps the dream field of reality, a truer place than any actual one, an enchanted spot in a magical village, the nation's home plate, the universal home town of the American imagination. It's the only proper place for a passionate fan and distinguished scholar of the game to repose.

After the readings and a gracious response from

Jennison scatters Seymour's ashes near first base, the historian's position in his sandlot and college days.

Seymour's widow, Dorothy, the crowd filed out of the grandstand and assembled near first base, the position Seymour himself had played as a youth. There an admirer, Chris Jennison, himself a baseball writer, scattered the ashes on the base path, where they would mix with the sacred earth of the field and with the remains of those who had preceded him: Doubleday Field is hallowed ground, indeed. The group then sang—what else?—"Take Me Out to the Ball Game." For the first time, what had always sounded like a carefree, exuberant invitation became something of a hymn, even something of a dirge, a sad song not only for Harold Seymour but for all the fans and players of all the games gone by, with perhaps the hint of hope that baseball really is forever, that they really do play the game in Heaven. If there's no baseball in Heaven, then what's a heaven for?

After the singing, the scattering of the ashes, and perhaps, for some, a few private words to the close and holy darkness, the ceremony ended. By way of benediction, the jovial Al Hall pronounced the last word. Now, he said, whenever he saw that famous, endlessly repeated, endlessly entertaining Abbot and Costello routine, he would always know who's on first. Anyone who goes to Cooperstown with the proper pilgrim attitude—as a devout Catholic would visit Rome or a Muslim journey to Mecca—should stop off in Doubleday Field and remember all those who play there in spirit; the visitor should also cast a glance toward first base and think for a moment of a player from the past who figured so importantly in the study of the game, remembering who's on first, remembering Harold Seymour.

The Megaphone Man

Robert Hardy

Baseball memories, like other memories of life, often take audible form, and these memories are sometimes even more vivid than their visual counterparts. These voices of baseball, from the musical calls of hot dog and peanut vendors, to the taunts and cheers of fellow fans, to the professional labors of ballpark announcers and radio and television sportscasters, all have origins that trace back to the early days of the game. A seminal voice from those early days belonged to a one-armed man with a megaphone named E. Lawrence Phillips, who was a fan favorite in Washington, D.C., long before the days of microphones and public address systems, much less of radio and television. Phillips is only dimly remembered now, but was one of the pioneering voices of baseball—Washington's original Megaphone Man.

The year 1901 marked the beginning of a long tradition of American League baseball in the nation's capital, a baseball tradition that picked up from clubs dating back to 1859 and that eventually stretched over most of the century, until the expansion-era Senators were uprooted and taken to Texas after the 1971 season. Nineteen-oh-one also marked the beginning of a great tradition of ballpark announcing, for it was during that season, at the newly opened American League Park, that Phillips, the scorecard concessionaire, decided that he could do a better job of announcing the batteries for the day than the home-plate umpire could.

The new ballpark, located at Florida Avenue Northeast between 12th and 13-1/2 Streets (what is now approximately the area bounded by 13th to 14th Streets and H Street and Bladensburg Road Northeast), was a boon to baseball in Washington. Phillips, who also ran a carnival nearby at 15th Street and Benning Road Northeast (only a few miles from where RFK Stadium stands today), had run the scorecard concession at the new park since it opened. As a vendor, he made fifteen percent of the price of all the scorecards he sold. Soon, though, he hired a team of neighborhood boys to sell the scorecards at ten percent, allowing him a chance to explore his other, new-found talents while still making a profit.

A stroll to the bleachers—The practice in major league baseball at the time was for the plate umpire to announce the home and visiting teams' batteries to the press box before the game. Not surprisingly, nobody in the park could understand what the umpire was saying, and the fans in the bleachers could barely hear him at all. Sometime during the 1901 season, as the Washington Nationals struggled toward what would be a not-uncommon sixth-place finish, Phillips brought a small brown megaphone to the park, strolled out to the bleachers, and in a smooth, booming voice announced the batteries to the fans in the cheap seats. He continued this practice until, toward the end of the season, as the crowds began to razz the umpires more and more for their unintelligible announcements and Phillips became more and more an entertaining fixture in the stands, the venerable man in blue, Tim Hurst, asked Phillips to stand in and announce the batteries to the press box. Some see this as the humble beginning of the illustrious profession of the sportscaster.

Robert Hardy *(6'1", 200 lbs.; BR, TR) is a writer and editor living in Washington, DC; a long-suffering Senators fan; and, despite that and everything else, a baseball optimist.*

Phillips began his routine on the first-base side of the field, make his way toward third base, then retrace his steps, making several of these trips before game time. He became noted among Washington fans for his dramatic rendering of the word "batteries," which he extravagantly prolonged into "*bat-ter-eeeze*," and for the syllable he added to the end of the players' names (*"John-son-ahh and Strr-eet-ahh"*). Phillips was a gregarious man, instantly recognizable to fans because of his missing arm, which he lost as a ten-year-old boy, falling under a freight car while hopping trains with the boys in his neighborhood in Southwest Washington.

Many fans knew Phillips only as "One Arm," or "One-Arm Phillips." The great Washington *Post* sportswriter Shirley Povich, who vividly remembers Phillips from the 1920s, recalls that he used to joke that they appointed him to do the collections at church because he couldn't steal with his free hand.

Settling in—Early in his career, Phillips was involved in an argument with Walter Hewitt, former president of the Washington club and then the head of concessions at American League Park. Hewitt, displeased with Phillips' announcing activities, and believing that he should concentrate on his scorecard concession, fired him. Ever the entrepreneur, Phillips quickly had his own scorecards printed, which he called "Phillips' New and Improved Score Card," and sent his boys outside the ballpark before games to sell them. The effect of this competition on Hewitt's inside-the-park concession was felt immediately, and Phillips was soon hired back—this time at a twenty-percent commission.

Throughout the early years of the twentieth century, E. L. Phillips plied his twin trades at the two great Washington ballparks. The original American League Park was abandoned in 1904 by the club's new owners, who moved the Nats back to the old National League Park (also known as Boundary Field, because it was situated at the end of the horse-drawn trolley line at 7th Street and Florida Avenue Northwest) and renamed it American League Park, which was usually referred to simply as League Park. In March, 1911, the wooden structure burned to the ground, but by the end of July it had been rebuilt at the same location. The new stadium had a truly pastoral outfield (421 feet to straight center field) and a capacity of nearly 20,000. It was renamed Griffith Stadium in 1922 for the premier figure in Washington baseball, Clark Griffith. A major league pitcher for various teams from 1891 to 1914, Griffith had been the Nationals' irascible manager and a minority stockholder since 1911. In 1920, he became owner and president of the Nats. This site was baseball's home in the nation's capital until it was abandoned for the new D.C. Stadium in 1961.

But while Griffith was the big name in the Washington dugout and the front office, the big name on the field in those early years of the century was Walter Johnson.

Johnson had not only Washington fans but fans everywhere talking about his dominating pitching. Although past his prime, his 1918 and 1919 seasons had been incredible, with 23 wins, 162 strikeouts, and a 1.27 ERA in 1918 and the next year a league-leading 1.49 ERA, 147 strikeouts, and an amazing seven shutouts. He was expected to have another outstanding year in 1920. On July 1 the Big Train pitched a no-hitter in Boston, and it was announced that he would pitch one of the games of a July 5 doubleheader against the Yankees in Washington. Washington won the first game, 4-3, and nearly 19,000 fans showed up for the second game expecting to see Johnson on the mound. As they settled into the stands, E.L. Phillips made his way onto the field and roared into his megaphone: *"Bat-ter-eeze for Washington-ahh—Ssschacht-ahh and Gharr-rityyy!"* The shocked fans howled their disapproval and disappointment, few suspecting that Griffith, "the Old Fox," had never intended to pitch Johnson, but had only planted the false hope in order to increase the day's gate after Johnson's no-hitter in Boston. It is not reported whether the fans that day attempted to take out any of their frustration on Phillips, as the bearer of bad news.

The end of the line—Phillips went on to perform his megaphone duties in Griffith Stadium for Washington's two consecutive World Series appearances in 1924 and 1925, by this time relaying not just batteries, but the entire home and visiting team lineups. Bill Werber, a major league player himself in the 1930s and 1940s, but in '24 and '25 a young shortstop for Tech High School in Washington and a great Nats fan, had the memorable privilege of ushering at the stadium during those two series. He remembers Phillips both as an announcer and a scorecard vendor, and recalls his cries of "Getcha scorecards here! You can't tell the players without a scorecard!" as "part of the game."

On July 4, 1928, the sports page of the Washington *Post* carried the following brief item:

> E. Lawrence Phillips, the silver-voiced announcer who has handled the megaphone for 28 years at Nats' home games, has resigned, and Lester L. Charlton has replaced him.

Phillips returned to Griffith Stadium to announce an exhibition matchup between Walter Johnson and veterans of the 1933 pennant-winning Senators team in support of a War Bonds drive in July, 1944, then faded from the public eye.

Although perhaps the most popular, Phillips may not have been the very first ballpark announcer. George Levy was a fixture in New York at both Yankees and

Giants games, relaying scores and player changes through a bright red megaphone from 1900 until 1940, and in Boston Wolfie Jacobs announced rule changes through a megaphone in 1901. But Phillips was nevertheless a pioneer and a true original. His is one of the great voices of the game, a voice still much loved from that golden era of baseball in Washington.

Sources

Morris A. Bealle, *The Washington Senators*, Columbia Publishing Co., Washington, DC, 1947

Shirley Povich, *The Washington Senators*, Putnam, New York, 1954

The Senators 1966 Souvenir Yearbook, *"The History of the Senators, 1859-1965"*

Bret Wills and Gwen Aldridge, *Baseball Archaeology*, Chronicle Books, San Francisco, 1993

Henry W. Thomas, *Walter Johnson: Baseball's Big Train*, Phenom Press, Arlington, Virginia, 1995

Donald Dewey and Nicholas Acocella, *The Biographical History of Baseball*, Carroll and Graf, New York, 1995

The Washington *Post,* 1901-1928

Shirley Povich, personal correspondence, 1995

William Werber, personal correspondence, 1995   (Thanks to Norman Macht for his introduction to Mr. Werber)

Walter Johnson's Fan Mail

Write a current major league star during the off-season for an autograph or advice and chances are pretty good you'll receive one of the following replies: none, request for money for the autograph, a rubber stamp signature, or your letter will be returned.

However, in a simpler time, during the Roarin' Twenties prosperity of Calvin Coolidge, future Hall of Famer Walter Johnson, with the help of his wife, Hazel, responded to each and every letter he received, many simply addressed to "Old Barney, Washington, D.C."

Even though he played in relative "obscurity" with the Washington Senators, Johnson had many fans throughout the country. Mrs. Johnson, writing in Liberty magazine in 1926, reported that Johnson "struggled mightily to keep up with his correspondences, with no assistance other than a tablet, some ink, a stub pen, and a determination to show some appreciation to people who were interested in him."

Eventually the Johnsons were aided by the purchase of a couple of portable typewriters, and they bought stationary wholesale. It was a monumental task, but, she said, "Walter had always felt that anyone who took the time and trouble to write him, a letter of congratulations or consolation, or anyone who wanted to ask a question was entitled to an answer."

Two-thirds of the fan mail came from boys from age 12 to 20. They requested an autograph, photograph, baseball, glove, old sweaters, "just one spike," and, most of all, advice.

They wanted to know how to pitch, how to break into the major leagues; what to eat and what not to eat; what time to go to bed; what to rub on their arms; and how about cigarettes.

The two most frequently asked questions of youths were, "How can I develop speed?" and "How do I throw a curve?" Johnson diplomatically replied that speed is a natural asset, and "don't throw a curve," believing that too many good young pitchers ruin their arms by the excessive use of the curve ball.

Of course, there were the job offers: real estate salesman, insurance agent, car salesman, and poolroom operator, and requests from towns for exhibition games.

Forty-nine fans wrote during 1924 and 1925 that they had named their son for Johnson. Usually the proud father wrote with the good news and requested an autographed photo or ball. They would usually reciprocate by sending a picture of the baby.

"Walter said he would like to have them lined up 20 years from now and have the privilege of selecting a ball team from among them," remembered Mrs. Johnson.

Then there were the fans who sent things: ginger ale, liniments, salves, ointments, overcoats, and inner tubes. Johnson was also the subject and recipient of numerous poems, and he had a special scrap book for them. He received several hundred good-luck charms before and during the 1924 and 1925 World Series. There were numerous religious emblems, four-leaf clovers, rabbit feet, horse chestnuts, bent pins, black cat hairs, shiny new dimes, rusty keys, and one horseshoe that was sent by inmates of the Illinois State Penitentiary.

"Now, I'm not superstitious," recalled Mrs. Johnson, "but I carried that horseshoe out to the last game of the 1924 World Series. And Walter won. And I did not carry it out to the last game of the 1925 World Series. And Walter lost. You may draw your own conclusion."

Interestingly, a number of ministers and priests wrote Johnson requesting information that can be used in their sermons. Sometimes they sent a list of specific questions, but generally asked that a statement on "clean living" or "playing the game" be sent them.

—Gary Hong

The legend is false, but the true story's not bad

Apocrypha in Pittsburgh

David Marasco

Baseball is about legends. The high point of the 1995 season was not Albert Belle's 50 home runs or Greg Maddux's pitching prowess, but Cal Ripken besting Lou Gehrig's famed streak. This appeal to myth is even stronger when it comes to Negro Leagues ball. One tall tale has Josh Gibson hitting a ball out of Forbes Field, only to be called out when it was caught the next day in Philadelphia. Not surprisingly Satchel Paige, as the Negro Leagues' most famous player, also stars in many such stories. One of these is recounted in his autobiography, *Maybe I'll Pitch Forever.*

> One day I pitched a no-hitter for the Crawfords against the Homestead Grays. That was on July 4. I remember because somebody kept shooting off firecrackers every time I got another batter out. Those firecrackers still were popping when I ran out of the park, hopped into my car, and drove all night to Chicago. I got there in time to beat Jim Trent and the Chicago American Giants one to nothing in twelve innings.

This seems more than a little unbelievable. A full nine innings followed by an all-night drive, to be topped with a twelve-inning shutout? Even if one does believe in Paige's pitching abilities, his memory might not be trusted. His autobiography was written in 1962, and

David Marasco *is a graduate student in physics at Northwestern University. He is a member of SABR's Negro Leagues Committee and is an associate editor of* Diamond Angle. *He can be reached via the internet at* marasco@nwu.edu. *This article was first published in SABR member Joe Wayman's estimable* Grandstand Baseball Review.

while that was only one year removed from his pitching for AAA Portland, it was nearly thirty years after the events in question. Also to be considered is that the only Trent that played for the Chicago American Giants was Ted Trent. This calls for a little digging. Fortunately both Chicago and Pittsburgh had very active press corps in their African-American communities, so many pieces of this puzzle could be found.

The Pittsburgh *Courier* splashed the banner head-line PAIGE HURLS NO-HIT CLASSIC across the top of their July 7, 1934, weekly edition. So the first part of Paige's story is accurate. This was a game for all time. Paige struck out 17 batters, and but for a walk and an error would have had a perfect game. Only four balls left the infield, one of them a low line drive by Harry Williams that was snagged on a diving catch by Vic Harris. The Crawfords were a loaded team, and they played like it that day. Cool Papa Bell led off their half of the first with a ball to left that was played into a speed-induced triple. He was plated by Josh Gibson's sacrifice fly. In the fifth Leroy Morney doubled, but when Paige sacrificed him over, nobody covered third. Morney took a wide turn and Buck Leonard, playing first, threw high to the man backing up the play. Morney scored on the error. In the seventh the Crawfords chased Homestead's starter and scored two more runs. All that was left was for Paige to complete the no-hitter. Despite pinch-hitting for the two last batters, the Grays could not stop Paige. To understand his dominance that day, observe his strikeout totals inning by inning: 3, 2, 3, 2, 1, 1, 1, 2, 2. According to the story, Paige was about to begin his overnight drive to Chicago.

The most popular newspaper of the Chicago African-

American community was the Chicago *Defender*. and it carried no next-day story about a Paige victory over Trent. Records from that era are spotty at best, but a Trent-Paige showdown would have received some press. Ted Trent was having a marvelous year in 1934, and would go on to start in the Negro Leagues' East-West All Star Game at Comiskey Park. Paige was so well known at the time that he often appeared simply as "Satchel" in box scores. He would win the East-West game that year. Given their fame, a twelve-inning duel between the two would have been news. The only twelve-inning game involving Trent was a match he won on the road at Nashville on June 24. That game was a Herculean effort, as recounted in the *Defender*:

> One of the finest efforts of Trent was his twelve-inning win over Nashville last week, played under a blazing southern sun. Trent was suffering from cramps from the first frame to the final, and yet continuing through to win. At the conclusion of the game and with the arrival of victory, Trent collapsed and had to be removed to the club house on the shoulders of his mates.

This does not resolve the mystery of the Trent-Paige showdown. The next week's edition of the *Defender* reveals some clues. A large picture of Satchel Paige was featured on the sports page with the title TWIRLS NO HIT GAME. Below the picture are details of his July 4 feat against the Grays. Also included is an account of Willie Cornelius' near no-hitter. Cornelius and Paige matched up for a pitchers' duel on July 8. The two put up zeros across the board for the first nine, but it was Cornelius who was the more effective. While Paige allowed six runners on five hits and a walk, Cornelius gave up no hits, allowing only walks to Bell and Gibson, with Bell reaching a second time via an error. However, in the tenth Cornelius fell apart, giving up five hits and three runs. Paige then shut down the American Giants in the bottom of the tenth to take the victory.

At this point Paige's actions in Pittsburgh on July 4 should be more closely examined. As it turns out, the Grays and the Crawfords actually played two games that day. After Paige had won the first game, the stadium was cleared for the second contest. With the Crawfords enjoying a 2-1 lead in the seventh, the Grays put two men on base. The Crawfords responded by bringing in from the bullpen—Satchel Paige! After striking out the first man he faced, Satchel gave up a double to the pitcher to plate two runs. Paige could not stop the bleeding and another run scored. While he recorded three more strikeouts for a day's total of 20, he was responsible for a blown save in the second game loss.

With Paige pitching twice on Wednesday, what were Trent's activities? After his twelve-inning effort the week before, Trent had pitched on Saturday June 30. He then came in and pitched three innings of relief on Monday, July 2. Finally he had a complete game against the Crawfords on July 7.

According to Paige, after he pitched his no-hitter he drove all night to Chicago and then beat Trent in a twelve-inning game. The reported facts support Trent pitching a twelve-inning game the week before in Nashville, and then Paige beating Cornelius in ten innings four days after his no-hitter. For Paige's version to be true, Trent would have had to achieve the following tasks: Sunday, the week previous, he had to pitch a twelve-inning game after which he had to be carried from the field. The following Saturday he started in a game against the Cleveland Red Sox, and then came in as relief on Monday night. According to Paige, on Thursday he was to have competed in yet another twelve-inning game, and then started yet again on Saturday. All but the twelve-inning game against Paige have been documented.

In addition to Trent's efforts, Paige would have had to pitch a nine-inning shutout, a twelve-inning shutout in the second game of a dokubleheader, and a ten-inning shutout over the span of five days. All of this and no reporting of the Trent-Paige twelve-inning affair. The historical truth would seem to be that after pitching his famed no-hitter, Paige blew a second game in relief the same day. Four days later he beat Cornelius with an extra-inning shutout, and after almost thirty years he would confuse not only the chronology of the events, but also Cornelius with the far better Trent.

The final piece of evidence comes from a comment in the July 14 edition of the Chicago *Defender*. It mentions the fact that Paige's victory over Cornelius was his third shutout over the Chicago American Giants that year. A quick search of that year's *Defender*s reveals the other two. On Chicago's opening weekend, Satchel and the Crawfords visited the American Giants and defeated Trent, 7-0. A month later Paige would return to Chicago and this time weave a one-hitter to once again triumph, 7-0. With the three shutouts verified, Satchel could not have posted a 1-0 victory over Trent and the Giants on July 5.

If Paige did not pitch against Trent, then what did he do between his no-hitter and his start against Chicago? These facts are revealed in the November 17 edition of the Pittsburgh *Courier*. According to an article that reviewed Satchel's season, after pitching on July 4, he left with Pittsburgh Crawfords owner Gus Greenlee for Marion, North Carolina, on the night of July 5. Leaving North Carolina on the night of July 6, Greenlee and Paige drove 1000 miles to Chicago, arriving on July 8, just forty-five minutes before the start of Satchel's game.

Satchel Paige's story is false. While this is regrettable, it does not detract from the fact that in a little over two weeks Ted Trent had a twelve-inning victory, Paige pitched a no-hitter, and Cornelius and Paige faced each other for ten innings with a near no-hitter.

While Satchel may not have had all of the facts straight, the greatness of these men is by no means exaggerated.

Boxscores of note

Sunday June 17, 1934 - 2nd Game

Paige's One-Hitter and second shutout of the season over Chicago

Pittsburgh	AB	R	H	P		Chicago	AB	R	H	P
J. Bell cf	5	2	3	3		Sterns cf	4	0	0	4
Crutchfield rf	4	0	0	1		Wells ss	4	0	0	2
Charleston 1b	2	2	0	0		Suttles 1b	4	0	1	11
Gibson c	4	1	3	9		Radcliff 3b	3	0	0	2
Johnson 3b	5	1	1	3		Hines c	3	0	0	2
V. Harris lf	4	1	4	2		Lilliard lf	3	0	0	3
Williams ss	3	0	1	4		Marshall rf	2	0	0	4
Morney 2b	4	0	2	3		Scott 2b	3	0	0	6
S. Paige p	3	0	0	5		Powell p	2	0	0	6
						Cornelius p	0	0	0	0
						x Rodgers	1	0	0	0
	34	**7**	**14**	**39**			**29**	**0**	**1**	**40**

x Rodgers batted for Powell in the 8th

Crawfords: 200 100 044-7

Chicago: 000 000 000-0

Errors: Scott, S. Paige 2. 2B-Johnson, Gibson 2. SB-J. Bell, Wells. Strikeouts: Paige 7, Powell 0, Cornelius 0. Walks: Paige 1, Powell 3, Cornelius 1. Hits: Paige 1, Cornelius 5, Powell 9. Runs: Paige 0, Cornelius 4, Powell 3. Balk: Paige in 8th. Umpires King and Kreig. Attendance: 2500.

Sunday June 24, 1934 - 1st Game

Trent's 12-inning victory over Nashville

Chicago	AB	R	H	P		Nashville	AB	R	H	P
Starns cf	4	0	3	4		Bank ss, cf	5	0	0	4
Radcliff 3b	5	3	1	1		Snow 3b	4	0	1	2
Wells ss	5	1	1	3		Huges 2b	5	0	1	4
Hines rf	5	1	1	3		Williams lf,c	4	0	1	8
Suttles 1b	4	1	2	10		Lyons 1b	5	0	0	14
Lilliard lf	5	1	1	5		Parker lf	5	0	0	0
Marshall 2b	5	1	2	2		B. Wright rf	5	0	1	0
Brown c	5	1	2	8		Walker ss	3	1	0	2
Trent p	4	0	0	0		Willis p	3	1	2	1
						H. Wright p	1	0	0	0
						x Dukes c	1	1	1	1
						Griffen p	0	0	0	0
						Miller p	1	0	0	0
	42	**12**	**10**	**36**			**42**	**3**	**7**	**36**

x Dukes batted for Walker in the 10th

Chicago: 200 000 000 109-12

Nashville: 002 000 000 100-3

2B: Hines. HR: Suttles, Dukes. Sac: Bankhead. LOB Chi 7 Nash 4. Walks: Trent 4, Willis 1, Wright 3. Strikeouts: Trent 7, Willis 6, Wright 2, Miller 1. Hits: Trent 7, Willis 6, Wright 4, Griffen 2. Winning Pitcher: Trent. Losing Pitcher: Willis. Umpires: Cleage and King. Time of Game: 2:27.

Boxsores of note (continued)

July 4, 1934 - 1st Game

Satchel Paige's No-Hitter

Grays	R	H	P	A		Crawfords	R	H	P	A
Lyles 2b	0	0	2	2		J. Bell cf	1	1	1	4
Binder 3b	0	0	12	2		Crutchfield rf	0	0	1	0
Leonard 1b	0	0	2	1		Charleston 1b	0	2	2	0
J. Williams rf	0	0	0	0		C. Harris 1b	0	0	2	0
Brown cf	0	0	0	0		Gibson c	0	0	17	0
H. Williams ss	0	0	0	5		Johnson 3b	0	0	0	1
Robinson lf	0	0	1	0		V. Harris lf	1	1	1	0
Burnett c	0	0	2	0		Williams 2b	0	1	3	0
Palm c	0	0	5	0		Morney ss	2	2	0	1
Dula p	0	0	0	2		S. Paige p	0	0	0	0
Stewart p	0	0	0	0						
x Jarnegan	0	0	0	0						
y Strong	0	0	0	0						
	0	**0**	**24**	**12**			**4**	**8**	**27**	**4**

x Jarnegan batted for Stewart in the 9th

y Strong bated for Lyles in the 9th

Grays: 000 000 000-0

Crawfords: 100 010 20X-4

Errors: Leonard, J. Williams, Morney. 3B: J. Bell, Charleston. Walks: Paige 1, Dula 1. Strikeouts: Paige 17, Dula 2, Stewart 2. Umpires: Young, Craige and W. Harris.

July 8, 1934 - 2nd game

Cornelius' near No-Hitter

Pittsburgh	AB	R	H	C		Chicago	AB	R	H	C
J. Bell cf	3	0	0	1		Sterns cf	4	0	0	5
Crutchfield rf	4	0	0	1		Radcliff 3b	4	0	2	3
G. Harris 1b	4	0	0	13		Suttles 1b	4	0	0	18
Gibson c	3	1	1	8		Wells ss	4	0	0	3
Johnson 3b	4	1	1	4		Hines rf	4	0	2	2
V. Harris lf	4	1	1	0		Lilliard lf	4	0	1	2
G. Williams 2b	4	0	0	5		Marshall 2b	3	0	0	7
Morney ss	4	0	1	8		Brown c	3	0	0	3
S. Paige p	4	0	1	2		Cornelius p	3	0	0	5
	34	**3**	**5**	**42**			**33**	**0**	**5**	**48**

Pittsburgh: 000 000 000 3-3

Chicago: 000 000 000 0-0

RBI: Johnson, Harris, Paige. Double plays: C. Harris to Morney. LOB Chi 3, Pit 3. Walks: Paige 2, Cornelius 1. Strikeouts: Paige 8, Cornelius 2.

Ed. Note:

Box scores misspell the names of Turkey Stearnes, Ted Radcliffe, Joe Lillard, and Sammy Hughes of Chicago. Pinch hitter "Rodgers" is probably Nat Rogers. In the Nashville lineup "Bank" is Sam Bankhead, and "Griffen" is probably Robert Griffith. SABR's Negro Leagues Book does not list "Stewart" in the 1934 Homestead roster, but this may be Riley Stewart. Totals don't add up for Pittsburgh's putouts in the first game, for Chicago's runs and hits in the second game, and for the Crawford's hits and assists in the third game.

The Supreme Compliment

Ev Parker

The baseball rule book is clear enough. An intentional walk is defined as one in which "the pitcher makes no attempt to throw the last pitch to the batter into the strike zone, but purposely throws the ball wide to the catcher outside the catcher's box."

For over a hundred years, baseball fans have witnessed the application of this rule in thousands of games. Ah, but add one ingredient and we have a tactical play that is anything but commonplace. In fact, we have the rarest tactical maneuver in the long history of the game. That ingredient is an intentional walk to a batter with the bases loaded—the "Supreme Compliment" any hitter can receive.

Records show that in the long history of the gamethis rare tactic has been employed just twice, once in the American League and once in the National League.

In Chicago on May 23, 1901—the maiden year of the American League—the White Sox were on their way to an easy victory over the Philadelphia Athletics. The score was 11-5 and the A's were batting in the bottom of the ninth inning. (In those days the home team captain had the choice of batting first or last, and the Sox had opted to bat first.) The A's rallied to score two runs, and with the bases loaded and none out, Sox manager Clark Griffith took over on the mound to face the great Napoleon Lajoie. Nap was setting the league on fire in 1901, and would go on to bat .426, the highest single-season batting average recorded in the twentieth century.

Griffith wanted no part of Lajoie in this situation, and to the astonishment of the announced crowd of 2,800, directed his catcher to stand and get ready to take four deliberate wide pitches. "Griff" then bore down, got three ground balls and preserved the Sox victory.

W. A. "Billy" Phelan, the old Chicago *Daily Journal* reporter, writing for the June 1 edition of *Sporting Life*, had this to say. "Many and many a time I have seen captains order a batter passed to first when there were two on base, but never have I seen a man deliberately take such a chance as forcing in a run with none out and good batters to follow." He also called it the "nerviest play ever turned on a local diamond and risky enough to scare an elephant."

Griffith's tactic went into mothballs after that spring day in 1901, and did not reappear for forty-three years. It was July 23, a hot and humid Sunday in 1944, when a fifteen- year-old kid was seated in the upper tier of the old Polo Grounds. From Section 20, between first base and home plate, the kid had watched the Chicago Cubs slugger, Bill "Swish" Nicholson, do a number on his Giants in the first game of a Sunday twin bill. The kid had seen the Giants' only decent pitcher, Bill Voiselle, take a pounding in the first game, which the Cubs won, 7-4. Worse yet, he had seen Swish Nicholson hit three home runs in his first three at bats in the opener. Nicholson had also hit a homer in his last at bat on Saturday, so he had slugged four in a row, and five so far in the series with one game still to go. To compound this reign of terror, this blizzard of homers had pushed him past the Giants' all-time hero, Mel Ott, now manager and still right fielder, in the National League home run derby.

Ev Parker *is a retired NYPD Inspector and lifelong baseball fan who turned to police work when he realized he would never play shortstop like "Rowdy Richard."*

In the nightcap, the Giants held a 10-7 lead in the eighth inning. Two Cubs were out and the bases were loaded, and once again Bill Nicholson strode into the batter's box. He had already stroked his sixth home run of the four-game series, and Ott on tired legs trotted to the mound for a word with his pitcher. Ott decided to seek the third out elsewhere, and "the Supreme Compliment" was resurrected after its forty-three-year sleep. Once again, it proved a winning strategy. The pitching-poor Giants held on for a 12-10 victory and sent the Polo Grounds crowd of nearly 24,000 home with at least half a loaf.

That 15-year-old boy left the old park, across the field and through the center field exit gate out onto Harlem's 8th Avenue, knowing he had seen something rare, but it took him nearly fifty years to realize just how rare. In the next day's papers James P. Dawson in the New York *Times* never even mentioned the event. *The Sporting News* that week gave it one line in the game story.

It took a "Fans Forum" letter to *Baseball Digest* in the early 1990s inquiring about the frequency of the intentional walk with bases loaded to whet the interest of a retiree, who as a boy had seen the very play.

Five years of research have turned up a few near misses and nothing else. Rumors that Ted Williams and later Willie McCovey were given this treatment went nowhere. No documented reports have been found. Joe "Ducky" Medwick was a hot rumor. *Baseball Digest* reported that Al Lopez "seemed to recall" Medwick getting the treatment in the late 1930s. This rumor was extensively pursued. Bob Broeg, the great St. Louis *Post-Dispatch* writer, seemed to recall it happening, but added that it never happened in St. Louis. The late great Cardinal centerfielder, Terry Moore, also seemed to recall the play but could not remember where or when. A canvass of players from the 1930s was interesting. Billy Jurges (Cubs and Giants) never heard of it. The late Burgess Whitehead (Cards and Giants) and the late Dick "Rowdy Richard" Bartell (Giants and Cubs) never heard of it. Harry Danning, the old 1930s Giants catcher, summed it up best. To the question on Medwick, Harry asked his own question. "If you were a rival manager in those days, would you walk Joe Medwick with the bases loaded to pitch to Johnny Mize?" Harry said it all.

The research turned up some near misses that had to be explored. Rumors had Babe Ruth, a likely candidate, receiving the "Supreme Compliment" twice in 1923, when he batted .393. Both rumors fell short. These turned out to be what might be classified as unintentional-intentional walks. In a June 14 game at Yankee Stadium against Hub Pruett of the St. Louis Browns, Ruth flailed weakly at Pruett's slow balls, according to the New York *Times*, before walking on a 3-2 count. The second Ruth sighting alleges an intentional bases loaded pass on September 26, again at the Yankee Stadium, in a game Ray Francis of the Tigers was winning 3-0. No mention of this rarest of plays showed up in the *Times*, The Detroit *News*, or the Detroit *Free Press*. H. G. Salinger, writing his "Tiger Tails" for the Detroit *News*, touched upon game highlights, but mentioned no bases-loaded intentional pass to Ruth. It never happened.

The last rumor involved, appropriately, the Giants' Mel Ott, who ordered the treatment for Bill Nicholson in 1944.

On October 5, 1929, in Philadelphia, the Phillies were hosting the Giants in a meaningless doubleheader near the end of the season. Ott was prevented from catching the Phillies' Chuck Klein for the home run crown that year by Phillies manager Burt Shotton ordering his pitchers to give Mel nothing good to hit. Ott walked six times in that double bill, the last time with bases loaded on a 3-2 count, in a 12-3 Giant win. Perhaps an unintentional-intentional walk, but not the "Supreme Compliment."

Five years of research have turned up only two pure instances of the "Supreme Compliment." A fine monument stands in Chestertown, Maryland, honoring the town's native son, Bill "Swish" Nicholson, who died in early 1996. The inscription mentions that baseball legend has it that only two men in major league history have ever been intentionally walked with the bases loaded: Babe Ruth and Chestertown's own Bill Nicholson. It's a fine memorial to a fine man, and the two count is correct. I can personally attest that Swish got the treatment (I was, of course, that kid in the stands). But the other guy was Lajoie, not Ruth.

Napoleon Lajoie—the other guy.

Transcendental Graphics

The Signal Tipping Scam of 1909

Kevin P. Kerr

This is a story about the art of signal tipping in the early part of the twentieth century. Signal tipping is the ability to read the catcher's signs and relay to the batter what the next pitch will be. Not unlike today, many players during the early 1900s had trouble with curveballs and various breaking pitches. If players knew what was coming they would be able to lay off the soft stuff and turn on the hard stuff. Signal tipping has been accomplished in a myriad of unique ways. Today it is most often done by a runner on second base. The runner is able to steal the signs from the catcher, and relay them to the hitter with everything from tapping a right or left leg or pulling on a piece of uniform. This particular signal tipping story was reported in the pages of the 1909 *Sporting Life*.

The Highlanders were the New York representative in the fledgling American League. The Highlanders, managed by George Stallings, who would achieve fame in 1914 as the skipper of the "Miracle Braves," would in that same year change their name in 1914 to the Yankees, but prior to the arrival of Babe Ruth they were not a very good team. The Hilltoppers, as they were also known, were fairly competitive for the first part of the 1909 season and the roller-coaster ride associated with many Highlander seasons was in the up-swing. Curiosity began to peak when the Highlanders finished the last month of the season with a terrific hitting exhibition. The media were quite surprised and the other teams were quite suspicious. How had the soft-hitting Highlanders suddenly become a hitting machine?

Kevin P. Kerr is a systems engineer with Microsoft by day and a Highlanders and Hal Chase researcher by night. A life-long Yankee fan, Kevin is near completion of his biography of Hal Chase.

The September 27 *Sporting Life* offered an explanation:

"HIGHLANDERS ACCUSED OF SIGNAL TIPPING"

Someone tipped off Detroit manager Hughie Jennings that the Highlanders had a signal tipping scam working. This accounted in part for the heavy hitting Highlanders for the past month. Jennings dispatched the team trainer, Tuthill, to see what he could find.

As the story goes it appears the Highlanders did have quite a scam going. In centerfield there was a hat advertising sign, the Highlanders placed a man up there with field glasses, he sat between the sign and the fence where he could not be seen. The crossbar from the 'H' in "Hat" had been cut out and painted white on one side and black on the other. When the man had figured out the opposing team's signs from the catcher, he would change the crossbar to black for fastball, white for curveball. Manager [Billy] Sullivan of Chicago was quoted as saying he had just left New York and suspected something was going on but couldn't catch them. It seems New York's batting decreased considerably after the discovery of the signal tipping plan. After the story broke, Tuthill and Jennings clammed up and refused to discuss it further. Ban Johnson sent Tuthill a letter demanding a full disclosure of the incident or he would be barred from the American League.

The man in the coop (behind the sign) remained at his post until he saw Tuthill coming over the fence. Tuthill says he knows who the individual was, but that he will not disclose his name because he only saw his back. He admits that he confiscated the glasses and tore the crossbar of the letter 'H' from the fence by the turning of which the New York players received the tip what was coming. He turned the entire paraphernalia over to Jennings, who does not deny he received the same. Tuthill in speaking of the matter said, 'I did not think it my place to make an expose, but since President Johnson wired me demanding the facts, I have written him all that I saw and did that day in New York. The peculiar feature of the whole thing was that no one ever tipped me off. Jennings sent Bill Donovan out to examine the fence, but he came back and reported that he could not find anything out of

George Stallings in later years.

the way. I was positive that Summers was being hit harder than he should have been in the first three innings, so I quietly walked out to the centerfield fence and looked it over. I thought I saw something that was wrong and jumped on top of the fence, but could not get over because of the barbed wire that had been stretched. I went to a point near the clubhouse, where I discovered that there was an opening, and finally got over. A man ran out of the coop as I came in. I think I know who it was, but I would not be positive.... I found a perfectly

equipped arrangement in the coop. There was a handle which moved the crossbar in the 'H', which I tore off, and the glasses I picked up, and when it was over I turned it over to Jennings. It was none of my affair after I had protected the Tigers, so I refrained from saying anything.' Several American League magnates insist that the statement of Tuthill, if proven true will mean the expulsion of Manager [George] Stallings from the American League.

Joe Cantillon, the manager of the Washington club, said he knew of the scam, but his team was out of the race so he never complained about it. Joe said the man who did the signaling from behind the fence was Gene McCann, the old Brooklyn pitcher [3-5 in 1901–1902]. During the winter meetings the league board of directors issued a statement that "after their investigation, they found no evidence of a signal tipping plan had been in effect in New York." They also stated that "if such a plan was discovered from any team in the league the manager or player responsible would be banned from the league for all time." (Actually, at the time there was no rule prohibiting the signal-tipping plan the Highlanders were using, but such a rule was implemented the following year.)

Stallings escaped persecution and went on to manage the world champion miracle Boston Braves of 1914.

We're Now A Baseball Town

Charles P. Treft

With the excitement of the Raptors bringing professional baseball back to Ogden, Utah, after a thirteen-year absence, many a memory of long-ago professional baseball heros in Ogden are being recalled. Memories abound of the heroics and the glory days of the Ogden Dodgers. Led by Tom Lasorda from 1966 through 1968 and Ray Malgradi in 1969, they won a league record four straight pennants. They are also remembering the times of the Ogden A's, the only AAA team to call Ogden home. The A's moving to Edmonton, Alberta, Canada, left a bad taste in the mouths of the Ogden city fathers, and in 1985 the city sold John Affleck Park, which was torn down to make way for business development.

There are some people who also remember the Ogden Reds, who in 1939 also broke a baseball drought of eleven years in the new Pioneer League. All these teams had a drive and zeal that has been mirrored by the new Ogden Raptors. But this type of spirit started in 1911, with a team that came to being with controversy, dreams of glory, and determination. These teams wanted to show that Ogden, no less than Salt Lake City, was a baseball town.

Ogden's first modern pro team was organized before the start of the 1912 season. The Union Association was less than a year old in 1911 when a couple of teams in the six-member league showed signs of trouble. One of these teams was John J. (Honest John) McCloskey's Butte Miners. McCloskey was having trouble getting

people to come to the home games, and was receiving little support from the local business community. McCloskey was impressed by the record crowds that attended the games of the Salt Lake City Skyscrapers. By the end of the 1911 baseball year, McCloskey was looking into the possibility of moving his franchise southward. He needed a town that was stable yet growing. The town had to have a good population to develop a large base of loyal fan support.

During the week of October 9, 1911, "Honest John" paid a visit to Utah's second largest city, Ogden. For two days, he looked over the railroad town and paid calls on civic and business leaders. The Salt Lake *Tribune* of October 9, 1911, reported, "While McCloskey did not divulge his plans at this time it is understood that he desires to come to Ogden and put up all the money necessary to purchase the franchise, put in the club, and defray whatever other expenses will be necessary. He will organize no stock company, but may ask the merchants and fans to purchase season tickets. Above all, he desires the goodwill of every citizen and businessman in his effort to give the city league baseball...."

On Tuesday, October 11, 1911, "Honest John" McCloskey announced that Mike Finn would take over the Butte team for the 1912 season, while he would lead the Ogden team. While the new arrangements were to be ratified by the directors of the league, the situation was presented to league president W. H. Lucas, before he made a trip east to attend the World Series. A survey of the directors of the Union Association conducted that fall showed that there was support for McCloskey's plan to expand the league.

Charles P. Treft *is a graduate of Southern Utah University with a B.S. in Social Sciences. His ongoing research is primarily with the history of professional baseball in Utah and with the Pioneer League and its predecessors. He lives in Layton, Utah, with his wife, Barbara.*

Though nothing had been finalized, McCloskey began the task of moving his franchise to the northern Utah city. Before heading home to Louisville, Kentucky, McCloskey requested that the people of Ogden show their support, not with the customary "donations" of the time, but by purchasing season tickets at $50 each. By November 24, 1911 McCloskey had moved his business affairs to the Marion Hotel in Ogden, and begun planning for the 1912 season.

John McCloskey was no novice in the world of professional baseball. The Louisville native had been connected with the game for thirty years by the time he came to Ogden. He was one of the founders of the Texas League in 1888. In 1895-96, he managed the Louisville team of the National League, and he skippered the St. Louis Cardinals 1906-1908. Later he was involved in owning or managing a number of teams in various leagues until his retirement in 1934.

On November 22, 1911 McCloskey visited with Union Association president Lucas in Ogden. The Ogden *Morning Examiner* of Friday, November 24, stated, "President Lucas expressed himself as well pleased with the outlook and believes that the business men and lovers of baseball will give McCloskey their unanimous support. In view of his decision in coming to Ogden, President Lucas has requested McCloskey to relinquish all claims to the Butte franchise, and this he will do before the annual meeting, which will be held within the next three weeks. President Lucas has been asked to hold the league meeting in this city, but he was unable to render a decision on this while here.

"Both of the Union officials returned to Salt Lake, but McCloskey will probably be back in the city within a few weeks. Immediately after the meeting he will take up his residence in Ogden and begin active preparations for the coming season."

By November 25 it was assumed that a Union League franchise also would be awarded to Pocatello, Idaho, making the Union Association an eight-team league. There were rumors that the owners of the Gate City team would be well-known baseball men from the east. It was also rumored that the manager would be a former Pacific Coast League man from Portland, Oregon.

President Lucas and McCloskey were to travel together to the Union Association winter meetings, slated to begin on December 14, in Missoula, Montana. On December 7 McCloskey received some bad news; he had no takers for the rights to the Butte franchise. Potential investors were worried that they would not be able to turn a profit. This was bad news for Ogden. McCloskey's plan would only work with a team in the Montana city.

McCloskey's membership was saved when J. W. Cody of Boise, Idaho, failed to show up. His Irragators were unceremoneously replaced by Ogden. Butte's status remained unclear. Details were left in the hands of McCloskey and president Lucas, who said, "If Butte comes in, Pocatello will be admitted also...." Butte, though represented, did not put up any of the necessary club guarantee money to remain in the league. The final details about Ogden and Butte's participation in the league were left in the hands of President Lucas and McCloskey.

One of the options possible for McCloskey was to take over the Boise franchise, with Chester N. Sutton, who was to get the Pocatello franchise, to take over the Ogden bid. But the Ogden fans wanted no part of any diversion from the original plan.

The final plan hammered out by the league directors at the Missoula meetings was to have a six-team circuit with Great Falls, Butte, Missoula, and Helena, Montana, plus Salt Lake City and Ogden. If different ownership for the Boise franchise could be found, then the Idaho capitol would help bring in Pocatello to make an eight-team circuit.[1] On December 21 McCloskey told the *Evening Standard*, "I gave my word that I was coming to Ogden and I intend to keep it. Just say for me that they couldn't hand me the Boise franchise on a silver platter."

With that "Honest John" began to build his Ogden team. On December 22 McCloskey announced that he had signed Arthur Laur of Milwaukee, Wisconsin, an infielder who could play at short or second. McCloskey also went after another experienced infielder, Alfred Robert (Dad) Clark. Clark was a former Chicago Cub (1902), and was under contract to the Columbus team of the American Association. At the time, though, he was held by the Akron team of the Ohio League, a team he did not want to play for.

Fielding players was not the only problem facing McCloskey; he needed a place to play. He leased property for his ballpark on 27th Street, between Washington Avenue and Grant Avenue. The entrance to the grounds was planned to be on the 27th Street side near Washington Avenue, with a twelve-foot high fence surrounding the grounds. The lease for the grounds was obtained from the estates of D. H. Perry, and the Thompson family.

Even with work in progress on Ogden's new field, the league had not settled the Boise question. President Lucas entertained the idea of granting the franchise to Hugh Kellacky. On January 15, 1912, Kellacky told Lucas that he had secured the necessary financial backing from the people of Boise to put up the forfeit money that Cody had earlier failed to pay the league. It seemed that the league directors and President Lucas were in favor of Kellacky's efforts. There was still no action from the people in Butte to secure the 1912 season for the Miners.

To settle the question of who would own what, McCloskey started to push for the sale of his Butte interest. Negotiations began between McCloskey and William Walsh of Butte, Montana. The *Evening Standard* of January 20 said: "According to McCloskey's last offer the former Butte manager should lose the $5,400 which he spent in building a ball park in Butte, two sets of uniforms and the members of last year's club, and yet Walsh did not see fit to take over the franchise and hold the berth in the Union Association. President Lucas has practically given up all hope of retaining an eight-team affair."

It seemed that McCloskey was to lose all he worked for in the Montana town. As another player in the Boise affair, D. F. McCoy of Salt Lake City, made a bid to place a franchise in Boise. But accusations of collusion were raised when it was reported that R. G. Cooley, owner of the Salt Lake City Skyscrapers, was involved in the deal. On the night of January 24, President Lucas decided to take matters in his own hands. He named Chester Sutton, former manager of the Orpheum Theater there, the new owner of the Butte franchise. Sutton immediately posted the $500 forfeit money.

Even with the Butte question resolved, problems still remained with Boise. On January 25 the *Evening Standard* reported, "Now that it is certain that Butte is to be in the league another city must be added or Boise dropped…All this, however, is dependent on whether or not Boise comes back into the league."

Support for the league in Boise was poor. The sentiment of the local fans was that president Lucas and "Honest John" McCloskey had all but destroyed their team with outside ownership.

In February Sutton announced that he wanted nothing to do with the Butte franchise. Walsh then dropped his bid for the Boise franchise and picked up the Butte bid. But with all the discussion going on with other towns, Ogden was not yet firmly in the league. McCloskey had set his headquarters at his pool hall located at 350 25th Street (now the site of the Ogden Federal Building).The new team had no nickname at the beginning of the season, but was named the Mackmen to honor McCloskey when new owners took over.

The league spring meetings were held in Ogden on April 3, 1912 to set the season schedule, and firm up the league. The opening game was to be a contest between the league champion, the Great Falls Electrics, and the new Ogden team. With the new diamond at Glenwood Park completed in April and hailed as one of the best in the league, opening day arrived. It was a typical northern Utah spring day, unpredictable. The weather delayed the opening contest one hour. When four o'clock rolled around, the new mayor, A. G. Felt, braved the chilly weather with 500 other fans and threw out the first pitch. The first season of professional baseball in Ogden was launched.

First Game Summary

Great Falls

	AB	R	H	PO	A	E
Murphy lf	4	2	2	1	0	0
Hisse ss	5	1	2	3	0	1
Huelsman rf	3	2	2	1	1	0
Tober 3b	5	1	1	0	2	0
Kelly cf	5	1	2	1	0	0
Hester 1b	5	1	2	11	1	0
Fats 2b	5	0	2	1	6	2
Shanbon c	4	0	0	8	0	0
Hildebrand p	3	0	0	1	3	1
TOTALS	40	8	13	27	14	4

Ogden

	AB	R	H	PO	A	E
O'Leary lf	3	1	0	3	0	0
Schimpff ss	5	2	3	1	3	0
Stevens rf	4	2	3	1	3	0
Clark 1b	2	1	0	13	0	0
Alexander c	5	1	1	5	1	0
Wesler 2b	4	0	1	4	3	0
Levy 3b	4	0	1	1	3	1
Murray cf	4	1	0	0	1	0
Jensen p	3	0	0	0	2	0
TOTALS	35	8	9	27	15	1

Scores By Innings

	1	2	3	4	5	6	7	8	9	TOTALS
Great Falls	0	0	2	1	0	0	1	0	4	8
Ogden	4	4	0	0	0	0	0	0	0	8

Two base hit: Murphy, Hester, Schimpff (3), Alexander, Levy. Three-base hits: Hester, Stevens. Home runs: Huelsman. Base-on-balls: off Jensen 3, off Hildebrand 7. Left on Base: Great Falls 8, Ogden 9. Double play: Schimpff to Wesler to Clark. Passed balls: Shannon. Hit by Pitched Ball: Huelsman. Sacrifice hits: Clark, Wesler, Levy. Hits: off Jensen 8, in 6 2/3 innings, off Kermeyer 0 in 1 inning. Time: One hour, fifty-five minutes. Umpire Hatlburt. Attendance: 400.

The game ended in an eight-to-eight tie in the ninth inning when it was called due to darkness.

Ed. note: Some of the totals from this Ogden Morning Examiner *boxscore of Thursday, April 25, 1912, are incorrect.*

Sources:

1. Interview with Dar Belnap by the author in the fall of 1993.
2. The Salt Lake *Tribune*, Wednesday, October 11, 1911, volume 83, number 180.
3. The Ogden *Morning Examiner*
4. The Ogden *Evening Standard*